Stars in a Dark Night

A History of Hornsea and the Great War

B. S. Barnes

Helion & Company Limited

Helion & Company Limited
Unit 8 Amherst Business Centre
Budbrooke Road
Warwick
CV34 5WE
England
Tel. 01926 499 619
Email: info@helion.co.uk
Website: www.helion.co.uk
Twitter: @helionbooks
Visit our blog http://blog.helion.co.uk/

Published by Helion & Company 2019
Designed and typeset by Versatile PreMedia Services. www.versatilepremedia.com
Photograph enhancement by Mach 3 Solutions Ltd (www.mach3solutions.co.uk)
Cover designed by Paul Hewitt, Battlefield Design (www.battlefield-design.co.uk)

Text © B. S. Barnes 2019
Illustrations © B. S. Barnes 2019

Every reasonable effort has been made to trace copyright holders and to obtain their permission for the use of copyright material. The author and publisher apologize for any errors or omissions in this work, and would be grateful if notified of any corrections that should be incorporated in future reprints or editions of this book.

ISBN 978-1-912174-99-7

British Library Cataloguing-in-Publication Data.
A catalogue record for this book is available from the British Library.

All rights reserved. No part of this publication may be reproduced, stored in a retrieval system, or transmitted, in any form, or by any means, electronic, mechanical, photocopying, recording or otherwise, without the express written consent of Helion & Company Limited.

For details of other military history titles published by Helion & Company
Limited contact the above address, or visit our website: http://www.helion.co.uk

We always welcome receiving book proposals from prospective authors.

This book is dedicated to the memory of Michael Sewell, a Hornsea historian who spent many years recording the sacrifices made by the people of Hornsea in the Great War of 1914–1918. His enthusiasm and dedication shines through in his work and as I began to get to grips with this subject his books guided me through the darkness like a bright light, shining into places I had never been before. I owe him a great debt and would have loved to have met him, sadly he passed away in 2009, a great loss. On 16 August 2016 I met his wife Pat in the Floral Hall Tea Rooms in Hornsea, we spent a pleasant hour chatting about Michael and the work I was doing on the town of Hornsea.

Contents

Acknowledgements		vii
Author's Introduction		ix
Foreword		xi
1	1914: A Call to Arms	1
2	1915: The War Comes Home	9
3	1916: Kitchener's Men and the Somme	23
4	1917: A Nation in Mourning	35
5	1918: When will it End?	47
6	1919 and Beyond: Better Days for Some	59
7	Stars in a Dark Night: The Forgotten Dead	67
8	The Persistence of Memory: Great War Memorials in Hornsea	143
9	Other First World War Graves in Hornsea: Men from other Counties	147
10	Hornsea Men who were Killed in the War but are not Listed on the Hornsea War Memorial	151
11	Men who Died in the Great War and had a Link to Hornsea but had no Right to be Included on the Hornsea War Memorial	155
Sources		163
Bibliography		164
Index		165

Acknowledgements

Many thanks to all the individuals and organisations below for their valued assistance in making this study:

Mike and Judy Galloway of the Carnegie Heritage Centre, Hull. For information on Sergeant Jack Galloway, Northumberland Fusiliers, who was stationed in Hornsea and met his wife there. They kindly provided a portrait picture of Jack Galloway.

The Staff of Hornsea Library. They were all very helpful and nothing was too much trouble for them.

Ted Gray of the Hornsea and District U3A. For his good company, interest and encouragement throughout my work on Hornsea. Without him this study would not have been complete.

The following members of the Hornsea and District U3A. They did the research that resulted in the production of an excellent book on the Hornsea war dead of First World War: *Hornsea Remembers*: Jennifer Cardiss, Rosemary Ellis, Ted Gray, Tim Hatchett, Susanne Jones, Christopher Parker and Ken Smith.

The volunteers at The Carnegie Heritage Centre. West Park, Hull. For their encouragement and help.

Joe Gelsthorpe of Mereside, Hornsea. His father served in the Royal Naval Air Service during the war. Joe provided a portrait of his father, Gladwin Webster Thomas Gelsthorpe and a picture of a Sopwith sea plane on Hornsea Mere.

Simon Dinsdale. For allowing me to use a portrait of Albert Teesdale from his own book: *First Gunshots of the Great War*.

Carol Harker of Hornsea, relative of George Frederick Harker, who died in Hornsea on 9 February 1916.

Michael Sewell. His superb body of work was essential as I struggled to come to grips with this multi-facetted subject.

David Brown of Hornsea. Whose relative, George Brown, is listed on the Hornsea War Memorial. He died of his wounds in November 1916 in Leith, Scotland, where he is buried. David also provided a portrait of George Brown's sister Elizabeth Brown.

Martin Lonsdale of Hornsea. His father, Arthur John Lonsdale, served in the Indian Army during the war. Martin kindly provided two portraits of his father and allowed me to use his letters and diaries.

Brenda Coneyworth of Leven. George Burgess was her grandfather and Frederick Burgess was her great uncle, they were brothers and both feature on the Hornsea War

Memorial. Brenda kindly provided a fine group picture of the Burgess children: Lucy, Winifred and Frances.

Collin and Joyce Brooks of Leven. They kindly allowed me to copy and reproduce the portrait of their relative Fred Brooks from their family archive.

Roger Montgomery. For his generosity in allowing me access to his excellent family tree and for giving me permission to use the portraits of William Oscar Montgomery and Leslie Montgomery Hulse.

The Hornsea Council Offices archive, Newbegin. I was given access to a general cemetery register on 22 September 2016, the information recorded in it was very scant and gave me nothing new. When I asked to see the more detailed registers for 1914–1918 I was refused permission to see them as I was told the Data Protection Act would not allow it. When I explained that the registers were over 100 years old and that the people in them had long been dead it made no difference and I was told by the Town Clerk that the DPA still applied, I was refused permission to see them.

St Nicholas Church, Hornsea. Just out of personnel interest I asked permission to view and photograph the memorial plaques from the Great War that are kept in the church and was asked to donate £50 towards the Peel of Bells Fund before I would be allowed to do so. I declined the offer.

The following portraits of the Fallen were published in *Green's Almanac* during the Great War. By kind permission of the Treasure House in Beverley: Harry Carr. Fred Burgess. Oscar Blanchard. Herbert Thomas Myers. Charles Davidson Brighouse. Thomas Whiting. George Herbert Dunn. Robert Tungate. Ralph Snowdon. Arthur Ernest Hobson and Arthur Pooley.

Other portraits of the Fallen were taken from the Hornsea and District U3A publication: *Hornsea Remembers*.

The following portraits were taken from the Beverley Guardian, by kind permission of The Treasure House, Beverley: Harold Anfield Robinson. Hubert Train. William Reynolds Parker. Philip Stewart Whipp. Edgar Hyde and Francis Frederick Beasley.

Michael Sewell produced an excellent study entitled His *Duty Nobly Done*, in it he featured portraits of Hornsea men who served and came home. Mrs Pat Sewell has kindly given me permission to use them in this study. Their names are: Robert Thomas Buttimer. Percy Hill Sykes. Thomas Arksey. Eric Parker. James Smith Usher and William Shaw.

The pictures of graves in Hornsea have been taken by the author. Also the picture of Ted Gray at the Hornsea War Memorial on Remembrance Sunday 2017.

All other pictures are from the author's personal postcard collection.

Author's Introduction

I worked on my last but one book, *Known unto God*, a history of Beverley and the Great War, for a number of years and as I trawled through the archives in the Treasure House in Beverley, I saw pictures of many Hornsea soldiers and noticed that the links between the people of Hornsea and the Beverley families' I was researching was very strong. The faces of these Hornsea men were burnt into my memory and I found I knew their names off by heart, I copied their photographs and filed them away in my study for future reference. I finished my next book on the Beverley war dead of the Second World War, The Infinite Debt, in 2016, and was wondering what to do next. As I browsed through the files in my study I came across the pictures and information I had collected many years before about the Fallen of Hornsea. I then went to Hornsea Library to view their local history collection, the staff there were very kind and helpful and nothing was too much trouble for them. I began to take numerous books on Hornsea home and read through them to give me a good background knowledge of the town. I was pleased to find some excellent publications and some relating to the war dead of the Great War in Hornsea. The Hornsea and District U3A had done good work on the Fallen and Michael Sewell had produced excellent in depth studies of the war dead and the town that covered the period I was working on and much more, I cannot thank them all enough for the efforts they have made over the years in recording the history of the town. However, I felt there was no detailed study of the Great War years, as was the case in Beverley, as experienced by civilians and I made it my goal for the future to track down all relevant records, any living relatives and first-hand accounts in diaries and letters I could find relating to the people of the town during those dark years. What I found was at once fascinating and deeply disturbing, the people of Hornsea, like the nation as a whole, suffered greatly both at the front and at home as the war dragged on and some of the most terrible battles in the history of mankind was fought over ruined towns and a desolate muddy landscape. The loss of the young men of Hornsea devastated families, Southgate stands out in particular when one looks at where in Hornsea these young men and their families lived.

This is a study of a small town on the East Coast of Yorkshire and how it suffered during the Great War, it is a microcosm of the experience of all the nation and reflects the experience not just of the servicemen that went away, but of all its citizens old and young during the war. Looking back 100 years later it is easy to view their world through a rose tinted lens, but life was hard for working people in those days with no welfare state, no national health service and very few luxuries in the home. Records show how 30–40% of the population lived in poverty and this kind of harsh poverty is unimaginable to most people today. For the working classes and rural labourers of 1914 conditions of poverty and ill health existed that we would now associate with the third world. At the turn of the century the death rate for children under the age of one was 200 in every 1,000 and the life expectancy of a working man was 51.5 years. People who could not afford a proper funeral were buried on the parish in an unmarked paupers grave and if any calamity befell a family the shame and disgrace of the Work House beckoned.

The working people of Hornsea came from conservative occupational categories now almost forgotten, one in seven worked as a domestic servant and one in four was a farm labourer. Most were surrounded by physical hardship and condemned to a life of hard monotonous work. In their world there was no radio, no television, no internet and very few of the new fangled cinemas. Many Hornsea men survived the war only to come home and die in the influenza epidemic that was raging world-wide in 1918 and 1919.

The graves of the Hornsea dead of the Great War, abroad and at home, stand as a silent witness to an event that was one of the greatest catastrophes of the twentieth Century. Within these pages they live again and their stories and sufferings can be understood for what they were. They were not an outstanding part of society and they were not supermen, ill-used they definitely were, but when their country called they stepped forward and played their part to varying degrees. Their experience has now passed from living memory and with the death of the last survivor, civilian or service personnel, a part of the life story of Hornsea has gone with them. Each day since the end of the Great War the cycle of renewal has continued and the pain and grief of that generation's loss has healed. Each year in the Memorial Gardens and in the churches of Hornsea the faithful gather to remember the dead of so long ago and it is also right and fitting that we continue to do so. The mantra 'We shall remember them' is repeated each year across the country as we struggle to keep their memory alive, but with the passing of each generation it makes our promise to remember much harder to keep. Who now knows the old names that were on everyone's lips in Britain during and after the Great War? Mons, Serre, Hill 60, the Somme, Passchendaele, Collincamps and all the rest that tripped so easily off the tongue. One wonders how much longer such books such as The Middle Parts of Fortune, the Patriot's Progress and All Quiet on the Western Front will have meaning to future generations.

Foreword

Hornsea is a pleasant town in which to live and there is little evidence to show that there has ever been an occasion when the relative peace of this quiet seaside town has been disturbed. The Mere provides residents and visitors alike with an area of natural beauty for quiet meditation, but the fact that for a short while it had a role to play in the defence of the realm has been lost in time. There are graves of servicemen from other counties in the towns' cemeteries and it is well documented that there were large numbers of troops billeted in and around Hornsea in both world wars. Their presence must have had an Impact on the tranquillity of the town but now there is little left to show where and why they were here.

Most people who visit the local Cottage Hospital for treatment or to visit a relative probably do not realise that the original building is a war memorial to commemorate the local men who lost their lives in the Great War. Likewise, when they hear the bells ringing out from the parish church are they even aware that the peal of eight bells was originally installed as an offering of thanks for peace and in grateful remembrance of the sacrifice that those same men made for their country and the town they lived in. The various rolls of honour, memorial tablets and other forms of remembrance around the town serve as a permanent reminder of those times, but the sad fact is that they are forgotten and unseen as we go about our daily lives.

The annual service held at St Nicholas Church and at the town's War Memorial every Remembrance Sunday enables the town to ensure that we will never forget that sacrifice. It is heart warming to see how large the gathering is on each occasion, the town's people come in numbers to remember those who lost their lives for their country in two world wars and in more recent conflicts.

During the time I was Chairman of the Hornsea and District U3A I had the honour to lay a wreath each year on behalf of the U3A and while I waited to lay the wreath my thoughts were inevitably with the servicemen who are commemorated on the memorial. As I scanned the names of so many men from such a relatively small town I wondered about the stories that lay behind the lettering on the memorial. They must have suffered unimaginable hardships before losing their lives in the most appalling circumstances. Back home their loved ones would have lived through very real and terrifying conflicts of their own, not least the news of their deaths.

The year 2014 marked the centenary of the outbreak of the Great War, which rekindled my interest seeking to find out more and was greatly assisted by the books written by a local historian, the late Michael Sewell, in particular his book entitle 'His Duty Nobly Done'. My interest intensified when I discovered excellent studies of those terrible times in the books written by Barrie Barnes that described in meticulously researched detail the history and influences of both world wars on the people of Hull and Beverley.

This led me to join with other members of the Hornsea and District U3A, to mark the commemoration of the Great War Centenary with the production of a book of our own called 'Hornsea Remembers', which was published by Hornsea Museum. The book tells a brief story of each of the men listed on the Hornsea War Memorial who lost their lives in the service of their country in the Great War. As my colleagues and I set about the onerous task of researching each man my admiration for Barrie's work was reinforced by the realisation of the level of commitment that was needed by each of us, even though that work was shared.

You can imagine my delight when I was subsequently contacted by Barrie Barnes, saying he was intending to follow up on his book on Beverley entitled Known unto God by writing a similar book on Hornsea. The fact that he was seeking my help was in itself humbling, but I have since had the privilege of witnessing at first hand the development of an outstanding work of research that will surely be forever regarded as the definitive study of this small East Yorkshire town and its people during a most turbulent period of time and its history.

Ted Gray, 2017

1

1914: A Call to Arms

Hornsea is a small town in a valley just 12 miles from Beverley, 15 miles from Hedon and 16 miles from Hull. As the nineteenth century ended and a new century began the town of Hornsea celebrated the new millennium with scenes of unbridled celebration. There were firework displays and church bells pealed out as the inhabitants of Hornsea looked to the future with hopeful exuberance. This was the heyday of a resort which was thriving as visitors flocked there in the Edwardian summer months, transported by the new railway system. At this time Britain was at the centre of a great empire that spanned the globe and celebrated the superiority of the white race and its right to colonise the world. We should not judge Edwardian man by our own standards, their class motivated world outlook was very different from ours today. The prosperity the empire gave and our superiority on land and sea was expected to go on indefinitely. However the storm clouds were gathering in Europe as the nations armed themselves, until in early August 1914 the headlines screamed out:

> England declares war against Germany.
> Army and Navy Mobilised.
> Railways under Government Control.

On 2 August the Royal Engineers of the West Riding Division, Territorial Force, arrived in Hornsea at Bridge Station for their annual camp, a contingent of 500 men and 120 horses. A large crowd of holiday makers and residents turned out to welcome them. But because of the imminent declaration of war they were re-called and left Hornsea by special train at 4:30 p.m. the 3 August 1914 in preparation for mobilisation. Amid the throng of holiday makers on a Bank Holiday in Hornsea on 3 August, panic stricken residents of the town bought non-perishable foods, sugar and newspapers in an effort to ensure they would have enough should shortages occur. At the start of hostilities on Tuesday 4 August retail shops opened as normal and were besieged by the women of Hornsea, shelves being cleared of food in quick time. As a result of such panic buying in the country wholesale prices rose quickly, the *Hull Daily Mail* reported that the price of flour had risen from 27 to 40 shillings for a 20 stone sack. The panic abated within days, though the problem of severe food shortages would be a major concern throughout the war.

On 4 August 1914 large crowds gathered at the police station where mobilisation orders were displayed. Already territorials and ex-soldiers still on the Special Reserve were in uniform and preparing to say goodbye to their families and friends. The Hornsea detachment of H Company, 1/5th Cyclist Battalion, East Yorkshire Regiment, Territorial Force, Officer Commanding Captain A E Butterfield, was mobilised at the Drill Hall at Back Southgate at mid-night, they were given an enthusiastic send off at the railway station as they went to join the other companies of the battalion, their home station in 1914 was Sutton-on-Sea, Lincolnshire. Thomas Allott of Hornsea was one of their number, he would be killed on the Somme in 1916.

Harold Anfield Robinson was born in Hornsea in 1897 and was the son of James Bethel Robinson and Mary Sarah Robinson of Hendon Villas, Newbegin, Hornsea. He joined the 1/5th Cyclists Battalion East Yorkshire Regiment at Hornsea on 24 February 1913, moving to the 6th Battalion East Yorkshire Regiment at some point, and served at home from 1914 to 1917, he was released from the army so he could join the Royal Naval Volunteer Reserve in 1917. He married Dorothy Johnson and in his later years resided at The Willows, Newbegin, Hornsea. Harold died at that address on 26 March 1984. Mrs Mary Sarah Robinson died on 29 July 1944. Mr James Bethel Robinson died on 28 June 1948. Their daughter, Florence Mary Hutchinson, died on 12 May 1932. The three of them are buried in Southgate Cemetery, Hornsea.

The railway station at Hornsea would be the scene of many a touching farewell in the next four years as wives, children and parents gave a last hug to their sons or husbands, all hoping for the best but knowing it may be the last time they shall meet again in this life. The mood in the town in the early months of the war was of confident expectation for the most part and the hope it would all be over by Christmas was on everyone's lips. This opinion was voiced with confidence by all the newspapers.

The large numbers of men enlisting meant there was a desperate shortage of facilities to turn these new recruits into soldiers, areas like parks and any open ground were commandeered to provide training areas. Such was the numbers of men stepping forward that the army could afford to be selective and rejected large numbers out of hand if they were too short, short sighted, flat footed or had bad teeth. The civilians of Hornsea watched the troop's intensive training with great interest, Alice Steel remembered:

> I and my friend Dora would be out shopping, getting something for tea, and all these young men were coming past like a regiment but still in their civilian clothes. They were calling out to us as they marched past three or four abreast. The next day we went to the park with the children and saw the same boys sticking bayonets into sacks of straw that were hanging from the trees. They were running towards the sack shouting and had been shown just where to stick the bayonet. Nobody stopped us looking and it was not long before it dawned on us that those sacks were supposed to be German boys, it wasn't so interesting after that.

In early August the Huntingdonshire Cyclist Battalion, Territorial Force, arrived in Hornsea for coastal defence duties, they were billeted in the town and the Congregational Church Schoolroom was opened for the rest and recreation of all uniformed personnel. By now the town was in a constant state of excitement and rumours began to spread, gun-fire was said to have been heard out to sea and a large number of wounded servicemen were expected to be arriving at any time. Troops of the Hull Service Battalions, Pals, arrived in Hornsea on 7 August to take part in rifle practise on the rifle range at Rolston Camp. The Commandant of the Hornsea Voluntary Aid Detachment [VAD], nursing, Dr H Johns, said premises for the treatment of wounded were being prepared in the town and the staff to work in them were being trained. The Children's Convalescent Home was converted into a 36 bed hospital and was staffed by No 12 East Yorkshire Voluntary Aid Detachment, the hospital was affiliated to the Humber Defences and was funded by private donations. Of course the war proper had not started yet for the British and the British Expeditionary Force was not yet in France, other troops were being called home from the far reaches of the Empire to aid the mother land in her hour of need.

Albert Teesdale, killed in action September 1914.

Trooper Sidney Hood was born in Hornsea in 1896 and was the son of John Jackson Hood and Sarah Ann Hood of Southgate, Hornsea. He joined the 10th Hussars in 1914 and survived the war. Sidney died in the East Riding in 1967.

On 23 August 1914 the British Expeditionary Force met a vastly superior German Army at the little town of Mons in Belgium, this their first action was a ferocious and bloody affair, but weight of numbers forced the whole Allied Line back. The British Expeditionary Force [BEF] was then in full retreat towards Paris and the situation was so desperate that plans were made to evacuate the whole of the British Army back to England. However the tide eventually turned as the Allies counter attacked the Germans before the gates of Paris and in September trench warfare began on the Marne.

The first casualty reported with a link to Hornsea was an ex-resident, Albert Teesdale, he was killed serving with the Coldstream Guards at the Battle of the Marne in September 1914 and is recorded on the Routh War Memorial with his brother Samuel who was killed in 1917. Albert and Samuel are also recorded on the hand written Roll of Honour in the Hornsea Wesleyan Methodist Chapel.

In the second half of 1914 the call had gone out for recruits for the Hull Service Battalions, Pals, and men from all over the East Riding travelled to Hull to enlist in this select unit. Many Hornsea men went to Hull and joined up in these battalions. Private 10/465 Robert Thomas Buttimer turned up in the first rush at the Hull City Hall to join 1st Hull or the Hull Commercials as they were known at the time, later to be the 10th Battalion East Yorkshire Regiment. This was an elite unit made up of teachers, clerks and others involve in the commercial world. Robert was born in Amble, Northumberland, in 1884 and worked as a Timber Merchant's Clerk in Hull. He was the son of William, retired Coast Guard, and Mary Jane Buttimer. The family had lived in Hornsea since the nineteenth century and resided at Armitage Terrace, Hornsea. Robert Thomas survived the war and died in The Memorial Hospital, Shooters Hill, London, on 3 December 1955. At the time of his death he was living at 24 Jenton Avenue, Bexley Heath, Kent. The brother of Robert Thomas, Charles Jose, died on 7 March 1903, aged 21 years. Mr William Buttimer died on 3 October 1925. Mrs Mary Jane Buttimer died on 12 November 1939. The three of them are buried in Southgate cemetery, Hornsea.

In local papers the censor tightened his grip and little was known in Hornsea, or indeed the country, of the true desperate situation on the continent. In October 1914 lighting restrictions were enforced in east coast areas as attack from the sea was a very real concern. Sabotage of essential services was also a worry and guards were posted at the Water Works at night and at 9:00 p.m. a curfew was imposed. During the winter months at least 1,000 troops would be billeted in the town.

Private Robert Thomas Buttimer.

In the same month the death of Thomas Boddy was announced, he was killed during the Battle of the Aisne on 13 October 1914 and his body was never recovered from the battle-field.

Thomas had been a regular soldier since 1905. He served at home until 1907 when he was posted to India until his discharge in 1913. He then moved to 31 Marlborough Avenue, Hornsea. He was the son of John Thomas and Mary Ann Artis Boddy of Hull.

In October a civilian volunteer company was raised in Hornsea for local defence, consisting of men over 35 and others too young to join the army. They had no uniforms but could be distinguished by a red arm-band with the cipher 'GR' on it. Mr Hugh Joseph Grummitt of Elim Lodge gave his tennis courts to be used as a parade ground. The men were to be trained in drill and rifle shooting, firearms were to be borrowed from civilian sources.

In late October 1914 the first Battle for Ypres began and would rumble on until 22 November. The massed ranks of the German army threw its weight repeatedly against the battered British force at Ypres and one of the bloodiest battles in human history began. The British Expeditionary Force would be destroyed on the anvil of Ypres in late 1914 and early 1915, it had suffered over 58,000 casualties since Mons. The old army had gone beyond recall and the stage was now set for Kitchener's Service Battalions and the Territorial Forces to make their appearance.

The next local man's death to be announced was Harry Carr of Hornsea, he was killed at First Ypres on 1 November 1914 serving with the 1st Battalion Northumberland Fusiliers. His body was lost to the battle-field. Harry was a bar tender in Hull in the early part of the twentieth century and he joined up in Hull on 10 November 1903.

He was posted to India and upon returning home was married to Edith Mary Carr in Hull in 1914, they had one child and resided at 4 Welbourne Terrace, Hornsea. Harry was the son of Louisa Carr of Hornsea.

On 17 November the Hull Commercials or 1st Hull Pals, 10th Battalion East Yorkshire Regiment, arrived at Hornsea Railway station and marched to Rolston Camp. Wooden barracks were still in the process of being erected and the whole area was ankle deep in thick mud. Private Aust remembers:

> An invasion scare caused us to move prematurely to this unfinished camp at Hornsea. It was a sea of mud and we were packed like sardines into the most inhabitable huts.

The move to Hornsea had been so rapid that the Army Service Corps had not yet brought up sufficient supplies to feed the troops properly. When leave from camp was finally granted the food shops in Hornsea did a roaring trade. Private Ronald Harrison recalls:

> Food and bedding was in short supply and we drank from a pale of water. When we got into Hornsea that night we were famished and spent most of our money on food and cigs, when we got back to the camp we felt a lot better.

The Hull Commercials in billets. Rolston Camp, Hornsea 1914.

A young soldier of the Hull Commercials on coastal duty, Atwick 1914.

The task the battalion was given was to guard the coast-line from Mappleton to Ulrome as the fear of a coastal invasion was very real.

The Hornsea Recruiting Committee, led by Councillor R P Maw, had been busy in the town and the men of Hornsea were not slow in responding. Dozens of recruits stepped forward and the town was buzzing with excitement. But soon an event would occur that would be a boost to the recruiting campaign and would bring home sharply to the civilian population the reality of war and foreshadow things to come.

In December 1914 the Dreadnaughts of the German Imperial Fleet were stalking the East Coast of Yorkshire. On Wednesday 16 December the people of Scarborough were going about their business as usual, a thick blanket of fog enveloped the coast in the early morning. People out for a walk or working on the beach could see strange dark shapes out to sea, then they saw belching flames emerging from them as large calibre shells began to scream over their heads and explode with deafening detonations in the town throwing flame and debris into the sky. As well as high explosive shells being used some were of the shrapnel variety, these exploded in the air above the town, throwing down a rain of death on the populace. Robert Clarkson Johnson remembers:

> Both my son and myself were injured by the same shell, shortly after the bombardment commenced the guns in the castle replied. The east end of the town came in for most attention at the hands of the enemy, when the firing ceased there were at least 100 homes in this part of the town in flames. Nearly all the largest buildings in the town were affected in one way or another. The Balmoral and Royal hotels were hit and nearly all the houses along the sea-front suffered varying degrees of damage.

The raid lasted for 30 minutes, after which 137 people lay dead with 455 maimed and wounded. The German Grand Fleet then moved unmolested up the coast to bombard Whitby and West Hartlepool.

The newspaper headlines reported:

Ruthless Ferocity!
Stigma of the baby killers!

The feeling of indignation in Hornsea was reflected throughout the country about this unprovoked attack on defenceless civilians. Recruiting posters appeared in Hornsea with the heading:

Men of Britain will you stand for this?

It depicted a young girl holding a baby and standing alone outside of her ruined home and had a great influence on the numbers of recruits coming forward in east coast towns.

The German Grand Fleet bombards Scarborough, 16 December 1914.

In late December Hornsea households were instructed on what action they should take in the event of invasion from the sea, Special Constables were sworn in and the numbers of the town guard increased. Rumours flew about regarding the stories of German atrocities in Belgium, refugees from that country were arriving in British towns and they all had terrible stories to tell of German barbarism.

In the local papers articles were featured complaining that the numbers of recruits in late 1914 was slowing down and of the so-called slackers that were hanging back. In the jingoistic attitude of the time draconian measures were proposed to force young men into the armed forces, press gangs at the Beverley races was one solution put forward, local poets were not slow in goading the young men to go to the Front:

English youths not yet recruited, perils threaten, dangers fall. You're not like these oak trees rooted, answer to your country's call. Would ye wait the laggards' fate and see the foe within the gate?

Many men who tried to join up were rejected for various reasons, but this did not put off the more determined individuals who would try again and again in different places. Arthur John Lonsdale of 1 Cliff Terrace, Hornsea, tried to enlist and was rejected because of his poor eye-sight. He travelled by train to York and was accepted at once into the Royal Army Ordnance Corps. He was to spend the war in Iraq and on the North West Frontier, was commissioned into the 2nd Battalion 33rd Punjabis, Indian Army, and did not return home until 1920.

Arthur John Lonsdale was born in Hornsea on 16 December 1894, educated at St Bede's College, Atwick Road, Hornsea, and left that establishment in 1910 to start work in the offices of the Hull Manufacturing Company Ltd. He was the son of John Henry and Sarah Elizabeth Lonsdale of 1 Cliff Terrace, Hornsea. After the war he was a founder member of the Hornsea Ex-Servicemen's Club and was Secretary to the Hornsea Branch of the British Legion. He married Phoebe Harrison and resided at Elim Lodge, Hornsea. Arthur John Lonsdale died on 15 December 1977. Phoebe Lonsdale died on 8 April 2004. They are buried with Phoebe's parents, Herbert and Marie Harrison, in Southgate, Cemetery, Hornsea. Mrs Sarah Elizabeth Lonsdale died on 7 January 1942. Mr John Henry Lonsdale died on 14 January 1943. They also are buried in Southgate Cemetery, Hornsea.

Private John Keith of Hornsea worked as a labourer in the Hornsea Brickyard before the war and was the son of George and Ellen Keith of Newbegin, Hornsea. He was the husband of Elizabeth Keith of 50 Southgate, Hornsea, they married in Hull in 1903. He was serving in the 3rd Battalion West Yorkshire Regiment in 1914, became ill and was sent to the Armstrong College Hospital in Newcastle, dying of bronchial pneumonia on 30 December 1914, aged 43 years. John was buried in Newcastle upon Tyne Cemetery.

At the end of 1914 the situation in France and Belgium was at a critical stage, the British Army had withstood the attacks of the German Army at First Ypres but the original British Expeditionary Force had been all but wiped out. The Ypres Salient would be one of the most infamous killing grounds of the Great War, thousands would perish and disappear in its mud in the coming years. But the German Army was not done yet and licked its wounds as it prepared for the next round in 1915. The wounded were arriving home in large numbers and the medical services in Hornsea would be stretched to the limit in the coming months.

The Hornsea men who joined up in large numbers in 1914 did so for many reasons, men from different backgrounds and occupations were thrown together and the only thing many of them had in common was their total ignorance of the horrors that lay ahead.

2

1915: The War Comes Home

In Hornsea on 2 January 1915 the year started with a happy event being reported in the local papers. Annie Gwendoline Bower married Harold D Wilkinson at St Nicholas Church, Hornsea, in December 1914. The event was well-attended and onlookers said it was a wonderful and heart-warming sight that gave a welcome break from the war news.

In the same edition pictures of advancing Tommies were seen with the caption:

Isn't he worth a packet a week for you?

The demand for cigarettes from the troops at the Front was a constant feature throughout the war and the people at home were generous in their concern for the soldiers of Hornsea. Other organisations in Hornsea were busy knitting socks, scarves and other items to send to the men at the Front. On the night of 2 January a great storm hit the Hornsea coast line and caused considerable damage. On the 9th the papers confidently told the populace:

The end in view.

The promise it would all be over by Christmas had turned out to be premature and casualties would soon be flooding into every town in Britain as the great battles of 1915 rumbled on.

In January the Imperial Hydro Hotel, Hornsea, was requisitioned as an Officer's School of Instruction and a military camp was established on the football field in Hull Road. On 21 January all foreign nationals arriving in the town were told to report their presence to the local police and locals were always on the look-out for anyone acting suspiciously.

Many articles reported in the papers were very much the same as today. On 23 January a former Hornsea resident, John William Adkin, was killed in an accident at Hurley's Flower Mill in Hull. The sad case of a young servant girl, Mildred Myers, 26, of Bridlington, was reported. She had an affair with her employer, Ernest Cooke,

Wine Merchant of Hull, and had got pregnant. She told no-one and gave birth to her illegitimate son in her backyard, the poor girl did not know who to turn to and left the child to die on a dustbin. She was charged with murder. In those days times were hard for girls in her tragic position, today she would have been cared for not punished.

Francis Henry Blackburn enlisted in Hull into the East Yorkshire Regiment in 1914, landing in France with the 2nd Battalion on 15 January 1915. He was killed in action one month later on 17 February, aged 20 years and his body was never found. Francis was the son of George Francis and Annabella Blackburn of Marlborough Avenue, Hornsea.

On 20 February lighting restrictions were rigorously enforced, no lights could be shown after 21:00 p.m. and some events in the town had to be postponed indefinitely. Street lights would not be turned on and all other lights had to be turned off or blacked out. A Red Cross Detachment was set up as a dressing station in the Public Rooms for use in the event of a Zeppelin raid. Troops continued to arrive in Hornsea and its surrounding areas and by mid-February 170 Hornsea men had joined up. Over 2,000 troops were now billeted in the town and surrounding areas.

On 6 March a soldier's concert was held at the Public Rooms in Hornsea for the Huntingdonshire Cyclist Battalion. The acts were of a high quality and George Ripley, Comedian, brought the house down. The same day a football match was played by the companies of the Hull Commercials on Mr Cammidge's Field, Skipsea.

Lieutenant Percy Hill-Sykes.

2nd Lieutenant Percy Hill Sykes joined the 5th Battalion Yorkshire Regiment in 1915, he was born in Hensall, Yorkshire, in 1897 and was the son of Herbert, School Master, and Rose Holland Sykes of Grove Place, Hornsea.

In 1911 he was a boarder in a York Private School and later worked as a School Master at St Peter's School, York, he was working here at the time of his enlistment. Percy landed in France in April 1916 and served with the 5th Battalion until the end of the war, he came home to resume his teaching career and married Gladys Frank in Ecclesall, Yorkshire, in 1922. He died in Saltburn by the Sea on 14 October 1957. Mr Herbert Sykes was born on 26 November 1863 and died on 19 October 1944. Mrs Rose Holland Sykes was born on 3 January 1870 and died on 16 February 1954. They are both buried in Southgate Cemetery, Hornsea.

On 10 March 1915 the Battle of Neuve Chapelle opened with a roar and lasted until 13 March. This was a supporting action to a much larger French action in Champagne aimed at capturing the high ground at Aubers Ridge. Although the British broke through the German defences and took the village of Neuve Chapelle German counter attacks prevented any further forward movement. The cost was 11,000 British and 4,200 Indian casualties.

On 22 April 1915 the 2nd Battle of Ypres opened with the use of poison gas by the Germans causing the Allies to fall back in confusion, the Germans advanced over the Allied Lines wearing respirators. On 23rd the Germans were still taking ground and used the gas cloud again to good effect. Canadian troops counter attacked the Germans on 24th at St Julien and checked their advance. Indian troops counter attacked the Germans on 25th despite the use of poison gas and the battle rumbled on into May. The Germans threw thousands of troops against the British Line continuously as the battle rolled back and forth but were checked each time. In the furnace of the Ypres Salient the old British Expeditionary Force was finally destroyed and the units who fought there were reduced to a ragged echo of what they had been. By the 25 May the British Army had suffered 60,000 casualties.

Bertram Smith of Hornsea lost his mother Harriet Smith of Wisbech in 1900, his father William Smith re-married to Mary Jane Smith and resided at the Cemetery Lodge, Southgate Cemetery, Hornsea. Mrs Mary Jane Smith died on 24 June 1902. Mr William Smith died on 11 March 1911. They are both buried in Southgate Cemetery, Hornsea. Bertram emigrated to Canada before the outbreak of war and promptly joined up into the 10th Battalion Canadian Infantry, Alberta Regiment, when war was declared. He was killed in action on 22 April 1915, first day of 2nd Ypres, aged 24 years. His body was never found and he is commemorated on the Menin Gate Memorial to the Missing of Ypres.

On 25 April the Allied armies landed at Gallipoli.

On 7 May 1915 the passenger liner *Lusitania* was sunk off the Irish coast by the U-20, resulting in the loss of 1,198 lives.

Private Cyril Chester Cookes emigrated to New Zealand before the war and was killed at Gallipoli on 7 August 1915, aged 34 years, serving with the Canterbury Regiment, New Zealand Expeditionary Force. His parents were Emily Elizabeth Cookes who died on 5 December 1901, and Thomas Stephen Cookes who died on 28 June 1923. They are buried in Southgate Cemetery, Hornsea, and their son, Cyril Chester, is commemorated on the headstone.

Many Hornsea residents had been ignoring the lighting restrictions now being enforced and had been warned about this on a number of occasions, after the bombardment of Scarborough the possibility of attack at night was all too real. Air Raid precautions had been issued to all households in Hornsea by the police who decreed that the alert would be the ringing of two church bells in rapid succession, upon hearing this people were told to stay indoors, in a cellar if possible. Zeppelins had already made raids on East Anglia. The authorities decided that enough was enough and began the first prosecutions under the new lighting regulations. On 4 May four Hornsea people found themselves in court at Leven for lighting offences. Mr T B Jackson and C E A Lyon were found guilty and fined 10 shillings plus costs. Quartermaster Sergeant Alfred Grindell, Hull Commercials, was billeted at

Cliff Terrace, Hornsea, and failed to obscure the light in his attic window. He was fined 10 shillings with costs. John Stephenson Kemp of Eastgate was prosecuted for burning thorn bushes in a field after 21:00 p.m. and was also fined 10 shillings with costs.

In May 1915 spy stories abounded around the country and the Hornsea Water Works was still under 24-hour guard in case of sabotage. Travellers had to register and those of a military age were put before tribunals and sent off to the army. Strange stories circulated throughout the war and were often reported as fact in the newspapers. One stated that Russian troops had been seen marching through towns on their way to assist the men already at the Front and that they still had snow on their boots. This of course was nonsense but people believed it and many other tall tales. The Hornsea Recruiting Committee was very active and held a series of meetings in the town demanding that more young men should take the King's Shilling.

More cases involving lighting offences were sent to Leven Court, Mary Bilton, Lodging House Keeper of Glen Dhoon, Hornsea, had been cautioned twice before and was found guilty and fined 10 shillings with costs, as was Marie Tong of Hornsea. The Magistrate, Justice Bethel commented that the cases so far seen had been leniently dealt with, but that others in the future would not be so lucky.

Men from Hornsea who had been wounded in action in France and Belgium were now arriving home. Mr William Hornsby, ex-East Yorkshire Regiment, received a letter from his son, Private Percy Hornsby, 21, 1/4th Battalion East Yorkshire Regiment, Territorial Force, who had been shot in the thigh and was recovering in hospital in London. Before the war he had been a Clerk at the Canister Works, Reckitt's Factory, Dansom Lane, Hull. He joined that firm on 12 March 1909.

In late March the Huntingdonshire Cyclists Battalion left Hornsea to take up their new station in Scarborough.

The first military funeral in Hornsea took place on 6 May 1915 in Southgate Cemetery, the ceremony being conducted by Father Flanagan of Marton. Private 6674 Thomas Doyle, 3rd Battalion Lancashire Fusiliers, aged 45 years, died of consumption/tuberculosis on 3 May at the VAD Hospital on Cliff Road, Hornsea. He was given a full military funeral with honours and a party from his own regiment fired volleys over the grave. In the same grave is Private 6767 Robert Steward, 3rd Battalion Manchester Regiment, he died at the VAD Hospital on Cliff Road on 13 September 1915, aged 33 years.

On 22 May the Hornsea Druids, Perseverance Lodge, met to discuss their contribution to the war effort, they felt more needed to be done and it was proposed they increase their members contributions, with the extra money going to the District War Fund. This was carried unanimously. The same day a happy event was celebrated, it was the Golden Wedding of Mr and Mrs Thomas Smith of Lake Cottage, Hornsea. They married in 1865.

News of men at the Front began to be reported in the local papers. Eric Leyburn, the son of Mr and Mrs Leyburn of Hornsea, had gone to South Africa in 1912 and was now serving with General Botha in South West Africa. Major C Eastern,

1/4th Battalion East Yorkshire Regiment, Territorial Force, had been wounded at Zonnebeke, Ypres, and was recovering in the Robert Lindsay Hospital, London, and had news of two Hornsea men. In the same hospital were Percy Hornsby and Henry Stephenson, who he said were on the mend. In the same letter he mentioned Bertie Smith of Hornsea who had come over with the Canadians but said he had no news of him. He could not know that Bertie had been killed on 22 April 1915.

Geoffrey William Seward England of 1 Alexander Road, Hornsea, was born in Hull on 23 December 1885. He enlisted as a 2nd lieutenant in the 11th Battalion East Yorkshire Regiment, 2nd Hull Pals, at the Hull City Hall in 1914. He was the son of William and Mary Jane England. Mr William England died in Hull. In 1911 the widowed Mary Jane, aged 60 years, resided at the above address with her son Geoffrey, who worked as the manager of a timber merchant, and daughter Enid. Living with them was Mary Jane's nephew, Kenneth Loftus, who worked as an accounts clerk. Kenneth went to Canada in 1911 and joined up on the outbreak of war, he was killed in 1915 and is recorded on the Hornsea War Memorial. Mrs Mary Jane England died on 15 October 1933, her address at the time of her death was 62 Park Road, Rochdale. She is remembered on a commemorative headstone in Southgate Cemetery, Hornsea, which was paid for by her son Geoffrey and his sister Enid.

On 6 June Margaret Elizabeth Strickland Constable, of Wassand Hall, was at home that evening and had put the children to bed, on the coast a heavy mist hung over the sea and land restricting visibility, when a terrible noise shook her and her family:

> At 10:50 p.m. came the most horrible buzzing and roaring noise just over our heads, we all said Zeppelin! Presently there came another much nearer. I woke Robert and picked up Hilary, white monkey and all, and put her to bed in the drawing room, then Gertie. I returned to the upper windows and sat listening, counting the bombs being dropped on poor old Hull and the gun-fire in return. Presently we saw an ominous red light in the sky. All was quiet by 12:00 p.m. and the thick white blanket of mist made everything look absolutely peaceful. It was a most curious feeling seeing nothing and hearing these sinister sounds overhead, it was dreadful too to sit listening to the bombs being dropped at regular intervals and to know that each meant death to many without the smallest possibility of defence. The same month the postman brought news of bombs being dropped on Driffield and that ambulances had been going back and forth from Hull all night. George sent up to ask if he could go and see if his parents were safe, at 11:00 a.m. he came back and reported that no-one was injured and that three bombs had been dropped, one in a field near the Driffield Station, one in a villa garden which had damaged some apple trees and another on the outskirts.

The Zeppelin raids that passed over the east coast on their way to Hull terrified the population of Hornsea and many thought it safer to leave their homes and look for open ground for some protection. Alice Burgess would go with her three children, Lucy, Winifred and Frances, and sister Ellen to the Mere and stand under a tree. They

The Burgess children. Left to right: Lucy, Winifred and Frances.

always took their pet duck with them held under someone's arm, which proceeded to quack throughout the time they were there. Alice would lose her husband Fred Burgess in August 1915 and Ellen would lose her husband, Fred's brother, George Burgess in September 1915.

On 13 June an incident occurred at the Imperial Hydro Hotel, Mr Edward Warner of 16 Clifton Street, Cliff Road, Hornsea, was the engineer at the hotel and in order to comply with the new blackout regulations had to return to the hotel at 10:30 p.m. to switch off the generator. On the night in question he finished work and returned home, there was a knock on the door and he was confronted by Colonel Beresford, Commandant of the Officer's Training School. He demanded that Mr Warner return to the hotel and turn off the generator, Warner told him that he had been instructed by the Hotel Manager, Mr C Morgan Graham, not to turn the lights off until midnight. The irate colonel then called two armed soldiers he had brought with him and arrested Mr Warner under the Defence of the Realm Act. He was taken to the Police Station and kept in the cells until noon the next day. In November Mr Warner sued the colonel for false imprisonment and was awarded 25 pounds in compensation at Beverley County Court.

In December 1915 Colonel Beresford and his wife told a slightly different version of this incident to Margaret Elizabeth Strickland Constable of Wassand:

After the first Zeppelin raid Colonel B told me that the Hydro Engineer was so frightened that he could understand nothing that was said, but went home and got into bed and took the key of the gas switch with him. Colonel B went with two soldiers and shouted him out and sent him to the police station for the night. Mrs B, whose hobby was Spies, 'the danger in our midst' as she used to say in a hollow voice, told us with glee they were sure the engineer was a real spy and that a German letter had been found in his rooms, which they thought was a cypher and conclusive proof. Colonel B said they could not quite make the letters out and the bits he quoted to me did not make sense and that he would like to show it to me, but he did not do so. The Judge disagreed and found for the engineer.

On 16 June a group of soldiers from the King's Own Yorkshire Light Infantry, stationed in Hull, were swimming in the sea off the Hornsea Coast. Private Mark Windle was swept out to sea and drowned. On 26 June more Hornsea residents found themselves before the Judge at Leven Petty Sessions charged with breaking the blackout regulations, they were: Annie Marie Bull, Sarah Musgrave, Thomas Richard Sizer and Alfred Mann. All were fined 10 shillings plus costs. Mr Charles Stanfield Wilson of the Esplanade Garage, Hornsea, was prosecuted by the Inland Revenue for failing to keep a Motor Spirit Stock Book and was fined five pounds.

Hornsea residents were encouraged to grow their own produce on allotments and to preserve the fruit and vegetables they produce so as not to waste them. The Women's Farm and Garden Union published a booklet showing the kinds of herbs that could be collected from the wild and how they could be preserved.

On 5 June the death at sea of Lord Kitchener was reported as HMS *Hampshire* struck a mine and sank, a great loss to the nation in its time of need. Memorial services were held at the Wesleyan Methodist Chapel and the Congregational Church, Hornsea.

On 8 June 1915 the local morning papers gave a very understated description of a Zeppelin raid on Hull, Margaret Elizabeth Strickland Constable wrote indignantly in her diary:

This considering there were 100 deaths, one whole street demolished and a number of smaller houses wrecked. We went to Hull, Edwin Davis's big drapery shop was a pile of smoking ashes, with two fire-engines still playing on it. We saw a house in Bright Street that had been completely burnt down and visited five other houses that were quite pathetic with their squalid interiors laid open and crumbled to powder. We spoke to a woman with a bandaged head who said quite proudly that everyone on this side of the street had been wounded. Then we felt we had seen enough that was depressing and came away.

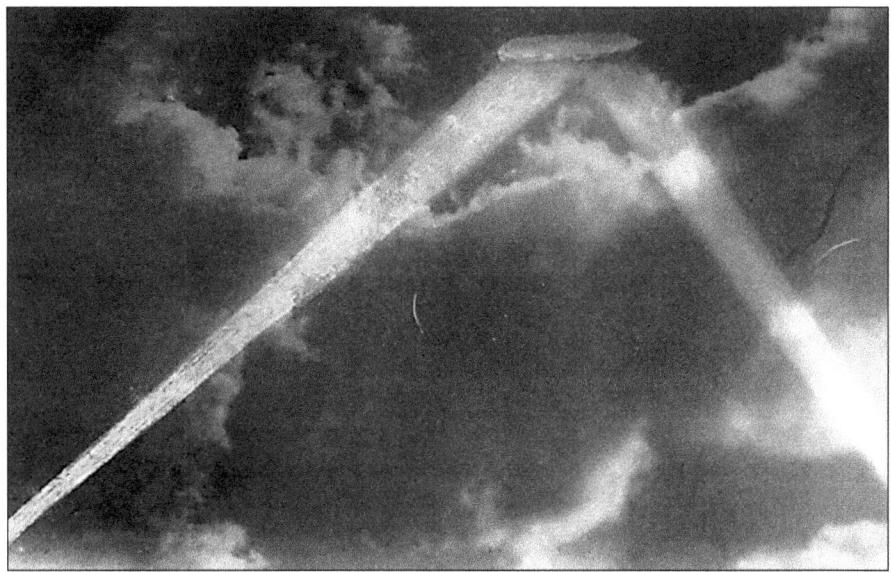

A Zeppelin caught in searchlights over Hull, 1915.

Two days later Margaret Elizabeth was in Hull again and found the population in a state of agitation and fear:

> Went to Spyvee Street, Hull, thought to have been destroyed but was ok. When we got back to the car a crowd of women had gathered around it declaring that we were spies. George only pacified them by telling them it was Colonel Constable's car. A police inspector came by and we asked him about the damage, he advised us not to go down any side streets as the people were so excited there is no knowing what they will do.

The Reverend John Harrington, Vicar of Hornsea, appeared at the Leven Petty Sessions on 7 June charged with contravening the blackout regulations on 24 May, a light was seen in his attic window which was open and the wind was blowing the blind. Harrington said the window was facing away from the sea and that in his experience the authorities tended to ignore such cases as the military authorities were the worst offenders for showing lights. The judge disagreed and fined the good reverend 10 shillings.

On 21 June the Hull Commercials, 10th Battalion East Yorkshire Regiment, left Rolston Camp and made a fine spectacle as they marched through the town to the Railway Station, large crowds turned out to bid them farewell. They were replaced by 20th Battalion Northumberland Fusiliers, 1st Tyneside Scottish, and 21st Battalion Northumberland Fusiliers, 2nd Tyneside Scottish.

With the massing of so many troops in the Hornsea area the water supply was under great strain and in early June the Hornsea District Council authorised the drilling of a new borehole. By July the situation had not improved, the Waterworks was intended to supply a population of 3,500 people with water, now it was working flat out to supply the requirements of over 10,000 people because of the numbers of troops encamped around and in the town.

Richard Douglas Dawson worked as a Commercial Traveller before the war and served for three years in the 1st Volunteer Battalion East Yorkshire Regiment. When war was declared he was recalled as he was still on the reserve and was considered a fully trained soldier. He was posted to the 7th Battalion the Rifle Brigade on 4 September 1914, promoted to sergeant and went to France with them in 1915. Richard was killed in action on 24 July 1915, aged 36 years. His body was never found. He was the son of Edward and Clara Jane Dawson of 6 Suffolk Terrace, Hornsea, and the husband of Maud Helen Dawson of Burton Lodge, Hornsea. Mrs Clara Jane Dawson died on 20 February 1914. Mr Edward Dawson died on 29 December 1929. They are buried together in Southgate Cemetery, Hornsea and Richard Douglas is commemorated on the family headstone.

On 7 August Mr Charles Thompson, painter of Hornsea, appeared in Beverley County Court, he claimed he had done work for Mr Richard Smith, builder of Hornsea, and had not been paid in full as the amount of 2 pounds 17 shillings and 6 pence was still owing. The Judge found in Mr Thompsons favour and ordered Mr Smith to pay the sum of two pounds immediately. That same day it was reported that Mr David Robinson fell from his yacht in Bridlington Bay on 16 July, his body was washed up near Hornsea in August.

Over the August Bank Holliday, on a bright and sunny day, large crowds came to the town in spite of the war. The beaches were packed and the Floral Hall concerts were playing to full houses.

On 18 August the 1st Tyneside Scottish paraded through the town with pipes playing and drums beating, it made a stirring sight. They marched to the Floral Hall and gave a demonstration of Highland Dancing. The two battalions left Hornsea the next day, the 23rd Reserve Battalion Durham Light Infantry taking their place.

Fred Burgess was a regular soldier before the war, serving abroad with the 2nd Battalion East Yorkshire Regiment. He left the army in 1908 and married Ellen Burgess in Beverley in 1909, they resided at 42 Beaver Road, Beverley and had three children. When war was declared Fred was still on the reserve and was called up immediately to join the 1st Battalion East Yorkshire Regiment. He was killed in action on 9 August 1915, aged 32 years. Fred was the son of John and Nancy Burgess of Brickyards, Hornsea. Mrs Nancy Burgess died on 22 December 1927. Mr John Burgess died on 20 January 1933. They are buried together in Southgate Cemetery, Hornsea. Mrs Ellen Burgess, wife of Fred, never re-married and died on 17 January 1961, she is buried in Queensgate New Cemetery, Beverley.

On 1 September a concert at the Floral Hall was seen to be offending against the black-out regulations, the police stepped in and cleared the hall at once to the displeasure of those attending. This was rectified later and the offending glass roof windows were painted with black paint at a cost of six pounds. By 21 September so many males had left the town to join up or on war work that there were only 695 men between the ages of 16 and 65 in the town, as opposed to 1,356 females.

George Burgess was the husband of Alice Burgess of Southgate, Hornsea, they had three children. He served with the 8th Battalion Seaforth Highlanders and was killed in action on 25 September 1915, aged 31 years. His brother Fred had been killed in August 1915. George was the son of John and Nancy Burgess of Brickyards, Hornsea.

As the year progressed there was always fund raising, flag days and appeals for cigarettes and comforts for the troops at the Front and Prisoners of War going on in the town. On Saturday 23 September the opening of the Girl's Patriotic Club was announced with a tea held to mark the event, it was held near the Public Rooms on land donated by Colonel Strickland-Constable. The club was part of the Young Women's Christian Association and was intended to be a place where young women between the ages of 13 and 19 could meet and socialise. It was opened by Lady Proctor, the National President of the YWCA, Colonel and Mrs Strickland-Constable of Wassand were invited to attend. Many Hornsea women were now sitting proficiency tests in nursing and first aid.

On 25 September, after a bombardment that lasted 25 days, the Battle of Loos began. It lasted until 8 October and cost the British army 61,000 casualties.

Unknown Hornsea nurse.

A strange case was brought before the Hull Police Court on 20 October 1915 and concerned Carl Imre Higton of Suffolk Terrace, Hornsea, aged 18 years. For some time he had been going around Hull in the dress of an officer of the King's Own Yorkshire Light Infantry who had been wounded at the Front. However his dress was not correct in its detail and he was soon spotted by other soldiers and reported to the police. The Hull Magistrate fined him 10 pounds and told him if it was not for his youth the punishment would have been much harsher. He seemed to learn no lesson from this and appeared in court at Stockport in February 1916 charged with the same offence, he was fined five pounds which he could not pay and was sentenced to one month in prison. While he was in prison another offence came to light and he was held on remand. In March 1916 he was back in court at Manchester for once again impersonating an officer and of obtaining items of military clothing under false pretenses. He had already spent weeks in prison on remand and was bound over and put on probation.

Captain Cyril Trevor Shaw was born in India and was the son of Henry James, Consular Official, and Hellen Marcia Shaw of Middleton Lodge, Eastbourne Road, Hornsea. The family left India for England in 1891 and settled in Croydon. In 1901 Cyril was residing in the Isle of Wight and was a 2nd lieutenant in the Sligo Militia. That same year he was posted to the York and Lancaster Regiment, serving with them until 1906. He was promoted to captain in 1908 because of his good work on the North West Frontier and posted to the 122nd Rajputana Infantry in Iraq, he was stationed there on the outbreak of war in 1914. At the age of 32 years he was killed in action on 22 November 1915 and is buried in Basra Memorial Cemetery,

Gunners of the Royal Artillery stationed on Hornsea Cliff Top, 1915.

Iraq. Mr Henry James Shaw died on 25 June 1921. Mrs Helen Marcia Shaw died on 22 February 1927. They are buried together in Southgate Cemetery, Hornsea, Cyril Trevor is commemorated on the family headstone.

In November 1915 a new gun for the defence of Hornsea had been put in position on the cliff top by troops stationed there and needed to be test fired. Margaret Elizabeth Strickland Constable remembers the distress caused to the inhabitants of Hornsea when it was discharged:

> On 27 November the new Stokes Gun was tested at Hornsea, the loud noise sent many people rushing to their cellars and one woman fainted. All the old people were much alarmed and asked 'Is it the bombardment?' At Sigglesthorne everyone was convinced that the great naval battle had come at last. All the windows at Hornsea and Sigglesthorne rattled.

The xenophobic atmosphere regarding people of German extraction brought out the worst in some people, Mrs Saville, the wife of the Reverend W H Saville, Vicar of St Mary's Church in Beverley, had been targeted and accused of spying and of being a danger to the security of the country because of her Germanic origins. Despite the fact that her father had become a naturalised Englishman in 1856 and had served as a British officer in the Crimean War. He then married an Englishwoman and Mrs Saville was the daughter of that marriage, she was brought up, educated and married in England and considered herself to be English. Rumours continued and the local papers reported the hurt felt by Mrs Saville at these unsubstantiated attacks upon her character and patriotism.

Wild rumours of spies abounded in Hornsea and its surrounding areas. A little grey motor-car was reported to have been seen guiding the Zeppelins to Hull. It was rumoured that it had been caught and the driver shot at Dalton. He was supposed to have had a flash-light on his wrist and wireless apparatus in the back of the car that he operated with his foot. A motor-bike rider was seen racing to Hull as the Zeppelins approached the city and it was reported with certainty that he was guiding them to their target. It turned out that the bike was driven by Arthur Coulson who was returning to Hull that night and was racing the Zeppelins to get to Hull first and warn the population. A Blacksmith from Coniston reported there was a car in a field making signals to a Zeppelin and that the car was full of Germans. When asked how he knew they were Germans he replied:

Well they weren't from anywhere here-abouts.

These rumours, like the rest, proved to be untrue.

As 1915 drew to a close numerous events were taking place in Hornsea, Flag Days were organised to raise funds for the war effort and street collections made, patriotic concerts were given by various organisations and the large hall in the Public Rooms was given over to showing films under the name of the Star Picture House.

Only towards the end of the year did it become apparent that the rapid enlistment of skilled and semi-skilled men into the army was causing great shortages in the labour market. Industrial and agricultural workers, essential for the prosecution and continuation of the war, were in ever shorter supply as men rushed off to join the new Kitchener battalions. In the first enthusiastic rush to join up before the war was over workers vital to the war effort were presenting themselves in large groups to enlist and serve together. The army had traditionally relied on the unemployed and hunger to fill the ranks, now the technically able and highly educated were enlisting too. The effect was to seriously undermine the economy, causing dislocation in essential industries. Women were now desperately needed to help rectify this situation and to fill in the gap in the labour market.

Mrs Elizabeth Brown in later life.

Miss Elizabeth Brown of Hornsea was a feisty practical girl and answered the call for women in the work-place. She volunteered to train as a carpenter and was trained in that trade which she enjoyed very much. She spent the rest of the war in France building hospitals and other non-permanent buildings for the troops. Her brother George would die of his wounds in November 1916.

By December 1915 the British Army had suffered tremendous casualties in numerous battles. In March the Battle of Neuve Chapelle had cost over 15,000 casualties. In April and May Second Ypres had cost 60,000 casualties. In April the Allied Armies had landed at Gallipoli, only to have to evacuate the peninsular in December at a cost of 473,000 casualties and in May the Battles of Aubers Ridge and Festubert were fought. In September–October the Battle of Loos had cost 61,000. The Old British Expeditionary Force had been destroyed on the anvil of Ypres and territorial units were already fighting in France. The scene was now set for Kitchener's New Army to take up an increasingly desperate fight in 1916 and they would soon be bloodied on the killing fields of the Somme. The strain was being felt keenly by the civilian population and the growing casualty lists that kept appearing in the local papers could not be ignored. All families with men at the front dreaded the knock on the door by the postman who would deliver the black bordered telegram that would shatter their world and change their lives forever.

3

1916: Kitchener's Men and the Somme

As 1916 opened the local papers were full of war news, the bloody battles of 1915 had not brought a conclusion to the conflict any nearer and the British army had suffered some important setbacks. The war now affected everybody and rationing meant food queues and shortages. The general mood of the public was not as accepting as it once was and hardships coming on top of bad war news made people more anxious as to what the future held. One result of this was the view that many young men were holding back from enlisting and any young man in Hornsea that was not in uniform came in for a hard time from families that had men at the Front.

One young Hornsea man, Gladwin Webster Thomas Gelsthorpe, had enlisted into the Royal Naval Air Service as a mechanic on 27 June 1916 and was fed-up of people criticising him and complaining he had not enlisted. He wrote off to the authorities demanding to know why he had not been sent for. The blunt reply informed him he would be sent for when they needed him at a fortnights notice but no date had been set so far. Gladwin put a notice in a local shop to answer his critics, it said: 'Gladwin Gelsthorpe wishes to thank his kind friends for their interest as regards his continued residence in this village'. He would eventually be sent for and would serve in the Royal Naval Air Service, stationed on Hornsea Mere, for the duration of the war.

On 1 January a well-attended service for the Fallen of Hornsea families in mourning was held at St Nicholas Church, Hornsea, events such as these would be a regular feature in the town in the coming months. The Hornsea Congregational Church entertained 120 troops at the Central Café, the vicar told them that 'it was the least we could do for our serving men'.

In January there was a minor spy scare when a man was arrested at the Alexandra Hotel, he was a Swedish timber importer called Gunnar Lindgrau. He arrived in Hornsea on the evening of the 21st but did not report to the police station as he should have done, he was placed under arrest and kept in the cells for two

Gladwin Webster Thomas Gelsthorpe, RNAS.

days before being brought before the Magistrates at Leven, where he was fined two pounds and two shillings for contravening the regulations.

On 5 January 2nd Lieutenant William Holmes Collinson was killed serving with the 6th Battalion Northumberland Fusiliers at the age of 26. He was the son of William Rowley Frederick Collinson and Sarah Haselwood Collinson of Cliff Road, Hornsea. The news arrived at the Collinson household on 19 January.

1916 would see a distinct shortage of officers at the Front due to the heavy casualties suffered in 1914 and 1915 and many men with a better education than most found themselves promoted from the ranks. Private Thomas Edward Anderson of Southgate, Hornsea, was serving at the Front with the 1st Battalion Coldstream Guards in 1915 and was promoted to the rank of 2nd lieutenant and later transferred to the East Yorkshire Regiment in January 1916. He was the son of Harriet and Thomas Barker Anderson of Southgate, Hornsea, and before the war had worked as a Shipping Clerk at Messrs G R Haller and Co, Hull. Thomas Edward survived the war and married Kathleen Anderson, they resided at 11 Hull Road, Hornsea. Kathleen Anderson was born on 5 December 1892 and died on 5 January 1956. Thomas Edward Anderson was born in 1893 and died on 3 December 1964. They are buried together in Southgate Cemetery, Hornsea. Mr Thomas Barker Anderson died on 24 July 1926. Mrs Harriet Anderson died on 13 October 1943. They too are buried in Southgate Cemetery, Hornsea.

Albert Train and his brother Hubert Train were the sons of George Edward and Mary Jane Train of 1 St Nicholas Mount, Newbigin, Hornsea. Albert served in the 7th Battalion King's Own Yorkshire Light Infantry and Hubert served in the 9th Lancers. Albert received gun-shot wounds to the thigh in December 1915 and was taken to No 7 Casualty Clearing Station at Merville where he died on 7 January 1916, aged 22 years. Hubert survived the war and died on 15 November 1934. Mr George Edward Train died on 7 November 1930. Mrs Mary Jane Train died on 22 January 1938. The three are buried in Southgate Cemetery, Hornsea. Albert is commemorated on the family headstone.

Early January saw more of the residents of Hornsea being brought before the authorities at Leven Petty Sessions. Mr W Bethel was in the chair. Hirst Barton, Gravel Catcher, of Southgate, Hornsea, was charged with allowing his donkeys to stray on the highway, many complaints had been received about this before and Mr Barton had been fined on numerous occasions for the same offence. He was fined five shillings. Harold H Gibson of Grosvenor Terrace, Hornsea, and James W Redman of Hornsea were fined five shillings each for showing a light in their windows after dark. Samuel Taylor was employed at the Victoria Hotel as a driver and was stopped one night by the police for driving with his headlights full on. Asked why he had done this he replied "I couldn't see where I was going." He was still fined 10 shillings.

On 22 February 1916 the Hornsea Council minutes record the selection of councillors to serve on the local Hornsea tribunal to scoop up any men still holding back from enlisting.

Frederick George Harker was serving with the Suffolk Yeomanry and contracted diphtheria, he was invalided home but died on 9 February 1916 at Middleton on the Wolds. He is buried in Southgate Cemetery, Hornsea. Frederick George was the son of John Clappison Harker and Pamela Jane Harker of The Whitehouse, Hornsea. Mr John Clappison Harker died on 8 April 1925. Mrs Pamela Jane Harker died on 31 December 1932. They are buried with their son in Southgate Cemetery, Hornsea.

On 21 February 1916 the Battle of Verdun opened as the Germans tried to break the French Line. It would not finish until 18 December and would cost the French 976,000 casualties.

Recruiting drives were a common occurrence at this time as the authorities demanded more and more men to make up for the losses taken in 1915. Tribunals were set up to gather in more men and those in protected occupations now found themselves liable for the call-up. Most of Kitchener's New Army Divisions were now abroad and it would not be long before they would begin moving to France to take part in the major event of 1916, the Battle of the Somme. But this was in the future and the citizens of Hornsea hoped that the New Year would bring better results than the old one had. The local papers relentlessly harangued the young men of the East Riding with regard to enlistment and numerous jingoistic poems appeared within their pages, telling men their fate on Judgement Day if they did not volunteer:

> And some who died in cause of right had sinned the Angel then. Their sins erased he wrote instead they died for other men. He saw his soul a craven thing marked with the brand of shame. His name was called, the Angel wrote: This is a coward's name.

Soon men would be compelled to join the forces and the papers were not slow in pointing out that this was the last chance to do the honourable thing and volunteer before the implementation of the Military Service Bill. Every day the casualty lists seemed to be getting bigger as the unreported deaths from 1915 were published, with many more maimed and wounded.

Private 10/1028 Edgar Hyde of the 10th Battalion East Yorkshire Regiment, Hull Commercials, was killed in action on 17 April 1916, aged 25 years. His grandmother, Mary Jane Fulston, died in Hornsea on 1 May 1924, she is buried in Southgate Cemetery, Hornsea, and Edgar is commemorated on her headstone.

Thomas Arksey was born in Hornsea in 1874 and lived at The Market Place, Hornsea, with his wife Emily Arksey, nee Jackson, and five children. They married in Hornsea in 1899. Thomas was a Boot and Shoe Maker and Retailer by trade. He joined up in 1916 into the Royal Engineers as Sapper 58689 and survived the war. He was the son of Thomas John and Mary Arksey, nee Robinson, of Hornsea. They married in Hornsea in 1866 and had six children. Thomas Arksey

Private Thomas Arksey.

Lightly wounded soldiers at the VAD Hospital, Cliff Top, Hornsea.
They are wearing the light blue uniforms issued to wounded men.

unveiled the memorial windows in the Primitive Methodist Chapel in 1921 and died in Riding, Northumberland in 1957.

Mr Thomas John Arksey died on 25 July 1902. Mrs Mary Arksey died on 25 November 1921. They are buried in Southgate Cemetery, Hornsea.

April 1916 saw a major influx of troops into Hornsea, three battalions of Northumberland Fusiliers and one battalion of the Durham Light Infantry were billeted in the town and surrounding areas.

With so many troops in Hornsea and a preponderance of females, romance was in the air, and many men found their future wives here. But not all men had honourable intentions as Margaret Elizabeth Strickland Constable remembers:

> A young woman called at the hospital and asked to see her fiancé, private so and so. We assured her he was a married man with children, but she insisted on seeing him. Presumably he admitted the facts for she came away in tears saying 'this is the third time I've been done in.

Oscar Blanchard was the son of John William and Elizabeth Blanchard of 3 Ocean Terrace, Hornsea. In 1914 he was living in London and working as a police constable in Y Division. He enlisted at St Pancras into the 2nd Battalion Gordon Highlanders and went to France on 10 October 1915. In May 1916 he received shrapnel wounds to the head and died on 13 May, aged 22 years.

A young Bugler in the 21st Reserve Battalion Durham Light Infantry called Wilfred Boagey was based in Hornsea and was found to be late coming back from leave. In 1915 and 1916 he had often fallen foul of the military authorities and had received numerous punishments for similar minor offences. He eventually turned up and was put under arrest and confined to camp. He had recently lost his mother and his comrades found him to be in a disturbed state of mind, telling them he was sick of life. On 16 May 1916 he sat in his tent and turned his rifle upon himself and was shot fatally through the left breast. A note was found that said 'dear Sir, I am too much of a coward to face my punishment'. His Next of Kin was given as his uncle Mr W E Wilford of 15 Lilly Street, Hartlepool, County Durham. He is buried in Southgate Cemetery, Hornsea.

Captain John Gay of the 30th Battalion Northumberland Fusiliers was in camp at Hornsea and died suddenly after taking a bath on 29 May 1916. He was a long serving officer with an honourable record and was on the retired list when war broke out but volunteered to enlist again and train men for the Front. His funeral was attended by numerous officers and the full strength of his battalion as he was much respected and very popular with the men. The coffin was borne on a gun-carriage covered with the Union Jack to St Nicholas Church where the service was conducted and after this the procession, which was of a considerable length, slow marched to Southgate Cemetery, the firing party with their arms reversed and the band playing the Death March. The population turned out in force to witness this impressive spectacle, after the body was committed to the earth the firing party fired volleys over the open grave and the last post was sounded.

On 31 May 1916 squadrons of the British and German Grand Fleets clashed head to head at Jutland in a bloody naval slogging match, the British Navy lost 14 ships and 6,000 men by the end of the day. People at home had no idea of the violent drama being played out as they went about their daily work. Many East Riding men perished at Jutland and one of them was a long serving seaman from Hornsea. His name was Thomas Herbert Myers and he had served for many years, joining the Navy in 1889.

Thomas was serving on HMS *Defence* at Jutland, she went down with all hands and 904 men were lost on this ship alone. He was the son of James and Ann Myers of Hornsea and the husband of Elizabeth Myers of 14 Marlborough Avenue, Hornsea.

Corporal John Arthur Hall emigrated to Canada before the war and was killed on 2 June 1916, serving with the 4th Canadian Mounted Rifles, aged 21 years. His brother, Lieutenant George Hall, Royal Naval Volunteer Reserve, would be killed on 1 May 1918, serving on HMS *Blackmore Vale*, They were the sons of George Hall, retired master mariner, who died on 21 July 1918 and Sarah Ann Hall who died on 28 January 1939. They are buried in Southgate Cemetery, Hornsea and both their sons are commemorated on the family headstone.

On 17 June 1916 an article appeared in the *Beverley Guardian* entitled: 'Hornsea Man Killed', He was J R Walker who was married with three children and worked at the Earl's Cement factory in Hull before the war. I can find no proof he lived in Hornsea.

In 1911 Charles Edwin Brighouse had emigrated from Hornsea to Canada, he returned home in 1915 to enlist and was killed in action serving with the 21st

Battalion King's Royal Rifle Corps on 22 June 1916 aged 23 years. He was the son of Charles Davidson Brighouse and Sarah Jessie Brighouse of Marine Drive, Hornsea.

For months now thousands of troops had been moving into Northern France in preparation for The Great Push on the Somme as it was known. On 1 July 1916 the good people of Hornsea sat down to their breakfast before going to work, they had no way of knowing the tragedy that was about to be played out on the fields of France. On a bright and sunny morning the soldiers of the British Army stood up and walked in lines towards the enemy, fully expecting there would be no opposition left after the weeks of artillery bombardment, they were mistaken and the Germans hurried out of their dug-outs to set up machine-guns and man the fire-step. The slow pace of the British advance gave them plenty of time to prepare a hot reception for the Tommies, the German troops looked on in amazement as they saw the British stand up and leave the relative protection of their trenches and advance in waves over the open countryside. The British were mown down like corn before the scythe and by the end of the first day 40,000 casualties had been taken. News of the great battle began to appear in the local papers but the casualty figures were not revealed by the censor. The Somme battle rumbled on into November at a terrible cost in lives lost and ruined, soon the casualty lists would be published in the papers and the true cost of this offensive would be obvious to the people at home. The papers generally reported an optimistic view of the Somme Battle:

> Heavy fighting in progress.
> Allies still advancing.
> Germans terrible losses.
> Fighting in the great battle.

Private James Harman of Hornsea, was serving in France with the 7th Battalion East Yorkshire Regiment when he was Killed in Action on 23 June 1916 at the age of 32 years. He was the son of Robinson Harman and Ann Valentine Harman of Hornsea.

Men who had served in the war and had been invalided out of the forces because of injury but had no outward sign they had anything wrong with them, were singled out as slackers and generally given a hard time by families who had men at the Front. Men that looked physically able could find themselves confronted in the street as to why they were not in uniform and white feathers were given to them by self-righteous women, the mark of a coward. Feelings and tempers were running high and house windows would be smashed or individuals became ostracised by their neighbours. The government stepped in and in late July the local papers reported the introduction of a silver wound badge to be worn on the lapel by all men who had served but were no longer fully fit, so saving them from humiliation.

On 5 July 1916 Private Montague William Potter, 32nd Reserve Battalion Northumberland Fusiliers, died in Hornsea and is buried in Southgate Cemetery, Hornsea. He has a civilian grave and not a War Graves headstone.

Captain Thomas Whiting.

Captain Thomas Whiting was born in Hornsea in 1879 and served with 20th Battalion King's Liverpool Regiment. He was killed in action on 30 July 1916 and is commemorated on the Thiepval Memorial to the Missing of the Somme. In the Wills and Probate records his address at the time of his death is given as Mount Street, Liverpool. Though the family are recorded as residing in Hornsea from 1881 to 1901, they must have left well before the war.

Men who were maimed or badly injured rarely featured in the papers, but many must have returned to Hornsea throughout the war and the people of Hornsea would have seen them in their own homes, in relatives' houses or in the streets, giving them a glimpse of the horrors being inflicted in the carnage.

The Collinson family, who had lost their son William Holmes Collinson on 5 January, had a stone memorial seat erected and dedicated to his memory in Eastgate, Hornsea, on 6 August. Mr William Collinson at that time was the Chairman of the Hornsea Rural District Council. The seat is still there to this day and has recently been refurbished.

The death of Thomas Allott was reported in the local papers in late August, aged 25 years, he was serving in the 1/5th Battalion East Yorkshire Regiment and had been wounded in the Somme battle, dying of his wounds in the South African General Hospital on 26 August. He was the son of John Charles and Mary Jane Allott.

Private George Christopher West of 3 East View, Hornsea, was killed in action on 16 September 1916, aged 20 years, serving with the 21st King's Royal Rifle Corps. He was the son of Frederick Augustus and Mary Rachel West of Back Southgate, Hornsea, later of Bridlington.

On 20 September George and Isabella Dunn of Headland View, Hornsea, were going about their daily business when the postman knocked on the door, as Mrs Dunn opened the door he gave her the dreaded black bordered telegram that all families hoped would never come to them. It informed them of the death of their son George Herbert, he had been killed in action serving with the 1st Battalion Coldstream Guards on 16 September during the battle of Flers/Courcelette, the Somme, aged 26 years. His body was never recovered from the battle-field.

In September 1916 a silent film, with piano accompaniment, was showing at the Marble Arch Picture Palace, Beverley, it was entitled The Battle of the Somme and would shock all who saw it. In the audience were people from Hornsea who were desperate to see exactly what the conditions the troops in France fought under was like, others had lost loved ones or friends. It showed scenes of happy and smiling Tommies gazing in wonder into the cameras, others waved to the camera as they marched to the slaughter in the hope that they would be seen by their relatives and wives at home, letting them know they were still safe and well. In the film tanks lumbered across the battle field, guns thundered and roared as they sent giant shells into the German Line. One scene was staged for the cameras but was believed to be real at the time, it showed a young officer leading his men over the top and one soldier is hit and falls back into the trench. Next Tommies are seen crossing a barbed wire entanglement, one is hit and falls into the wire as his comrades disappear into the smoke. To the generation that watched and was only just getting used to the new cinemas, these were upsetting scenes, never before had British troops been seen to fall in battle. The effect on the audience was traumatic, many wept in the darkened room while others looked on in stunned silence. The film drew large audiences in 1916.

In late September 1916 the magistrates at Leven found themselves busy as people, both civilian and military, were brought before them charged with stealing army stores. Most cases were minor but John Henry Jarman, a civilian canteen manager employed by the military in Hornsea, was sentenced to four months hard labour in prison. He had been found guilty of stealing 68 pounds of bacon, 23 pounds of tea, large amounts of sugar and items of clothing. The stolen items were found in his home in Scunthorpe. The most heavily punished Hornsea man was Amos Fortis, a gas stoker, the authorities found large amounts of bacon, tea and army blankets at his house in Marlborough Avenue, Hornsea.

Private Percy Seddon served with the 10th Battalion King's Own Yorkshire Light Infantry and was killed on 25 September 1916. He was the son of Susan Elizabeth Seddon who died on 23 April 1946 and Walter Seddon who died on 20 November 1952. They are buried together in Southgate Cemetery, Hornsea.

The bad news continued to arrive regularly in Hornsea, 2nd Lieutenant Walter Harold Griffiths of Hornsea was killed serving with the Royal West Kent Regiment on 30 September 1916, aged 20 years. He was the son of Walter Gould Griffiths and Olive Hicks Griffiths of Berkley House, Burton Road, Hornsea.

The local papers featured ever growing lists of the Fallen and wounded, families feared looking in the papers in case they should see a familiar name listed as a casualty. The glib headlines gave no hint of the scale and ferocity of the Battle of the Somme and the increasing sacrifices being made. Most papers reported glorious advances made by the British and huge German reversals. However, in every village, town and city in Britain the casualty lists became longer and more frequent and could not be ignored by an increasingly traumatised public.

Company Sergeant Major William Reynolds Parker, of the Yorkshire Regiment worked at his father's grocery business in Hornsea before the war, he was born in Hornsea in 1896 and enlisted in Hull on 1 September 1914. In the Battle of the Somme at Contalmaison on 10 July 1916 his unit was mauled badly, his company officer was killed and two junior officers wounded. Parker took charge and led the assault to a successful conclusion showing great bravery amid a perfect storm of lead and steel. For this act of selflessness he was awarded the Distinguished Conduct Medal, because of his obvious

Company Sergeant Major William Reynolds Parker. DCM.

leadership qualities he was commissioned into the 8th Battalion Yorkshire Regiment on 17 December 1916 and survived the war.

He married Bertha Anderson in Leeds on 22 March 1934 and had a son: Denis, and was the son of William, grocer and baker, and Sarah Ann Parker of Hazelholme, 7 Cliff Road, Hornsea. William Reynolds Parker died on 13 October 1938. Mr William Parker died in Hornsea on 12 May 1948 and Mrs Sarah Ann Parker died in Hornsea on 13 May 1952. They are all buried together in Southgate Cemetery, Hornsea.

Private Eric Parker.

Private Eric Parker was born in Hornsea in 1900 and was the brother of William Reynolds Parker. He joined the East Yorkshire Regiment in 1918, survived the war and married Florence Emma Parker. They resided at 34 Burton Road, Hornsea. Eric died in Hornsea on 4 May 1956. Florence Emma died in Hornsea on 20 January 1989. They now lie together in Southgate Cemetery, Hornsea.

Arthur Stanton Lyon was educated at Hymer's College, Hull, and worked for 17 years as a bank clerk at the Birmingham Branch of the National Provincial Bank. He was the son of Charles Edward Augustus and Betsy Milicah Rafton Lyon of Victoria Avenue, Hornsea. In 1915 he enlisted into a Pals Bankers Battalion, 26th Royal Fusiliers, which was made up of clerks and accountants. The 26th Battalion Royal Fusiliers took part in the Battle of the Ancre Heights and he was killed in action between the 4 and 10 October 1916, aged 34 years. His body was never found and Arthur is commemorated on the Thiepval Memorial to the Missing of the Somme, France. Mrs Betsy M R Lyon died on 11 September 1917. Mr Charles E A Lyon died on 5 September 1931. They are buried in Southgate Cemetery, Hornsea.

In mid-October 1916 Thomas Barr was recorded in the casualty lists as having been killed in action on 26 August 1916 serving with the 6th Battalion East Kent Regiment, aged 31 years. He was the son of William Kemplay Barr and Sarah Barr of Eastgate Hornsea. His body was never recovered from the battle-field and he is commemorated on the Thiepval Memorial to the Missing of the Somme, France. Mrs Sarah Barr died on 9 February 1912. Mr William K Barr died on 12 April 1917. They are buried in Southgate Cemetery, Hornsea.

Private Philip Stuart Whipp was born in Hornsea in 1896 and was the son of Albert Edward and Emily Marion Whipp. In 1881 they were living at Etton, moving to Hornsea by 1891. In the late 1890s they moved to Croydon, London. Philip was a clerk before the war and enlisted in Essex on 28 April 1916 into the Hertfordshire Regiment. He was transferred to the 1/5th West Riding Regiment on 10 September 1916 and was killed serving with them on 13 October that year.

The *Hull Times* reported the wounding of Private Peter Allen Dunn, Yorkshire Regiment, on 21 October 1916. He was a regular soldier before the war and had served for 15 years. Peter was wounded on 12 July 1916 on the Somme, a picture of him was featured in *Green's Almanac* in 1916. He was born in Hornsea and was the son of George and Isabella Dunn of 6 Headland View, Hornsea. His Brother, George

Three unnamed Hornsea nurses.

Herbert Dunn, had been killed on 16 September 1916. Peter Allen survived the war and died in Hornsea on 15 February 1950.

Lieutenant Henry Douglas Jackson, MC, of Hornsea, had served with the 1/4th Battalion East Yorkshire Regiment in 1916 and was killed in action on the Somme on 26 October that year, aged 22 years. He was the son of Henry Ollershaw Jackson and Bertha Amelia Jackson of 4 Clifford Street, Hornsea.

2nd Lieutenant Ralph Noel Heathcote served with the 12th Battalion East Yorkshire Regiment, 3rd Hull Pals, and was in action with them as they attacked the village of Serre on the Somme on 13 November 1916. He was badly wounded and was taken to hospital but died on the operating table on 17 November. He was the son of Ralph George and Emily Victoria Julia Heathcote of Manchester. Ralph Noel married Eva Mary Reynolds at St Nicholas Church, Hornsea, on 18 December 1915, they resided in Manchester. Eva Mary was the daughter of Robert, Principal of St Bede's School, Hornsea, and Eva Agnes Reynolds of Hornsea. The Reynolds family would lose their son Roland at sea in 1919 during the Russian War of Intervention, he is recorded on the Hornsea War Memorial.

George Brown worked as a wagoner before the war at Nunkeeling, Seaton. He joined up into the 9th Battalion King's Own Yorkshire Light Infantry, was wounded on the Somme and sent to Leith Hospital, Edinburgh. George died of his wounds on 29 November 1916, aged 26 years and was buried in Edinburgh Cemetery, Leith. He was the son of Christopher and Isabella Brown of Bewholme near Hornsea.

As 1916 drew to a close the newspapers, under scrutiny from the censor, gave no clue as to the realities of the military situation in France and painted an optimistic picture of the various stages of the Battle of the Somme, the aim of which it was claimed was to relieve the pressure on the hard pressed French at Verdun and to break out and defeat the German Army in the field bringing the war to a hasty conclusion. By the end of the year it was obvious that the German Army had not been defeated.

The sight of wounded and maimed men arriving in Hornsea and the ever growing casualty lists were having a disastrous effect on civilian morale, by the end of 1916 28 Hornsea men had been killed with at least three times that number maimed or wounded. No-one who lived through those times ever forgot the terrible casualty lists. By the end of the Battle of the Somme the British Army had suffered 420,000 casualties, this toll was never revealed to the population at the time as the authorities feared a backlash against the war and a total breakdown of civilian morale. The people of Hornsea looked to the future and it was hoped a final and successful conclusion to the war, they had no idea of what lay in store for them and the country. The civilian populace were being affected in numerous ways, the burden of high taxation, air raids, lighting restrictions, shortages of food and materials, the movement of women out of the home and into the factories and fields and the continuing and ever growing casualty lists. The mood was bleak and the people were just beginning to realise the magnitude of the struggle that they and the nation were involved in.

4

1917: A Nation in Mourning

The New Year brought with it casualty lists containing men who had been killed in 1916 but not yet reported.

Troops continued to be billeted in and around Hornsea, many of them were men who had been wounded in action and were being re-trained for other units. Many fell in love during their time in Hornsea and married before they went back to the Front. One such young man was Sergeant Jack Galloway of the 26th Reserve Battalion Northumberland Fusiliers, Tyneside Irish, he had transferred to the Machine-Gun Corps and was living in a barn to the rear of what is now the Hornsea Museum on Newbigin. He met a young woman from Hull while he was at Hornsea, Elizabeth Ellen, they married on 8 September 1917, Jack survived the war and died in Hull in 1974, Elizabeth Ellen died in Hull in 1970. They are both buried in Hull Eastern Cemetery.

Sergeant Jack Galloway.

Private William Walker of the 21st Reserve Battalion Durham Light Infantry enlisted in County Durham in July 1915 and was sent to Catterick Camp. His battalion was moved to Hornsea in April 1916 and re-designated 87th Training Reserve Battalion. He later went to the Front but survived the war.

Fund raising for comforts for the men at the Front was a continuous activity in Hornsea, this could be anything from cigarettes, knitted items and food. On 20 January 1917 a letter appeared in the *Beverley Guardian* from a group of Hornsea men serving in Egypt thanking the good people of Hornsea for their kindness, it was sent to the Vicar of St Nicholas Church:

Private William Walker.

> I beg to thank you and those friends who have so thoughtfully sent the Christmas parcels. The contents are very acceptable out here in the desert and it is nice to think we are not

forgotten though so far from the old place. We are at present in a pretty camp situated in a grove of palm trees. The other Hornsea lads and myself are in the best of health. I wish the war was over and that we were back in dear old Blighty, with best wishes to all Hornsea friends.

Private James Smith Usher.

James Smith Usher was born in Hornsea in 1898 and in 1901, he and his mother, Teresa, were living with his grandparents, George and Betsy Usher, nee Smith, at Beach Villa, New Road, Hornsea. Their other son Francis also lived with them and they all ran a Café on the beach end of New Road. Betsy Usher died on 3 May 1906 and in 1911 the family were living at the same address. James served with the Sherwood Foresters and survived the war. He married Lillian Violet Hogg in Brigg, Lincs, in 1924 and died in Hull on 31 January 1933. His grandparents and his mother are buried in Southgate Cemetery, Hornsea.

Spare Hand Albert Henry Norton was born in Hornsea on 29 June 1893 and served on the Trawler Shakespeare from Hull. He married Ellen O'Connell in Hull in 1914 and was the son of Ralph and Jennie O'Connell of Hull. The Shakespeare was torpedoed off Whitby on 2 February 1917, Albert Henry was killed in the explosion.

The Hornsea tribunals, in connection with conscription, were kept busy weeding out fit men for the Front who had been called up but thought they should not have to go for various reasons, the decisions of the Hornsea tribunals could be challenged at the Hull tribunals and many Hornsea men appeared before them in April 1917. Names were not given in the papers, the manager of the Hornsea branch of Jackson's the Grocers, aged 38, appealed against the decision of the Hornsea tribunal. He was refused exemption in Hull and was told to join up. His employer was not happy at this decision but the head of the Hull tribunal said:

> It is a serious thing but that is the unpleasant part of our duty, if these men are to be in the army they must get in it now or the war will drag on.

Claude Stanley Fullam, was serving as an Apprentice at the age of 17 years in the Merchant Navy aboard the Collier SS *Okement* in February 1917. His ship was torpedoed on 17 February and sunk by the U-64 140 nautical miles from Malta with the loss of 11 crew members. His body was lost to the sea and he is commemorated on the Tower Hill Memorial, London. Claude was the son of Alfred and Mary Ann Fullam of The Elms, Chambers Lane, Hornsea.

The unrestricted submarine warfare that was now raging was beginning to have a serious effect on the civilian population, food stuffs and materials were in ever shorter supply. The outward sign of this was the ever present queues outside of shops. People were encouraged to save bones, tins and waste paper for re-cycling. Exhibitions were given in the town for housewives about the production of economic meals and how to ration their family's weekly food intake. This situation would only get worse as the war dragged on and a committee would be appointed in Hornsea, the Local Food Control Committee, to prevent shortages as far as possible and to prevent profiteering by the unscrupulous.

William Shaw was born in Hull on 8 September 1899 and was the son of William Crossland Shaw and Emma Harding Shaw of Back Westgate, Hornsea. William Crossland Shaw was a Publican in Hull in 1891 and 1901, by 1911 he had moved the family to Hornsea and worked as a Painter and Decorator. William Shaw joined the Royal Naval Reserve in 1917 as Able Seaman number Z/11865 and served until the end of the war.

Mrs Emma H Shaw died on 21 August 1943. Mr William C Shaw died on 30 September 1961. They are buried together in Southgate, Cemetery, Hornsea.

On 9 April 1917 the great and bloody Battle of Arras opened with the Canadians successfully storming Vimy Ridge, it lasted until 24 May and cost the British forces 158,000 thousand casualties. Though it was to be of shorter duration than the Somme Battle the daily loss of life was to be much greater in this vicious killing ground. The news of casualties soon began to filter through to the populace.

John Frederick Wilson Lord of Hornsea had been a volunteer in the East Riding Yeomanry before war broke out, in September 1916 he was commissioned as a 2nd lieutenant in the 1/5th Battalion King's Own Yorkshire Light Infantry and was killed in action serving with that unit on 9 April 1917, aged 34 years. He was the son of Mr Frederick Lord who died on 12 September 1937, and Mrs Jane Lord who died on 30 June 1932, of Belvedere, the Esplanade, Hornsea. They are buried together in Southgate Cemetery, Hornsea. Their son, John Frederick Wilson Lord, is commemorated on the family headstone.

John Bertram Bradforth worked as a clerk at Hornsea Bridge Railway Station, North Eastern Railways, before the war and was the husband of Evelyn Boyston Bradforth. They lived at Back Westgate, Hornsea and had two children, a boy and a girl, the boy died the same year he was born in 1916. John Bertram enlisted at Hull in 1915 into the 8th Battalion East Yorkshire Regiment, his unit was involved in the 1st Battle of the Scarpe, Arras, which started on 9 April and he was wounded on the first day of this action which lasted until 14 April. He died of his wounds on 9 April aged 32 years. He was the son of George and Margaret Bradforth of Masham, Yorkshire.

In the Battle of Arras the Hull 92nd Brigade, or Hull Pals, found them-selves in action at a little village called Oppy. It was their task to take the wood and the ruins of the village. Many Hornsea men had enlisted in the Hull Pals in the early months of the war, this was thought to be an elite local unit and men took pride in being amongst its ranks. Private George Ernest Binning of Hornsea took part in the Oppy Battle on 3 May 1917 and was wounded in the melee. He was in the 12th Battalion East Yorkshire Regiment, 3rd Hull Pals, and died of his wounds on 5 May aged 25 years. He was the son of Mr George Binning who died on 8 October 1942, and Mrs Esther

Ellen Binning who died on 3 April 1945, of 37 Southgate, Hornsea. They are buried together in Southgate Cemetery, Hornsea.

The memorial at Oppy, France, dedicated to the men of Kingston upon Hull and local units who gave their lives in the Great War. In grateful remembrance from the French people, completed in 1927.

Thomas Edward Anderson was born in Hornsea on 5 December 1892 and joined the Coldstream Guards in September 1914, going to France with them in January 1915. He was later commissioned into the 10th Battalion East Yorkshire Regiment, 1st Hull Pals. In May 1917 his parents, Harriet and Thomas Barker Anderson, received a telegram from him from a hospital in England as he recovered from severe wounds to his left shoulder and right hand. He was invalided out of the army, survived the war and married Kathleen Anderson. They lived at 11 Hull Road, Hornsea. He died in Hornsea on 5 January 1956 and Kathleen died in Hornsea on 3 December 1964, they lie together in Southgate Cemetery, Hornsea. Mr Thomas Barker Anderson died on 24 July 1926. Mrs Harriet Anderson died on 13 October 1943. They also are buried in Southgate Cemetery, Hornsea.

On 30 May a YMCA hut was opened opposite the Wesleyan Methodist Chapel, Newbegin, the money for this building was raised by Pudsey town, West Yorkshire, and the Mayor of Pudsey presided over the opening. The hut could hold 400 people and was designed to provide recreational facilities for troops stationed in Hornsea.

Charles Waudby Stephenson of Hornsea worked as a Draper before the war and joined up in the Royal Artillery in 1915. At Arras in May 1917 his unit was part of the Royal Naval Division when he was wounded in action on 4 May, he was evacuated to Etaples Military Hospital where he died of his wounds on 6 May aged 20 years. He was the son of Joseph Samuel Stephenson who died on 3 January 1937 and Ada Rachel Stephenson who died on 12 July 1913, of 1 Rise Terrace, Hornsea. They are buried in Southgate Cemetery, Hornsea, and their son, Charles Waudby Stephenson, is commemorated on the headstone.

Harold Willows Jackson of Hornsea joined up at the Hull City Hall in 1914 into the 1st Hull Pals, Hull Commercials, later to be the 10th Battalion East Yorkshire Regiment, as a ranker. He was given a commission in March 1915 and transferred to the 1/4th Battalion East Yorkshire Regiment. Harold was wounded in the Battle of Arras in 1917 and died of his wounds on 14 May that year, aged 20 years.

He was the son of John Henry Jackson who was born on 3 November 1856 and died on 16 January 1911 and Caroline Maud Jackson who was born on 23 October 1863 and died on 3 January 1936, of 12 Grosvenor Terrace, Hornsea. They are buried in Southgate Cemetery, Hornsea, and their son, Harold Willows Jackson, is commemorated on the headstone.

In the local papers letters were being published from troops in numerous postings throughout the world, they wrote home to their families and told them as much as they dared as all mail was censored before it reached home. Lieutenant Arthur John Lonsdale of Hornsea sent home news of his present situation in warmer climes:

> Our camp is nothing but a dust heap, without exaggeration in some places we are over our boot tops in it and of course we have to sleep on it. We eat dust, breath dust and are clothed in it amid the heat. It is winter out here so what must it be like in the summer, I dare not think. I don't know if I asked you to send me socks but please do. I washed mine last night, they were hanging outside the tent all day drying and tonight when I went to fetch them they had gone, Interval for five minutes while I fetch a broom to sweep away my tears. Our nights rest is somewhat disturbed by mosquitoes, the little beggars. You can hear them buzzing around all night and in the morning you see the results of their nights work.

The men of the Royal Naval Air Service were kept busy on Hornsea Mere working on the sea-planes and making sure they were kept in running order. When not working in the workshops they would often be required to perform guard duty around the Mere, the station and roadway. The blackout made it quite a frightening experience. One compensation was that they could collect duck and other wildfowl eggs for their breakfast in the reeds around the Mere. Quite often a relief guard would turn up at a post but would find no sign of the man he was relieving, who had gone off into the fog with a local girl. A special plan was devised to remedy this problem, a hook was fixed to a tree where the guard's rifle was to be hung, if it was hanging there when the relief turned up they would know he had gone off with a local girl. The RNAS was known locally as the Rather Naughty after Mid-Night Brigade.

Air Mechanic Gladwin Webster Thomas Gelsthorpe, RNAS, was on guard duty one night at the Mere when he heard a splashing and loud rumbling noise in the reeds to the north-east of the Guard Room. He moved toward the noise with his empty rifle and gave the challenge 'halt who goes there'. A small voice replied: It's only me Mr Gelsthorpe, it's George Veaney. He recognised the voice as one of his Sea-Cadets. When asked what he was doing he replied stealing cans of petrol. The Veaney family ran the Victoria Hotel and were the first people in Hornsea to run a taxi service. As petrol was so scarce they resorted to stealing what they needed to keep the taxi service running. Air Mechanic Gelsthorpe helped young George to carry the petrol home and was given a pint of ale before returning to duty.

The local papers carried news of men from the front that had been killed or wounded with many poignant photographs provided by their families. On 2 June the *Beverley Guardian* reported: 'Hornsea soldiers killed and missing'. Charles W Stephenson and Albert Sutherby were reported as killed. George Jordan of the East Yorkshire Regiment was reported missing since 23 April. He was the son of Richard and Jane Jordan of Southgate, Hornsea. Denis Habbershaw of the East Yorkshire Regiment was reported as missing, he also lived in Southgate. Private W Clark of the East Yorkshire Regiment was also reported as missing, his parents lived at Mill Lane, Hornsea. They all later turned up as prisoners of war and survived the war. Many men reported missing would remain in this limbo throughout the war, until their deaths were confirmed in 1918 or 1919. Their families lived in hope for years of the deliverance of their loved ones until their hopes were dashed by a formal telegram from the authorities.

On 7 June Haig's next great offensive started, numerous mines were detonated under Messines Ridge, after which the British forces attacked and took this important high ground. Messines was a great victory, from this ridge the Germans had a clear view of the entire British Line and if any movement was spotted they could direct their artillery fire down on any position at will. The newspapers reported this important event:

Great Battle in Flanders.
Violent explosion heard in England.
Over 5,000 prisoners taken.

This gain was not capitalised on and on 31 July the 3rd Battle of Ypres opened and lasted until 10 November, this battle is known generally as Passchendaele with all its doom laden connotations. The British forces advanced out of the Ypres Salient as a ferocious barrage moved before them, the first German Line fell but it was not long before resistance stiffened and the attack sank into the Flanders mud as the battle dragged on into the winter months. The battle cost the British 250,000 casualties.

In the summer months the East Yorkshire Volunteer Royal Reserve Engineers was formed in Hornsea, it was to be a signal section made up of local men with some experience of engineering and telephone communications. The fact that skilled men were allowed to do their service at home did not go down well with all of the population and a rather sarcastic little ditty appeared in the local papers aimed at the Amalgamated Society of Engineers:

Don't send me in the army George, I'm in the ASE, take all the bloody labourers but for God's sake don't send me. You want me for a soldier George but that can never be, a man of my ability I'm in the ASE.

The scare of invasion from the sea was very real in 1917 and this unit was empowered to take over and defend telephone exchanges should the Germans arrive on our shores. In July 1917 there were fewer holiday makers coming to Hornsea because of war weariness and food shortages but concerts were still being held in the town at the Floral Hall to raise funds for men who had become prisoners of war, these concerts were always well-attended by the people of Hornsea and surrounding areas.

Richard Miller was born in South Africa and lived with his mother, Mrs Sarah Miller and sister, at Lynton Cottage, Burton Road, Hornsea. When war broke out he enlisted at the Hull City Hall into the 1st Hull Pals or Hull Commercials, later to be the 10th Battalion East Yorkshire Regiment, serving with them in Egypt in 1915 and on the Somme in 1916. He was killed in action on 29 June 1917, aged 24 years.

Herbert Edward Simpson of Hornsea worked as a postman before the war and joined up into the Army Service Corps in 1915, in 1917 his unit was attached to 84th Heavy Artillery Group in the Ypres Salient. The German artillery found the position of the 84th and bombarded it for a number of hours on 11 July. Herbert Edward was killed in the barrage on that day, aged 37 years. He was the son of Robert and Jane Elizabeth Simpson and the husband of Annie Simpson of Sandringham House, New Road, Hornsea, they had one child.

Lieutenant Colonel John Ralph Hedley, DSO, MID, of Hornsea, served in the 6th Battalion Northumberland Fusiliers and was awarded the Distinguished Service Order for his bravery on the Somme in 1916. He was the husband of Mrs Ada Marie Walker of Westgate, Hornsea, they had two children. He died of a heart-attack in France on 15 July 1917 aged 46 years.

2nd Lieutenant Frank Kemp served with the 11th Battalion King's Own Yorkshire Light Infantry and in July 1916 was attached to the Machine-Gun Corps. Before the war he worked as an apprentice fitter and was the son of William and Ada Ellen Kemp of Rockleigh, Wilton Road, Hornsea, Frank was killed in action on 22 July aged 24 years. His body was never found and he is commemorated on the Thiepval Memorial to the Missing of the Somme.

> Mr William Kemp died on 20 May 1938. Mrs Ada Ellen Kemp died on 11 September 1945. They are buried in Southgate Cemetery, Hornsea, and their son Frank is commemorated on the headstone.

Among all the grim war news that was being reported there were lots of local interest stories concerning the residents of the East Riding which of course included Hornsea. A young man called Thomas Henry Jackson was a farm servant and was employed at Mr Barnfather's farm on Bewholme Road. One day he was feeding the cows when a bull attacked him, as it tried to gore him its horns became hooked in his trousers and he was tossed into the air like a rag-doll. Other farm workers came to his rescue but not before he had suffered a fractured shoulder and cuts to his face. Thomas Henry Jackson died on 13 June 1937, his wife, Mary Agnes Jackson, died on 13 June 1957. They are buried together in Southgate Cemetery, Hornsea.

Robert Tungate worked as a police constable in Beverley before the war and enlisted in the 4th Battalion Coldstream Guards. He was wounded in action in early August 1917 and died of his wounds on 3 August, aged 26 years, during 3rd Battle of Ypres or Passchendaele. He was the son of Charles and Eliza Tungate of 13 Brickyard Cottages, Hornsea and the husband of Nancy Tungate of Hornsea, they had one child.

On 27 September 1917 Private Conrad Clark Fletcher, 1/4th Battalion East Yorkshire Regiment, died of Sickness at the VAD Hospital on Cliff Road, Hornsea, aged 32 years. He is buried in Southgate Cemetery, Hornsea.

On 30 September Margaret Elizabeth Strickland Constable and her friend Hillary were taking a walk around Hornsea Mere when they noticed something strange at the waters' edge just below the surface:

> I saw a dark object in the lake and I poked it with my umbrella, it was a sea-plane, under water but for the top of one wing. We tried to tow it in with the handle of the umbrella but it was too firmly aground. Further on we saw another sea-plane aground in the reeds on the south-side. There were eight planes in and on the Mere making the water oily. I talked to a pilot the next day in the hospital, he was very much disappointed at having crashed on his very first patrol flight. In October Dr Hawke says that a sixth sea-plane had fallen into the Mere. The Hornsea people say charitably that the men are all so drunk they don't know what they are doing.

Ralph Snowdon of Hornsea worked as the Manager of the Hull Savings Bank before the war and enlisted in Hull in 1914 at the Hull City Hall into the 1st Hull Pals, Hull Commercials, regimental number 10/1070. He served with them in Egypt in 1915 and on the Somme in 1916 until he was gassed. He recovered and was commissioned into the 1/4th Battalion East Yorkshire Regiment in July 1917 and was killed in action serving with them on 2 October 1917, aged 36 years. He was the son of William Snowden who died on 30 December 1913, and Charlotte Snowdon who died on 10 July 1912, of 1 Clifford Terrace, Hornsea. They are buried together in Southgate Cemetery, Hornsea. Their son Ralph is commemorated on the family headstone.

In October a mobile war cinema visited Hornsea, a large screen was fixed to the side of the school house on Mereside and large crowds gathered to watch film of the various war fronts and the fleet at sea.

George William Cooper attested in Hornsea on 6 December 1915 and was sent to France in 1916 with 7th Battalion East Yorkshire Regiment, later being posted to 1st Battalion. His unit was heavily involved in the Battle of Broodseinde, Passchendaele, on 4 October 1917. George William was killed in action that day aged 36 years. He was the son of Benjamin and Phoebe Cooper of Hull and the husband of Mary Jane Cooper of 49 Southgate, Hornsea, they had one son.

Arthur Keith served with the 7th Battalion East Yorkshire Regiment during the war and was killed in action at Passchendaele on 12 October 1917, aged 31 years. He was the son of Michael and Sarah Ann Keith of Ocean Terrace, Southgate, Hornsea. Arthur's brother, Herbert, would be killed in 1918, neither of them are recorded on the Hornsea War Memorial.

Mr Harry Raymond Burrows was a local assistant schoolmaster in Hornsea before he enlisted in the 8th Battalion West Yorkshire Regiment. He was commissioned during the war and was wounded twice at the Front and awarded the Military Cross for bravery. On 19 October 1918 the *Beverley Guardian* listed him under 'The Stricken

Brave' after his second wounding. He was the son of Eleanor and Joseph Thomas Burrows of Weeton, near Leeds. Harry survived the war.

On 12 November troops were receiving arms training in the Drill Hall, Back Southgate, when a round was left in a rifle which duly went off by accident and hit Private Edward Bradley in the arm. He was taken to the VAD Hospital on Cliff Road, where what was left of his badly damaged arm was amputated. Margaret Elizabeth Strickland Constable arrived at the hospital in time to help with the operation:

> Went to Hornsea Hospital and found them about to cut off young Bradley's arm, he is a volunteer and it was shattered by a bullet from a machine-gun during instruction. I stayed to see and helped to hold him down, there was at least a foot of muscle and nerves hanging out, there was no bone left. It took 20 minutes, was glad of tea at Mrs Clifford's afterwards.

Fred Brooks of 30 Southgate, Hornsea, was married to Rose Brooks, they had eight children. He worked as a Plate Layer for the North Eastern Railway before the war. Fred enlisted in 17th Battalion Northumberland Fusiliers and served with them in France and Belgium, he was killed in action on 19 November 1917 aged 36 years. He was the son of John and Emily Brooks of Brantingham, and the husband of Rose Brooks of Hornsea. Rose died on 21 May 1943 and is buried in Southgate Cemetery, Hornsea. Her husband Fred is commemorated on the family headstone.

On 20 November the Battle of Cambrai opened as British troops and cavalry attacked with the support of tanks. Great advances were made as the Germans fell back before this new mechanised warfare. They soon recovered and learnt how to deal with these iron monsters, on 30 November to 4 December the German forces counter-attacked and drove the British from the field, costing them 40,000 casualties by 8 December. The local papers tried to give a gloss to this deep disappointment:

> British consolidate new positions. Village near Cambrai won and lost.

Richard Alma Dry was the son of Annie Elizabeth and James Thomas Dry of Newbegin, Hornsea, before the war he worked as a servant at the Commercial Hotel, Withernsea, and enlisted into 13th Battalion Yorkshire Regiment. This was known as a Bantam Battalion and recruited men of a smaller stature, the army was so desperate for recruits in 1917 that physical and medical requirements for soldiers had been lowered. Richard was the husband of Sarah Ellen Dry, they had one son and lived in Barnsley Street, Hull. It was reported in the local papers that he had died of wounds received in action on 24 November 1917 aged 29 years.

Richard Arthur Grantham worked as a bricklayer before the war and resided at Westgate, Hornsea, with his wife Elizabeth Jane Grantham. He was the son of George and Sarah Ann Grantham of Westgate, Hornsea. Richard joined the 3rd Battalion East Yorkshire Regiment in Beverley on 16 May 1917 and was later posted to the 8th Battalion. He was wounded in November 1917 and died of his wounds on the

Private Arthur Ernest Hobson, MM.

28th of that month, aged 42 years. Mr George Grantham died in Hull in 1901 and Mrs Sarah Ann Grantham died in Bridlington in 1919.

On 21 December 1917 Lieutenant Colonel Frederick Charles Strickland Constable of Wassand Hall tried to take his own life by cutting his throat in a London hotel. At the start of the war he commanded the 3rd Battalion East Yorkshire Regiment. He was a major landowner in Hornsea and owner of the Mere and took a great interest in the town. He obtained a staff appointment in France during the war, but suffering from depression he had been brought back from France and admitted to a London hospital. A few days after the unsuccessful attempt to take his own life he contracted pneumonia and died. He was buried with full military honours at Sigglesthorne.

Arthur Ernest Hobson was born in Hornsea in 1890 and was the son of John and Edith Emma Hobson of 6 Eastgate View, Hornsea. Before the war he worked as a house decorator. He joined the East Yorkshire Regiment early in the war and was wounded and sent home to recover. After his recovery he was posted to the 20th Battalion Northumberland Fusiliers, Tyneside Scottish, and was awarded the Military Medal for bravery in 1917.

His picture was featured in *Green's Almanac* in 1917. Arthur survived the war and returned to Hornsea, marrying Ann Ellen Knaggs in 1927. He died on 18 November 1977, Ann Ellen died on 5 June 1977. They are buried together in Southgate Cemetery, Hornsea. Mr John Hobson died on 18 September 1930. Mrs Edith Emma Hobson died on 16 March 1948. They also are buried in Southgate Cemetery, Hornsea. At the time of Edith Ellen's death her address was 'Dunroamin', Victoria Gardens, Hornsea.

For the population of Hornsea, as for the nation, 1917 was a grim year for many reasons. News of great victories on land or sea was rare, German U-Boats were waging a ruthless war that deprived the civilian population of many commodities. British arms had prospered in only a few peripheral campaigns as the successes at Vimy and Messines were soon put in the shade by the protracted blood baths of Arras and 3rd Ypres or Passchendaele, these disappointments were crowned by the military blunder of Cambrai. The bad news from the Front was compounded by the misery felt by families that still had men in the trenches or had already lost one or more loved ones. By the end of 1917 51 Hornsea men had been killed with many more wounded and maimed.

Lighting restrictions saw many Hornsea residents hauled before the courts, darkened streets were the cause of much genuine concern, in numerous ways simple pleasures disappeared. Race meetings and the football league went into limbo. Coal was rationed and paper was running short. At the end of 1917 the shortages in foodstuffs came with a rush as bread became less palatable as substances not usually found in a loaf were put in to the mix to make it go further. All of this had a detrimental effect on the war weary population of Hornsea, the great offensives of 1917 had brought the end of the war no nearer and every week the casualty lists grew bigger with little to show for the sacrifices. The events in the first half of 1918 would do little to relieve their suffering, as the people of Hornsea looked to the future and it was hoped an end to the killing, they had no idea of the storm that was about to break over their men in France.

5

1918: When will it End?

As the year 1918 opened cold and bleak the people of Hornsea looked to an uncertain future, this terrible war that had taken so many of their young men seemed to be endless and those that had men and women at the Front were ever fearful that soon the postman might bring to them the bad news that everyone dreaded. Men that had been killed in late 1917 began to be reported in the local papers in early 1918. Those who had been prisoners of the Germans and were too badly injured to be a future threat began to arrive home in Hornsea and its surrounding areas, bringing with them stories of starvation rations and poor treatment. The Germans were glad to be rid of them as they could hardly afford to feed themselves. Services of Thanksgiving were held in local churches and many families celebrated the homecoming of one thought lost forever.

On a cold, wet and stormy day in late December 1917 a body was washed ashore on Hornsea beach, it had no papers on it and was in a poor state of preservation and so could not be identified. This unknown man was buried in a pauper's grave in Southgate Cemetery, Hornsea, on 1 January 1918.

In 1917 there had been a great deal of industrial unrest in the country due to shortages of commodities and poor wage levels. The local papers featured letters from soldiers at the Front complaining about the strikers, but many of the serving men knew the poor wages and conditions labouring men had to put up with and knew the same conditions would be waiting for them when they got home. Public meetings were held locally concerning the food situation which was now very urgent. The food distribution system was increasingly unreliable and its delivery sporadic, rural areas like Hornsea suffered worst with shops running out of basic items. Most imported food was now directed towards the centres of population where it was most needed and village stores could find themselves with little or nothing to sell, much of what it did have was beyond the pockets of ordinary folk. Families were going without and young children perished without the diet that would give them the nutrition they needed to survive. The age old traditions of poaching, pilfering and collecting nature's bounty came into their own, in the hedgerows and fields there was an abundance of food. Wild fruit, birds' eggs, mushrooms, vegetables and nuts were among the favourites. Rabbits and birds appeared in many a home, helping to keep the poorest families alive.

Russia was now out of the war and millions of German troops were now free to move to the Western Front in preparation for one last throw of the dice before the Americans could arrive in numbers that would decide the outcome of the war. General Ludendorf marshalled his forces between Arras and St Quentin, the new offensive was to be called Operation Michael. In the early hours of 21 March 1918, as the people of Hornsea went about their daily routines, the storm broke over the Allied Lines, 6,000 German guns opened up on the British firing gas and high explosives, continuing for five hours. 3,000 mortars bombarded the British Line to be followed up by bands of elite storm troops who infiltrated between strong points, the stunned and dazed defenders could see little as the main body of the German army, 76 divisions, attacked frontally. With storm troopers to their rear and massed formations attacking to their front the British had little choice, many surrendered, others fought to the last, but most fled for their lives before the violence of the assault. On that one day the British suffered 17,000 casualties with over 21,000 being taken prisoner. The British fell back seven miles and the stalemate of the trenches was broken, on 21 March 1918 Blitzkrieg was born.

2nd Lieutenant George Stanley Mansfield enlisted as a ranker at the Hull City Hall in 1914, into the 1st Hull, Pals, or Hull Commercials. He was commissioned into the 1/4th Battalion East Yorkshire Regiment in 1917 and went to France with them in December 1917. George Stanley was killed in the Great German Offensive on the 22 March 1918 serving with the 1st Battalion East Yorkshire Regiment, aged 22 years. He was the son of George and Emily Mansfield of 5 Grosvenor Terrace, Hornsea. His body was never found and he is commemorated on the Pozieres Memorial to the Missing of the Somme. Mr George Mansfield died on 7 April 1918. Mrs Emily Mansfield died on 19 March 1928. They are buried together in Southgate Cemetery, Hornsea. Their son George Stanley is commemorated on the family headstone.

The *Beverley Guardian* reported heavy fighting along the whole British Front south of the Somme and north east of Arras, according to the reporter the Germans had very little to show for their efforts and that our line had only slightly been withdrawn east of Arras. By 30 March thousands of our wounded and maimed began to pour into Britain, bringing with them stories that did not quite tally with the newspaper reports.

The Zeppelin raids on Hull continued unabated and the people of Hornsea and its surrounding areas had a grand-stand view of events. Mrs Margaret Elizabeth Strickland Constable of Wassand Hall wrote in her diary on 12 March:

> At 8:30 p.m. Robert and I put on our boots and fur coats and sat on the terrace to await events, almost at once we heard the Zepp droning up the Humber. Presently both Hedon and Hull seemed to be having a terrific bombardment which we watched for half an hour. Then the Zepp came back over Hornsea and the lake was most beautifully lit up by the flashes of the guns, bombs and searchlights. About 10:00 p.m. there was a fresh

tremendous outburst of firing and bombing, some of the bombs falling in Hornsea and making quite an alarming noise. I began to think about fragments of shrapnel and took Robert into the library where we could watch from the windows and brought Hilary down, but she was very much disgusted because nothing more happened. There are a great many complaints in Hornsea today about the barrage fire, which they declare attracted the Zepps. Elsie Bird is said to have picked up a piece of shrapnel in Sigglesthorne but I have not seen it yet.

Bomb damage after a Zeppelin raid, Waller Street, Hull.

On 25 April firing was heard out to sea off the Hornsea coast, the next day there was a glut of drift wood on the beach, the inhabitants of Hornsea quickly gathered up this bonanza for fire-wood. When a ship foundered at Filey the shore from Reighton to Hornsea, was strewn with cases full of butter, it is not recorded if any residents of Hornsea supplemented their diets with this treasure trove but it would be very surprising if they did not. That same day two mines came ashore on Hornsea Beach.

On 6 April 1918 the *Beverley Guardian* reported that Captain Kenneth Philip of Bank Terrace, Hornsea, 1/4th Battalion East Yorkshire Regiment, had been missing since 27 March. He was the son of Robert Harris Philip and Lilly Elizabeth Philip of 447 Beverley Road, Hull. He was born in Hull in 1888 and worked as a Merchant Clerk before the war. His parents had hoped he was still alive and a prisoner of war, but his death was later confirmed as being on 27 March 1918, aged 30 years. The Wills and Probate records confirm his address as Hornsea but he is not recorded on the Hornsea War Memorial.

On 6 April 1918 the next German hammer blow fell on the British Line from around Neuve Chapelle, the Portuguese troops in the area were swept away in the violence of the assault and the British Line was pushed back three miles by mid-day. The British defences crumbled before the victorious Germans and by 7 April 24 miles of the British Front had been engulfed in a crushing storm of shells and men. The situation was now serious and there was a very real chance that this offensive would win the war for the Germans. Haig issued a desperate order of the day:

> There is no other course open to us but to fight it out. every position must be held to the last man. With our backs to the wall and believing in the justice of our cause. Each one of us must fight to the end.

The local papers featured long lists of the dead and wounded and men who had been taken prisoner, under the title of: Local men and the Great Offensive. The battle rolled on into May and the casualty lists grew longer.

Herbert Keith was a wagoner at Catwick before the war and served with 1st Battalion East Yorkshire Regiment. He was the son of Michael and Sarah Ann Keith of Ocean Terrace, Southgate, Hornsea, and was killed in action on 9 April 1918, aged 31 years. His brother Arthur had been killed in 1917, neither of them are recorded on the Hornsea War Memorial.

Private Cyril Pexton Pitchford was killed on 10 April 1918 serving with the 8th Battalion the Border Regiment, aged 21 years. He was the son of The Reverend John Pitchford who died on 9 February 1935 and Ada Fanny Pitchford who died on 5 February 1943. They are buried together in Southgate Cemetery, Hornsea, and their son, Cyril Pexton Pitchford, is commemorated on the family headstone.

Private Geoffrey Nevill Hetherington was a schoolboy before 1917 and was a Sea Scout watching the coast for submarine activity in 1915 and 1916. He was a very keen Sea Scout and won a number of good conduct awards for his enthusiasm. He joined-up on his 18th birthday in Beverley on 28 September 1917, and was sent for training to the Durham Light Infantry. He went to France and was posted to 15th Battalion Durham Light Infantry on 3 April 1918 and was wounded in the chest the same day. He lingered for 18 days before dying of his wounds on 21 April, aged 18 years. Geoffrey was the son of Walter Hudswell Hetherington and Gertrude Annie Margaret Hetherington of 20 Clifford Street, Hornsea.

Ernest Ford lived in Hornsea with his parents, John and Dinah Ford, at Ivy Cottage, Newbegin, Hornsea. John Ford was a sergeant in the East Yorkshire Regiment before retiring in 1908. Ernest was called up in 1917 and posted to the 10th Battalion East Yorkshire, Regiment, or 1st Hull Pals. On the night of 26/27 April he took part in a trench raid on the German Lines at La Becque, he never returned to his own lines and was posted missing believed killed aged 19 years. His body was never found and was lost to the battle field. Mrs Dinah Ford died in March 1951 and is buried in Southgate Cemetery, Hornsea. Mr John Ford died in Beverley in 1962.

Herbert Blanchard worked as the footman to the Earl of Ancaster at Grimthorpe, Lincs, before the war and he enlisted at Paddington, London, in 1915 into the 2/14th

London Scottish. His brother Oscar had been killed in 1916 serving with the Gordon Highlanders. In April 1918 Herbert was mortally wounded and died on 30 April, aged 21 years. Both men were the sons of John William and Elizabeth Blanchard of 3 Ocean Villas, Southgate, Hornsea.

The badly mauled British and French Armies in France were holding the line but they had taken a terrible beating, thousands of men had become casualties or taken prisoner, but their troubles were not over yet. At 1:00 a.m. on 27 May a terrible storm of fire burst upon the British/Franco Front between Reims and Soissons as an overwhelming torrent of German troops swept over the Allied Line. The need for more men at the Front was now urgent as the Germans pushed back the Allied Armies 40 miles, medical requirements for recruits were lowered and 50 year old men now faced the call-up. The tribunals looked again at past cases and men previously given exemption were now forced into the armed forces.

Driver Peter Harold Blanchard was a wagoner before the war and served in the Royal Field Artillery, he was wounded in May 1918 and taken to Casualty Clearing Station 49, where he died of his wounds on 13 May, aged 27 years. He was the son of Jane Blanchard of South Cave.

On 30 May Hornsea saw the formation of 451 Flight of the Royal Naval Air Service on the Mere, the aircraft, Sopwith Baby Floatplanes, would be employed in anti-submarine patrols. Hangars were constructed on Kirkholme Point, floatplanes based in Killingholme had been landing on the Mere since 1915, but this was the first permanent base.

Sopwith float plane on Hornsea Mere.

The 30 May 1918 was an important day for labouring agricultural workers as it saw the formation of the Hornsea Branch of the Agricultural Labourer's Union. The horse lads, who lived on the farms, were not represented by this union as it was primarily for men on weekly or daily contracts with their employers. The open air meeting took place on Mereside and was presided over by Mt T B Anderson of the Hornsea Druids Society. Mr G W Rayson of the Yorkshire Agricultural Wages Committee was a guest speaker appealing for men to join the union, who were at that time negotiating standard wage rates and overtime payments. 23 men put their names forward.

Directions were issued to Hornsea dog owners regarding the use of dog hair, from St John's Ambulance and from the Red Cross, they asked owners to collect it as it was required from certain breeds for spinning, hair from the shorter haired breeds was to be used to stuff pillows. Human hair was not required but hair from Persian Cats was to be kept and used.

John Francis Fridlington worked as an oil mill worker in Stoneferry, Hull, before the war and was the son of William James and Agnes Cordelia Fridlington. The family originated in Hull but by 1911 had moved to Mill Lane, Hornsea, and later to 42 Southgate, Hornsea. John Francis enlisted into the 7th Battalion East Yorkshire Regiment and was killed in action with them on 8 June 1918, aged 35 years.

2nd Lieutenant Hugh Stewart McDowall enrolled as a ships officer for the Ellerman Line of Hull before the war but became ill on his first voyage and was released when he got home. He made a full recovery and enlisted into the Royal Flying Corps in 1917. He trained as a pilot and was stationed in England training other pilots. He died in a flying accident on 28 June 1918, aged 19 years, and was buried in Southgate Cemetery, Hornsea. Hugh was the son of Robert Moffat McDowall who was born on 19 April 1853 and died on 31 May 1940, and Helen Murdock McDowall who was born on 19 January 1869 and died on 31 May 1946, of Victoria Street, Hornsea. They are buried with their son in Southgate Cemetery, Hornsea.

The Influenza epidemic had taken a firm grip by June 1918 and the nursing staff at the Hornsea Hospital were finding it hard to cope with the number of cases being admitted. Margaret Elizabeth Strickland Constable recalls:

> All the nurses at Hornsea have got the flu so I volunteered to help, there were seven cases in my ward and two of them turned to pneumonia. One patient, Mr McLeod, was violently delirious and pulled our veils off. About 12-hours before he died it required two people to hold him down, one nurse was hurt dreadfully, if he got hold of one's hand or hit someone it could result in injury. We were all kept busy about his death-bed until the end. Last night I heard windows shaking and saw searchlights and gun flashes all over Hull. Numbers of star shells went up, two Majors in the hospital suffering from shell-shock hid under their beds. An aeroplane dropped a red star shell then roared over this house, it was a plane from Lincoln and made a bad landing at Atwick, one man was killed.

Lance Corporal Harry Bulson was the son of David and Leith Emma Bulson of 50 Southgate, Hornsea, and worked as a mechanic before the war for W H Johnson's Motor Garage, Hornsea. He married Nora Anderson in Hornsea in 1915 and moved with his new wife to 58 Winchester Road, Armley, Leeds. Harry enlisted in Leeds into the Army Service Corps on 9 December 1915 and went to France on 22 May 1917. While riding a motor-bike as a Dispatch Rider he collided with a lorry and was badly injured and taken to the 2nd Lowland Field Hospital where he died of his wounds on 11 June 1918, aged 26 years.

By June 1918 the German offensive had finally run out of steam and their epic advances stemmed. The ragged Allied Line had only just held but now a new optimism was in the air. On 18 July French and American troops attacked on a front of 27 miles and pushed the Germans back eight miles. This was not a decisive action but it was the first taste of victory after such deep and bitter defeats in 1918. On 8 August the Allies counter attacked and set in motion a course of events that would lead to the end of the Great War. However the Germans where still full of fight and thousands more casualties would be reported in the next four months as the German forces were pushed back to the Fatherland inch by bloody inch.

One name on the Hornsea War Memorial is a curious inclusion, that of Alexander Curtin. His grandfather, Francis Catley Curtin, was born in Hull and emigrated with his family to Australia in 1855. Alexander was born in Australia in 1893 and was the son of Frederick Faulding Curtin and Margaret Curtin of Australia. He was married to Esther Jane Curtin and they had two children and resided in Adelaide, Australia. While serving with the 27th Battalion Australian Infantry Force he was killed in action on 9 August 1918 at the age of 25 years. One of his brothers was killed and the other gassed. In Southgate Cemetery, Hornsea, lie the remains of Richard Curtin who died in 1905, his wife Alberta Mary Curtin who died in 1928 and Mary Walker who died in 1944. Their son Harry, who was lost at sea in 1909, aged 23, is commemorated on the headstone. I assume it was Alberta Mary Curtin who put Alexander's name forward to be included on the war memorial.

Sergeant Walter Cecil Cannell worked as a Furnisher's Assistant before the war and enlisted at the Hull City Hall on 16 November 1914, into the 4th Hull Pals, later to be the 13th Battalion East Yorkshire Regiment. He served with them in Egypt 1915, on the Somme in 1916 and at Arras in 1917. When the 13th Battalion was disbanded in early 1918 he was transferred to the 22nd Battalion Northumberland Fusiliers and then to the 1st Battalion East Yorkshire Regiment. In September 1918 the Germans were in full retreat and the 1st Battalion was ordered to attack Chapel Hill in the early hours of 10 September. The attack was a failure and Walter was killed along with many other good men on 10 September aged 27 years. His body was never recovered from the battle field. He was the son of Robert Holmes Cannell and Eleanor Cannell of 9 Clifford Street, Hornsea.

Thomas William Wiles was a member of the Ancient Order of Druids, Hornsea Perseverance Lodge, and married Mary Elizabeth Beilby in Hornsea in 1901. They had four children and resided at Ocean Terrace, Hornsea. He was the son of William and Sarah Ann Wiles of Village Street, Bewholme, Hornsea. Thomas William was killed in action during the final advance on 18 September 1918, serving with the 6th Battalion Leicester Regiment at the age of 42 years. Mr William Wiles died in Bridlington in 1882. Mrs Sarah Ann Wiles died in Hornsea in 1925. Mary Elizabeth Wiles, wife of Thomas William, never re-married and died in Hornsea on 7 August 1955 and is buried, with three of her children, in Southgate Cemetery, Hornsea.

George Mathew Evans worked as a Chimney Sweep in Hornsea before the war and was the husband of Annie Ellen Evans of Southgate, Hornsea, they had three children. He enlisted into the 7th Battalion East Yorkshire Regiment and at some point was sent home wounded. He returned to his regiment in 1918 and was killed in action during the final advance to victory at the Battle of Amiens on 12 August 1918, aged 32 years. He was the son of George Henry and Lucy Jane Evans of Southgate, Hornsea, they had 12 children.

Thomas Fowler worked as a clerk for a Hull timber firm before the war. He enlisted into the Lincolnshire Yeomanry and was later transferred to the 10th Battalion Essex Regiment. He was killed in action on 2 September 1918 aged 19 years and his body was never found. Thomas was the son of William Fowler who died on 29 April 1929 and Clara Elizabeth Fowler who died on 15 December 1950, of St Nicholas Mount, Hornsea. They are buried in Southgate Cemetery, Hornsea, and their son Thomas is commemorated on the headstone.

On 29 October 1918 Albert Ernest Holmes died in Hutton Cranswick, aged 29 years, and is buried in Southgate Cemetery, Hornsea. He was the husband of Sarah Ann Holmes of Mill Lane, Hornsea. I mention this man because in the cemetery register he is recorded as having been a soldier by occupation. I can find no proof of this and the Commonwealth War Graves Commission does not record him as a war casualty.

Kenneth Loftus was the son of Alfred and Isabella Loftus, both his parents died in Leeds in 1902 and in 1911 Kenneth was living with his aunt, Mary English, at 1 Alexandra Terrace, Railway Street, Hornsea, and worked as an accountant's clerk. He left the shores of England for Canada in 1911 and landed at St John, Brunswick. When war broke out he joined up in a Canadian unit as a private and arrived in France with the Canadian contingent on 22 September 1915. In 1917 he was commissioned as a 2nd lieutenant in the Royal Field Artillery. Kenneth was wounded in the final advance in November 1918 and was sent home to England where he died of his wounds at the Royal Free Hospital, London, on 9 November. He is buried in Brookwood Military Cemetery, Pirbright, Surrey.

Joseph Roland Grummitt emigrated to Canada from Hornsea in 1914 and joined up in Canada as a Private, he was commissioned into the 1/4th Battalion East Yorkshire Regiment in 1916 in France. Joseph caught influenza and died in Colchester Military Hospital on 14 November 1918, aged 24 years. He is buried in Southgate Cemetery, Hornsea. He was the son of Hugh Joseph and Bertha Grummitt of Elim Lodge, Cliff Road, Hornsea. They would lose two sons in the war. Mr Hugh Joseph Grummitt died on 9 March 1919 and is buried in Southgate Cemetery, Hornsea, with his two soldier sons, Joseph Roland and Hugh Cecil [died 1919], both died of influenza. Mrs Bertha Grummitt died in New South Wales, Australia, on 4 July 1942.

In early November 1918 the Great War was still raging as the German army was pushed back, rumours began to spread of an Armistice but for many it was thought to be too good to be true, especially by the men fighting and dying at the Front. But the Great War was fast drawing to a violent and bloody close, on 11 November 1918 the Armistice was signed and the Great War came to an end, if it was not the final peace treaty then at least the killing had stopped. It felt good to be alive on that cold November morning. The newspapers reported no wild celebrations in Hornsea and the good news arrived in the town with a whimper rather than a celebratory roar. A church service for all denominations was held at St Nicholas Church and in the evening a bonfire was lit at Mereside and rockets were let off amid snow showers. Like the men at the Front the people felt a dazed relief but there were no mad celebrations. Margaret Elizabeth Strickland Constable remembers the day well:

> On 11 November 1918 I was sitting writing a letter on the Terrace when I found out the Armistice had been signed. I drove down to Hornsea Post Office to read the telegraph. A band in Newbegin was playing Tipperary and there were a few flags out. The patients at the hospital were having ham and eggs for their tea. Everyone was too much taken by surprise to have made any adequate preparations. Personally I felt terribly sad all Armistice Day thinking it could have all been so terribly different.

Many Hornsea men were still at the Front, some had been listed as missing for quite some time, some of them had been taken prisoner and would later return home. Families that had men listed as missing hoped against hope that their loved ones would soon be back home and struggled to come to terms with the last four years. No one who had lived through the war and had lost a loved one was able to ignore the moments of false hope which were still capable of flaring up. The sound of the postman rattling the letter box, the click of the garden gate latch and the knock on the door, hope flourished in the context where there was no proper proof of death. Annie Spivey lost her husband Arthur in the war, he was posted missing later presumed killed and his body was never found:

> The Armistice was signed and we all breathed a sigh of relief, the slaughter was over at last. The next agonising months of waiting, hoping that Arthur would return with all the other prisoners of war, was he in hospital or had he lost his memory? If we knew he was dead it would have been a mercy, but he was missing, even after such a long period of time those years of waiting and hoping still don't bear thinking about.

For others in Hornsea the end of the war with its banners, flags and pealing bells, meant very little. They would not take part in even the most muted of celebrations but went home and closed their doors to be left alone with their memories of happier days gone by.

In late November a self-appointed War Memorial Committee was formed in Hornsea, they planned to raise money by local subscription for the building of a War Memorial Hospital which would leave a practical and lasting legacy for the town. On 2 December the Hornsea Rural District Council proposed a Roll of Honour be made of all men who served in the war, when it was found that 450 Hornsea men had served it was decided that a roll of the Fallen should be placed in the parish church. On 19 December the Parish Council started to raise money for a peal of bells for St Nicholas Church to act as a war memorial for the Fallen. Other religious denominations made their intentions clear to erect their own memorials.

On 25 November 1918 Private William Henry Mellish, 1/4th Battalion East Yorkshire Regiment, died of pneumonia in the VAD Hospital on Cliff Road, Hornsea. He had served in France and had come home wounded to recuperate. He is buried in Southgate Cemetery, Hornsea.

Lieutenant Arthur John Lonsdale was in Sabatha, India, when the news came, he wrote home to Hornsea:

> At last it has come! *Der Tag* has arrived. What do you think of the turn events have taken, I'm afraid my feelings are very, very hard to express in words. I can't realise that the end has actually come. It seems far too good to be true. My feeling is of supreme happiness. There is one thing makes me feel sad, that those who have lost someone in the war will now feel that loss as they have never felt it before. I wonder how you are all feeling at home.

Leonard Frankish worked in Hornsea as a bricklayer before the war, he was the husband of Helena Frankish of Back Westgate, Hornsea, and they had one child. Leonard was the son of Thomas and Betsy Jane Frankish of Atwick and enlisted in December 1915. He went to France in July 1916, his erratic behaviour brought him to the attention of the medical services and he was admitted to hospital in August 1916 because he was now unable to precisely control his bodily movements. It was thought he was always an unstable character but that his experience at the Front had aggravated the situation. Leonard was sent home to Bethnal Green Hospital, he was discharged from the hospital and the army in September 1916 as being unfit for military service. In 1917 he worked for the Steam Laundry, Cliff Road, Hornsea, but after a while his condition grew worse until he was admitted to the East Riding Asylum in May 1917 as a lunatic/pauper. Leonard died at the asylum on 3 December 1918 and is buried in an unmarked grave in Southgate Cemetery, Hornsea.

Private Arthur Pooley of Hornsea worked at the British Oil and Cake Mills in Stoneferry, Hull, before the war and his job of pressing gun-cotton was classed as a reserved occupation because of its importance to the armed forces. He was the son of Jane Marlow Pooley of 34 Southgate, Hornsea, Jane never married. Arthur married Cecelia Agnes Sutton in St Nickolas Church, Hornsea, on 14 December 1915. They resided at Middleburg Street, Hull, and had one child, a daughter, Cecelia Agnes, who died in childbirth on 7 December 1916. Arthur joined up and was posted to the 1st Battalion East Yorkshire Regiment, later being transferred to the 12th Battalion, 3rd Hull Pals. His unit took part in the Battle of Oppy Wood on 3 May 1917 and he was taken prisoner, spending the rest of the war in a Prisoner of War Camp at Limberg, Germany. He was on his way home by sea on the SS *La Cour* when he caught influenza and died on 31 December 1918, aged 24 years, he was buried in Copenhagen Western Cemetery, Denmark.

For many returning servicemen the reality of being a civilian again did not always match up to expectations, they returned home hoping to pick up the threads of their past lives where they had left off. Many thought they would walk into their old jobs, some of which had been promised to them when they left. Others were lucky and found employment straight away, most found only unemployment and took years to find work. They would be deeply scarred by the long search for a job of any kind. As unemployment began to rise the women who had been recruited into the workplace during the war and refused to give up their jobs came in for criticism.

For men who had been killing Germans at the front for years adjusting to civilian life was difficult, the army had paid, fed and clothed them, now that responsibility was on their shoulders. Young children who were born just before or during the war and did not know their fathers and suddenly found a stranger in the house, they had to tread carefully as the men who returned home were not always the easy going men who had left to fight for their country. Ex-soldiers would have horrendous nightmares as terrible visions they had witnessed returned to haunt them, and many would jump at any loud bang as a door slammed shut or an engine backfired. Others came home wanting only to get back to normality, marry and raise children, they put the war behind them and looked to the future. Relationships were often shaky as men who had been away from home would worry about the fidelity of their wives who they may not have seen for months or years. Men away from home for so long would not always be faithful and many brought home with them sexually transmitted diseases, though this aspect of life was kept quiet at the time.

6

1919 and Beyond: Better Days for Some

By January 1919 most Hornsea men who had been prisoners of war had returned to the town, however no official reception was been held as the men did not arrive together. Later that month the VAD Hospital on Cliff Road was closed and in March 248 Squadron, Royal Naval Air Service, was disbanded at Hornsea Mere. The influenza epidemic was still raging at this time and continued to take a steady toll of the population of Britain. Some men who had served throughout the war came home only to die in this virulent epidemic.

Lieutenant John Francis Gresham of Hornsea served in the 1/4th Battalion East Yorkshire Regiment and died in the Influenza epidemic on 16 February 1919, aged 26 years. He was the son of Frank and Helena Gresham of La Estancia, South Cliff, Bridlington, and is buried in Dieppe Cemetery, France. Frank and Helena lost two other sons in the war.

To mark the closure of the military hospital on Cliff Road an event to celebrate its achievements during the war was held at the Wesleyan Methodist Schoolroom on 21 March. Mrs F S Broderick, the Superintendent, stated that the hospital had treated nearly 5,000 patients during its working life.

Lieutenant Hugh Cecil Grummitt served in the 1/4th Battalion East Yorkshire Regiment with his brother, Joseph Roland, he died of influenza at the Brooklands Military Hospital, Newland, Hull, on 29 March 1919, aged 20 years, and is buried in Southgate Cemetery, Hornsea. His brother died in the influenza epidemic in 1918. They were the sons of Hugh Joseph and Bertha Grummitt of Elim Lodge, Cliff Road, Hornsea.

On 24 April a service was held in St Nicholas Church, Hornsea, in which a memorial window was dedicated to the memory of Lieutenant Colonel John Ralph Hedley, DSO, who had died in 1917.

By late April all troops stationed in and around Hornsea had left their postings and returned home for demobilisation.

Lieutenant William Oscar Montgomery, MC and Bar, 13th Battalion East Yorkshire Regiment, 4th Hull Pals, Hull 92nd Brigade Trench Mortar Battery, 31st Pals Division, was decorated for gallantry in action more than once. His Military

Cross was awarded for the following: He was in charge of a trench mortar section as the Germans advanced and had lost all but three of his men, he re-sited the mortar and crew in a good position and directed a withering fire onto the Germans delaying their advance temporarily. The Germans pushed forward around both flanks and cut them off from their battery and eventually surrounded the mortar team, in the melee two more men were hit leaving only Lieutenant Montgomery and an NCO still standing. The young officer guided them both through the German Lines and back to their own unit.

Lieutenant William Oskar Montgomery, MC and bar.

Lieutenant Montgomery was the son of William Ashton Montgomery and Emily Montgomery, nee Greenham, of Hull, they married in that city in 1878. Mr William Ashton Montgomery died in Hull in 1891.

Henry Hulse was born in Arnold, Notts, in 1844 and married Mary Balding at Holy Trinity Church, Hull, on 18 October 1869. Mary was born in Horncastle, Lincoln, in 1833 and died in Hornsea on 16 April 1891. Henry re-married to Emily Montgomery at Sculcoates Registry Office, Hull, in 1893. He died in Hornsea on 24 October 1925 and is buried with Mary Hulse in Southgate Cemetery, Hornsea. Emily died in Hull in November 1928 and is buried in the Great Western Cemetery, Hull. William Oscar was born in Hull on 16 October 1888 and in 1911 worked as a Stockbroker's Clerk, living at 9 Alexandra Road, Hornsea, with his mother and step-father. On 24 February 1917 he married Maud Marie Watts in the Methodist Chapel, Coltman Street, Hull, and in 1921 they resided at Farago, Wilton Road, Hornsea. He died in Hull Royal on 19 August 1959. Maud Marie Montgomery was born on 5 April 1897, she died in the War Memorial Cottage Hospital, Hornsea, on 29 May 1938. They now lie together in Southgate Cemetery, Hornsea.

Lieutenant Leslie Montgomery Hulse.

Leslie Montgomery Hulse was born in Nottingham in 1896 and was the son of Henry and Emily Hulse [nee Montgomery] and the half-brother of William Oscar Montgomery of 9 Alexander Road, Hornsea.

He joined up into the East Yorkshire Regiment, regimental number 1064, and was commissioned as a 2nd lieutenant into the West Riding Regiment. He landed with them in France on 14 January 1917 and survived the war. He married Ida Watson Harrison in Hull in September 1923, served in the Observer Corps in the Second World War and died in the East Riding in 1967.

Sergeant Geoffrey Bowen joined up at the Hull City Hall in 1914 into the 2nd Hull Pals, later to be the 11th Battalion East Yorkshire Regiment. He served with them in Egypt in

1915, on the Somme in 1916, at Arras in 1917 and in the German offensive in 1918 through to the advance to final victory. When the 11th Battalion was disbanded he decided to remain in the army and was transferred to the 6th Battalion Royal Dublin Fusiliers as part of the Army of Occupation in 1919. He was laid low in the influenza epidemic and died of this illness on 7 May 1919, aged 23 years. He was the son of Joseph and Eleanor Kate Bowen of 2 Park Row, Hornsea, and is buried in Dunkirk Cemetery, France.

Post war improvement schemes and their costs were announced by the Hornsea Council, 30 council houses were to be built at a cost of nearly 17,000 pounds. The Public Rooms were purchased for 3,500 pounds and the Floral Hall was to be enlarged at a cost of 3,000 pounds. The Hall Garths were to be bought for 4,000 pounds and turned into a public park for the recreation of the people of Hornsea and its visitors.

A public meeting was held in the school at Mereside on 21 February 1919 to discuss the present progress of the funds being raised for the War Memorial Cottage Hospital. Members of the audience voiced feelings of discontent that certain individuals had taken it upon themselves to decide the nature of the war memorial without consulting the majority of the people of Hornsea. Mr Hollis, the Chairman, apologised and stated there was no intention of offending anyone but sufficient money for the construction of the hospital had been promised and that there was no need for any further meetings of the War Memorial Committee.

19 July 1919 was designated Peace Day, Hornsea was decorated with flags and bunting, a detailed programme of events was organised and the people of Hornsea joined enthusiastically into the celebrations. The Central Café provided a free lunch for ex-servicemen, sports of all kinds were organised for adults and children and dances and concerts were given until 8:00 p.m. At 11:00 p.m. a bonfire was lit at Hornsea Burton and many fireworks lit up the night sky. The streets of Hornsea were thronged with people until well after mid-night.

In August 1919 the body of Able Seaman William John Rodgers was washed ashore on Hornsea beach. He had been in the Royal Navy since 1889, had served throughout the war and was 39 years old. William was serving on HMS *Holderness* which was part of a mine clearance flotilla working in the North Sea. His date of death is given as 16 August 1919 as this is the last date his shipmates saw him, he is buried in Southgate Cemetery, Hornsea.

Lieutenant Roland Reynolds of Hornsea served in the Royal Navy and was the son of Robert and Eva Agnes Reynolds of Railway Street, Hornsea. Mr Robert Reynolds was the founder and principal of Brampton School for Boys, Railway Street, Hornsea, and would later take over St Bede's School on Atwick Road, Hornsea. Roland was mentioned in despatches during the Great War on 8 January 1918 for attacking a U-Boat, he was serving on HMS *Cyclamen* at the time. In 1919 he was serving on HM Drifter Catspaw, minesweeper, during the Russian War of Intervention, 1919/20 and was taking part in coastal patrols in the Baltic. Extremely bad weather hit the Catspaw and as she tried to get to Copenhagen harbour the raging seas overwhelmed the vessel and she was lost with all hands on 31 December 1919. Roland was 21 years old, his body was washed ashore in Sweden and he was buried in Kvigberg Cemetery, Sweden.

Many men felt a distinct lack of purpose now the war was over, men who had been in positions of power and influence went home to the same hum-drum life they had known before the war, if they were lucky. Lieutenant Norman L Thompson was a friend of Lieutenant Arthur John Lonsdale of Hornsea and wrote to him in 1920:

> Since I've been back I've gone slightly mad in one way or another. I decided to go back to my old job as I couldn't get anything better, and on the whole they haven't treated me badly. In addition I bought a Tailor's business with my gratuity. It's the limit I reckon when Indian Army nobs have to take up tailoring for a living. I had a day in London with Fitton before he went up north, but have not heard from him since. We met Farley and ran across Tug Wilson looking like a lost sheep in the Strand. It hardly seems possible that just over two months ago I was climbing the Heights at Chora, I feel now I have been a business weed all my life, it's a sad end to a military career, but I never expected any more.

Lieutenant Arthur John Lonsdale.

Lieutenant Thompson commented bitterly "I suppose they won't want us till the next war, then we shall be somebody again."

The Peace Celebrations of the summer of 1919 showed a people determined to forget that horrid war and the horrors of the past four years, but beneath the surface the psychological wounds were still wide open under this façade of celebratory optimism. The scars of war were not to be erased in such a short space of time and in the first year of peace there was more national unrest than had been seen in Britain for many years. A way for the populace to remember and honour the sacrifices of the past four years had to be found, so they could feel the deaths had not been in vain, and a profusion of memorial building began across the country. Most people could not afford to travel to foreign lands to visit the grave of a loved one, memorials, in churches or public places, gave them a place where they could grieve. Out of this the Great Silence was born, at the 11th hour of the 11th day of the 11th month the nation would stand in silence and remember its Fallen sons and daughters.

This eloquence of silence.

In November 1919 people prepared themselves for the first Armistice Day, ex-soldiers polished their medals and photographs on the mantelpiece and sideboard of a lost loved one were taken down and dusted, invoking once again old memories and heightening the pain of loss. People who would be spending the two minutes silence in their church or chapel ironed their Sunday best and shined their boots. On Armistice Day 11 November 1919 the first two minutes silence was observed nationwide, at 10:58 a.m. the church bells of Hornsea rang out in a clear clarion call that was understood by all, when the bells fell silent at 11:00 a.m. the life of Hornsea and the country ceased, school lessons were suspended, shops and factories stopped work, vehicles and people stopped where they happened to be, men removed their hats and bowed their heads, old soldiers stood to attention as they recalled friends who had never returned. Black clad women wept openly as the memories of lost loved ones rushed upon them and men found it hard to remain unemotional at this most poignant of moments as the two minutes ticked slowly by. For those two minutes time stood still and the dead returned home once again. There was no formal war memorial in Hornsea at this time where people could grieve but it was no less important that the missing men of Hornsea should be remembered and their sacrifice recognised. Others, whose lives had been shattered by their loss, never came to terms with the last four years and chose to stay at home, withdrawing from the world in their grief, sitting in a silent darkened room with their memories and the thought of what might have been.

By 1921 unemployment was biting hard in the East Riding, numerous families found it hard to cope and relief funds were set up to help them. However the poverty was so great and the funds available so few that many people went without food and adequate clothing in the winter months. Some men who came home from the war with injuries or suffering the effects of gas poisoning found only unemployment and hardship, their mental traumas went untreated and being unable to find regular work many took their own lives. Women who had lost their husbands and had no man in employment in the family were in a desperate situation. Their plight touched the hearts of many who tried to help. Mr John Fox, first Labour Mayor of Beverley, wrote:

> We feel sure the public have only to know the great need that exists to elicit a generous response. Grants of groceries and milk have been given to 170 families and 21 pairs of boots to necessitous children. The need is still very great. The sub-committee had to refuse 92 applications, all needy cases, at their last meeting because of a lack of funds.

The treatment of returning soldiers was a sore point which angered many officials, Mr Lockwood Huntley, Head Librarian of Beverley, had the following letter published in the *Beverley Guardian* on 30 July 1921:

> There are many men who stemmed the advancing Bosche at the most critical times of the war, some severely wounded more than once and are now simply starving between periods of casual work, he and his young wife and children. What a reward! Where now is the wave of gratitude that rose to such mighty power in the early days of the war. Yes there is plenty of distress and the Distress Committee are in dire need of funds to carry

out their work. Cases roll in every day, some of them exceptionally hard. Plenty have to be refused, not for lack of sympathy but for lack of funds, there are some actually needing the most basic necessities who fought for England throughout the horrors of this ghastly war, whose praises at one time were in the hearts and minds of the nation at large. [Lockwood Huntley lost a son in the war.]

The local Labour Party was concerned about the growing numbers of unemployed and the distinct lack of any fair relief they were getting. In 1921 some unemployed had been walking the streets for a year looking for work, those that had saved their money had used it to feed and clothe their families and the relief they did get was not enough to keep body and soul together. Men did not want charity, they wanted work. Others were so desperate for work they started selling trinkets from door to door, posing as employees of the Ministry of Labour, to earn a crust. Official warnings were issued to stamp out this activity.

The generation that fought the Great War never found the Land fit for Heroes they were promised and the War to end Wars proved to be nothing of the kind. They headed helter-skelter into the Great Depression and mass unemployment. In the 1930s the rise of the fascist dictators saw aggressive regimes on the march, which led in turn to a second great war even more terrible than the first. The sons of the soldiers

Mr Ted Gray at the Hornsea War Memorial, Remembrance Sunday, 12 November 2017.

of the Great War generation would find themselves having to fight a military regime they thought had been consigned to the dustbin of history long ago.

The last act. 12 November 2017.

The morning of Sunday 12 November 2017 was cold and windy with the promise of rain in the air. Just after 10:00 a.m. Brigitte and I drove from our home in Market Weighton to Hornsea, arriving there before 11:00 a.m. The heavens opened and we promptly drove to the sea front, found a nice café and ordered coffee. Looking out over the sea front we could see people, totally undeterred by the weather, braving the wind and rain. The sky was dark and stormy and the waves were breaking against the shore defences sending plumes of spray high into the air, quite an impressive scene. At 11:30 a.m. we left the warmth of the café in the rain and headed for the car park on New Road near the Memorial Gardens. As we walked up New Road the rain eased off and numerous people could be seen waiting for the coming parade that would march down the road from St Nicholas Church where the service of remembrance had been held. The crowd had grown larger by this time and at 11:45 a.m. the sounds of a military band could be heard in the distance, people lined the road at the entrance to the Memorial Gardens and it was not long before the parade came swinging round the bend to the strains of martial music. They made a fine colourful spectacle and were made up of people of all ages. After a short pause on New Road the parade was dismissed and then entered the Memorial Gardens where each organisation and individual took up their allotted places before the black granite war memorial, each clutching a beautiful wreath of blood red poppies that stood out in sharp contrast against the black granite.

The commemorations began as the gathering stood in reverential silence listening to the words that we all knew so well. At a given point the standard bearers lowered their colourful banners and the two minutes silence began. All stood with heads bowed and I thought of the faces of the Fallen I had been researching and of the mostly forgotten history of that town I had unearthed. The sky was grey again and above us only the plaintive cries of the wheeling seagulls could be heard. At the end of the silence the banners and all heads were raised and wreaths were laid before the memorial as people stepped forward to add their own dedication to the Hornsea war dead of so long ago, a moving and poignant moment.

The Great War generation and their children have now passed into history, taking with them the pain and grief that this war memorial represents to present and future generations. This very recent war memorial, 2008, stands now as a silent witness to momentous events in all its grim splendour in the Memorial Gardens. The men recorded on it came from all walks of life and with their passing a part of the history of this fine little town has died with them. No formal war memorial was erected in Hornsea after the Great War, their war memorial was the Cottage Hospital, a practical and sensible choice, and various memorial plaques in chapels and churches. Each year since 2008 the faithful have gathered in large numbers at this new monument keeping their promise to remember and to honour their fallen sons. In between these times the memorial slumbers silently with only individuals like myself taking an interest as the town in general goes about its daily life. Often I have visited the town over the last two years as my work progressed, many times sitting in the memorial Gardens alone as I felt the ghosts of that time flitting around me. The cemeteries of Hornsea also have memorial inscriptions on family headstones to lost sons and husbands as people tried to keep alive the memory of their loved ones who fell so far from home. Others died at home and are buried with their parents in Hornsea, the pain inflicted on parents that lived longer than their children can only be guessed at. The heartfelt headstone inscriptions give a clue to their grief. For two years I would visit these places searching for families and every visit produced more and more information.

Since the end of the Great War the cycle of renewal and healing has continued and what was once a memory too painful to bear has become just another faraway distant conflict to many. The Hornsea men who died overseas are still buried in the ground they once contested. The cemeteries they lie in have a sad beauty all their own and are meticulously kept by the Commonwealth War Graves Commission. On the 11th hour of the 11th day of the 11th month 1918 the Armistice was signed, as a stillness that was heard around world descended across the front. The numerous Hornsea men that survived and returned home left behind them their comrades buried in mass graves, if they were found at all. Many bore the scars of battle, others were badly maimed and the majority carried with them mental scars that were slow to heal, if they ever did. They came home to a world greatly changed from the one they knew, a world not renewed.

The new war memorial is a fitting tribute to the sacrifices that the Hornsea war dead and service people made and it is to the credit of those people of Hornsea who worked so hard to get funding for its completion. Individuals in Hornsea have worked quietly and tirelessly in the background to keep the memory of that time alive and without their help I could not have succeeded so fully in recording the events depicted in this study. Completing this work and meeting so many Hornsea residents has been my privilege and I hope they approve of the final result.

Barrie Samuel Barnes.

7

Stars in a Dark Night: The Forgotten Dead

Allott. Thomas.
Private 1329. 1/5th Cyclist Battalion East Yorkshire Regiment. Attached to 8th Battalion East Yorkshire Regiment. 8th Brigade, 3rd Division.
Died of Wounds at No 1 South African General Hospital, Abbeville, on 26 August 1916, aged 25 years. Buried in Abbeville Communal Cemetery, France.

Private Thomas Allott.

He was born in Willerby, Nr Hull, in 1891 and was the son of John Charles Allott and Mary Jane Allott, nee Dean, of Howden Dyke, one mile south of Howden. They had two other children: Maud born 1896 and Doris born 1900.

At the time of his son's death John Charles was living at Balkholme, two miles east of Howden.

Thomas was a single- man, he worked as a farm servant and enlisted in Hull on 28 August 1915 at the Hull City Hall. He went to France on 26 July 1916 and received a gun-shot wound to the thigh on 18 August 1916. It turned septic and resulted in his death on 26th. His personal effects were sent to his sister Doris Allott of Westgate, Hornsea, in 1919.

The death of Thomas Allott was reported in the *Hull Daily Mail* on 31 August 1916 and he featured in a Roll of Honour in the *Beverley Guardian* on 2 September 1916.

Southgate Cemetery, Hornsea.

John Charles Allott: Born in 1864 and died in Hornsea in 1926. He is buried in the Pooley plot in Southgate Cemetery, Hornsea.

Mary Jane Allott: Born in Hornsea in 1871 and died in Hull in 1902.

Thomas Allott is commemorated on:
The War Memorial, Memorial Gardens, New Road, Hornsea.
The War Memorial in St Nicholas Church, Hornsea.
The War Memorial, brass plaque, and hand written Roll of Honour in the Wesleyan Methodist Chapel, Hornsea.

The War Memorial in the Old Drill Hall, Back Southgate, Hornsea. Now the Ex-Servicemen's Club.

Corporal John William Andrew.

Andrew. John William.
Corporal 25680. 1st Battalion Machine Gun Corps.
   Killed in Action 20 March 1918, aged 23 years. Buried in Minty Farm Cemetery, Belgium.
   He was killed in the bombardment of the British Lines that preceded Ludendorf's great offensive that began on 21 March 1918.
   John William was born in Sigglesthorne in 1895 and was the son of John Andrew, golf labourer, and Georgina Andrew, nee Myers, of 4 Welbourne Terrace, Back Southgate, Hornsea. They married in Hornsea in 1890 and had eight other children: Mary Elizabeth born in Sigglesthorne in 1889, Annie Elizabeth born in Sigglesthorne in 1890, Edith Mary born in Sigglesthorne in 1892, George Arthur born in Hornsea in 1896, Louisa Alice born in Hornsea in 1898, Lillian born in Hornsea in 1901, Thomas Henry born in Hornsea in 1902 and Doris May born in Hornsea in 1903.
   By 1901 the family was living at 4 Welbourne Terrace, Back Southgate, Hornsea. The make-up of the household at that time was: John Andrew 33, Farm Labourer, Georgina Andrew 33, Mary Elizabeth Andrew 11, Annie Elizabeth Andrew 10, Edith Mary Andrew 8, John William Andrew 6, George Arthur Andrew 4, Louisa Alice Andrew 11 months and Mary Dale Andrew, mother of John, 63.
   Mrs Georgina Andrew died in Hornsea in 1910.
   In 1911 the family resided at the same address. The make-up of the household was: John Andrew 43, Golf Labourer, Annie Elizabeth 20, John William Andrew 16, Golf Labourer, George Arthur Andrew 14, Louisa Alice Andrew12, Lillian Andrew 10, Doris May Andrew 7 and George Bilany Myers 3, nephew.
   John Andrew married again in 1913 to Annie Keith of Hornsea.
   John William joined up in 1914 into the 1st Battalion Royal Munster Fusiliers and served with them in the disastrous Gallipoli Campaign where he was wounded.
   The death of John William by shell-fire was reported in the *Hull Daily Mail* on 5 April 1918 and 16 January 1919.
   He featured in a Local Roll of Honour, with picture, in the *Beverley Guardian* on 13 April 1918.
   His photograph appeared in *Green's Almanac* in 1919.
   In August 1918 Mr John Andrew attended a ceremony to receive an award that had been given to his son posthumously, the French Croix de Guerre, in recognition of his gallant service.

Georgina Andrew: Born in Sigglesthorne in 1868 and died in Hornsea in 1910. John Andrew married for a second time in Hornsea in 1913 to Annie Keith. Annie Keith: Born in Garton on the Wolds on 17 September 1871, she married Marmaduke Medley in Hull in 1888 and had a son, Fred Medley, born in Hull on 3 May 1906. Marmaduke died in Hull in July 1911, Annie died in Hornsea in October 1915 and lost her brother, Fred Keith, in the Great War, he is recorded on the Hornsea War Memorial. Mr John Andrew: Born in Arnold in 1868 and died in Hornsea in 1937.

John William Andrew is commemorated on:
The War Memorial, Memorial Gardens, New Road, Hornsea.
The War Memorial in St Nicholas Church, Hornsea.
The hand written Roll of Honour in the Wesleyan Methodist Chapel, Hornsea.
The War Memorial in the Old Drill Hall, Back Southgate, Hornsea. Now the Ex-Servicemen's Club.

Barr. Thomas.
Private G/8567. 6th Battalion East Kent Regiment. The Buffs. 37th Brigade, 12th Eastern Division.
Killed in Action 7 October 1916, aged 31 years. He has no known grave but is commemorated on the Thiepval Memorial to the Missing of the Somme, France.

Thomas was killed in the Battle of the Ancre Heights, the Somme. The 6th East Kents were in the Line with Gueudecourt to their rear. The 6th Battalion and the 8th and 9th Battalion Royal Fusiliers attacked through a hail of machine-gun fire, their objectives, Rainbow and Bayonet Trenches, were achieved but they never had enough men left to hold these positions and were forced back with great loss of life.

He was born in Hornsea in 1884 and was the son of Sarah Barr, nee Collinson and William Kemplay Barr, joiner, of 1 Eastgate, Hornsea. They married in Bridlington in 1871 and had eight other children: Annie born 1874, later to be Annie Carter, Emma born 1876, later to be Emma Wray, William and Mathew born 1878, Henry born 1880, James born 1881, John born 1883 and died 1887 and Harold born 1889. All the children were born in Hornsea.

In 1891 the family was in residence at 1 Eastgate, Hornsea. The make-up of the household was: William Kemplay 62, Sarah 53, Annie 16, Emma 14, William 13, Henry 11, James 9, Thomas 6 and Harold 2.

Harold Barr served with the Hull Heavy Battery, Royal Artillery, and survived the Great War.

In 1911 Thomas was working as a manufacture's clerk in London and was a lodger at the house of Hannah Mills at 6 and 7 Guilford Street, Russell Square, London. He attested at Shoreham, Sussex, on 9 November 1915 and arrived at the Infantry Base Depot at Etaples on 9 April 1916. On 12 August 1916 he was admitted to hospital with trench foot and re-joined his unit on 11 September 1916. Thomas was reported as missing on 7 October 1916.

His personal effects were sent home to his sister, Lillian Barr, at 1 Eastgate, Hornsea, on 16 February 1918.

The death of Thomas Barr was reported in the *Beverley Guardian* on 11 August 1917.

Southgate Cemetery, Hornsea.

Mr William Kemplay Barr: Born Hornsea in March 1839 and died in Hornsea on 12 April 1917. Mrs Sarah Barr: Born Flamborough in 1847 and died in Hornsea on 9 February 1912. They lie together in Southgate Cemetery, Hornsea.

In the same family plot are: John Barr, died 20 April 1887, aged 4 years and James Barr, died 9 December 1959, aged 78 years. Annie Carter, nee Barr, died on 6 September 1964, aged 89 years. Thomas Barr is commemorated on the family headstone.

In the same cemetery are buried the following:

Henry Barr, brother of Thomas, died on 16 November 1960, aged 80 years. His wife Alice Gertrude Barr who died on 13 February 1828, aged 47 years, and their daughter Ada Margery Hadland who died on 30 November 1983, aged 72 years.

Also:

William Barr, brother of Thomas, who died on 17 November 1952, aged 74 years. His wife Alice Blanche Barr who died on 23 October 1967, aged 91 years, and their daughter Marion Barr who died on 12 May 2001, aged 91 years.

Also:

Harold Barr, brother of Thomas, who died on 1 November 1964, aged 75 years and his wife Doris Barr who died on 19 May 1978, aged 81 years.

Thomas Barr is commemorated on:
The War Memorial, Memorial Gardens, New Road, Hornsea.
The Thiepval Memorial to the Missing of the Somme.
The family headstone, Southgate Cemetery, Hornsea.

Binning. George Ernest.
Private 12/442. 12th Battalion East Yorkshire Regiment. 92nd Hull Brigade. 31st Pals Division.

Died of wounds 5 May 1917, aged 25 years. Buried in Aubigny Communal Cemetery Extension, France.

George Ernest was wounded as the Hull 92nd Brigade attacked Oppy Wood, part of the Battle of Arras, on 3 May 1917, he died of his wounds two days later.

He was born in Atwick in October 1891 and was the son of George Binning, General Carrier, and Esther Ellen Binning, nee Staveley, of Atwick, later of 37 Southgate, Hornsea. They married in Hornsea in 1890 and had one other son: Christopher William born 3 April 1895.

In 1901 and 1911 the family resided at Atwick.

George Ernest was a Joiner/Wheelright by trade and enlisted at the Hull City Hall into the 3rd Hull Pals Battalion of the East Yorkshire Regiment on 19 September 1914. His unit went to Egypt in 1915 and to France in March 1916 to take part in the

Battle of the Somme. On 3 May 1917 the Hull 92nd Brigade moved into the Line opposite Oppy Wood in preparation for the attack as part of the Battle of Arras. In this action George Ernest received gun-shot wounds to the back, arm and buttocks and died of his wounds two days later. His personal effects were sent home to his father on 21 January 1918.

The death of George Ernest Binning was reported in the *Hull Daily Mail* in June 1917.

Southgate Cemetery, Hornsea.

Mr George Binning: Born in Atwick in 1860 and died in Hornsea on 8 October1942. Mrs Esther Ellen Binning: born in North Bewholme in April 1859 and died in Hornsea on 3 April 1945. They lie together in Southgate Cemetery, Hornsea. In the same plot is Mrs Ellen Burgess, daughter of John and Nancy Burgess, they lost two sons in the war, she was born on 29 May 1878 and who died 3 June 1964.

George Ernest Binning is commemorated on:
The War Memorial, Memorial Gardens, New Road, Hornsea.
The War Memorial in St Nicholas Church, Hornsea.
The War Memorial in the Old Drill Hall, Back Southgate, Hornsea. Now the Ex-Servicemen's Club.
The Druids Roll of Honour, 22 Albion Street, Hull.
The Atwick War Memorial.
The Roll of Honour inside Atwick Church.

Blackburn. Francis Henry.
Private 9369. 2nd Battalion East Yorkshire Regiment. 83rd Brigade, 28th Division.

Killed in Action 17 February 1915, aged 20 years. He has no known grave and is commemorated on the Menin Gate Memorial to the Missing, Ypres, Belgium.

In early February 1915 the 2nd Battalion was in the trenches north and south of the Yser Canal, in the heavy shell-fire they had to endure Francis Henry lost his life.

He was born in Hull in January 1895 and was the son of George Francis and Annabella Blackburn, nee Rowan, of Hull, later of Marlborough Avenue, Hornsea. They married in Hull in 1891 and had two other children: Matilda Jane born in Hull in 1892 and George Frederick born in Hull in 1897.

In 1901 the family resided at 61 Peel Street, Hull. The make-up of the house-hold was: George Francis 33 Building Contractor, Annabella 34, Matilda Jane 9, Francis Henry 6 and George Frederick 4.

By 1911 the family had made the move to Marlborough Avenue, Hornsea. George Francis was employed as a Rifle Range Warden. Matilda Jane and George Frederick were still living with their parents. Francis Henry had left home by then.

In 1911 Francis Henry was working as a servant at Rydal Mount, Parsonage Road, Brighouse, West Yorkshire. This was the house of Daniel, United Methodist Minister, and Annie Patterson.

He enlisted in Hull in 1914 and landed in France on 15 January 1915.

Mr George Francis Blackburn: Born at 7 Charlotte Terrace, Beeton Street, Hull, on 25 March 1868 and died in the Poor Law Institution Hospital, Anlaby Road, Hull, on 6 March 1929. Mrs Annabella Blackburn: Born in Hull in 1867 and died in Hull in 1915.

Francis Henry Blackburn is commemorated on:
The War Memorial, Memorial Gardens, New Road, Hornsea.
The War Memorial in St Nicholas Church, Hornsea.
The War Memorial in the Old Drill Hall, Back Southgate, Hornsea. Now the Ex-Servicemen's Club.
The Menin Gate Memorial to the Missing, Belgium.
Blanchard. Peter Harold
Driver 2296/755521. C Battery. 223 Brigade, Royal Field Artillery.

Died of Wounds at 49th Casualty Clearing Station, France, on 13 May 1918, aged 27 years. Buried in St Riquier British Cemetery, France.

He was born in North Cave on 6 October 1891 and was the son of Sarah Jane Blanchard.

In 1901 Peter Harold was living in North Cave with his grandmother, Annie Blanchard, 58, and her son, Robert Blanchard, 24. His grandfather, Peter B Blanchard, died in North Cave in 1899. In 1911 Harold was working as a wagoner on the farm of Thomas and Sarah Jane Davey of Hotham.

He joined the Royal Field Artillery at Hull in 1916, after his death his belongings were sent home to his uncle, John Blanchard.

I can find no record of Sarah Jane Blanchard ever marrying.

North Cave Cemetery.

Peter B Blanchard. Born in North Cave in 1831, died in North Cave on 1 November 1899.

Annie Blanchard. Born in Newbald in 1842, died in North Cave on 18 February 1905.

They now lie together in North Cave Cemetery.

Sarah Jane Blanchard. Born in North Cave in 1873, death unknown.

Peter Harold Blanchard is commemorated on:
The War Memorial, Memorial Gardens, New Road, Hornsea.
The hand written Roll of Honour in the Wesleyan Methodist Chapel, Hornsea.

Private Herbert Blanchard.

Blanchard. Herbert.
Private 512182. 2/14th Battalion. London Scottish Regiment. 179th Brigade, 60th 2/2nd London) Division.
Died of Wounds on 30 April 1918, aged 21 years. Buried in Jerusalem War Cemetery, Israel.

He was born in Hornsea in 1897 and was the son of John William and Elizabeth Blanchard, nee Banks, of 3 Ocean Terrace, Southgate, Hornsea. They had three other children: Oscar born 1894- killed 1916, Tom born 1904 and Hilda born 1905.

Before the war he worked as Second Footman to the Earl of Ancaster at Grimthorpe, Lincs, and enlisted at Paddington, London, in 1915.

In a Local Roll of Honour the *Beverley Guardian* reported the death of Herbert Blanchard with picture. Herbert and his brother Oscar were listed 'In Memoriam' from their mother in the *Beverley Guardian* on 17 May 1919.

Herbert Blanchard is commemorated on:

The War Memorial, Memorial Gardens, New Road, Hornsea.
The hand written Roll of Honour in the Wesleyan Methodist Chapel, Hornsea.
The War Memorial in the Old Drill Hall, Back Southgate, Hornsea. Now the Ex-Servicemen's Club.

Private Oscar Blanchard.

Blanchard. Oscar. Brother of the above.
Private S/10989. 2nd Battalion Gordon Highlanders. 20th Brigade, 7th Division.
Died of Wounds to the head on 13 May 1916, aged 22 years. Buried in La Neuville Communal Cemetery, France.

He was born in Malton in 1894 and was the son of John William and Elizabeth Blanchard, nee Banks, of 3 Ocean Terrace, Southgate, Hornsea. They married in Malton in 1892 and lost two sons in the war but had two other children: Tom Lowson Blanchard born 1904 and Hilda Blanchard born 1905.

By 1901 the family had left Malton and were living at 3 Ocean Terrace, Hornsea. The make-up of the family was: John William 34, Elizabeth 30, Oscar 7 and Herbert 3.

In 1911 Oscar was a Farm Servant on the farm of Mrs Mary Helen Holmes of Bewholme Road, Hornsea. Just before his enlistment in 1914 he was a serving Police Constable in Y Division, London. He enlisted in St Pancras, London, in 1915 and went to France on 10 October 1915.

A photograph of Oscar Blanchard was featured in the *Beverley Guardian* on 20 May 1916 under the title of: 'Hornsea soldier killed', he was also featured 'In Memoriam' in the same publication on 17 May 1917.

His photograph appeared in *Green's Almanac* in 1916 and 1917.

Oscar and his brother Herbert were listed In Memoriam from their mother in the *Beverley Guardian* on 17 May 1919 and 15 May 1920.

Mr John William Blanchard: Born in Malton in 1867 and died in Hornsea in 1932. Mrs Elizabeth Blanchard: Born in Malton in 1871 and died in Hull in 1928.

Oscar Blanchard is commemorated on:
The War Memorial, Memorial Gardens, New Road, Hornsea.
The War Memorial in St Nicholas Church, Hornsea.
The handwritten Roll of Honour in the Wesleyan Methodist Chapel, Hornsea.
The War Memorial in the Old Drill Hall, Back Southgate, Hornsea. Now the Ex-Servicemen's Club.

Private Thomas Boddy.

Boddy. Thomas.
Private 8170. 1st Battalion East Yorkshire Regiment. 18th Brigade, 6th Division.

Killed in Action at La Couronne, Battle of the Aisne, on 13 October 1914, aged 27 years. He has no known grave and is commemorated on the Ploegsteert Memorial to the Missing, Belgium.

He was born in Hull in 1887 and was the son of John Thomas Boddy and Mary Ann Artis Boddy, nee White, of 69 West Parade, Hull. They married in Hull in 1899 and had seven other children: Herbert born 1879, Harold born 1883, Kate born 1885, Albert born 1886, Sam born 1888, Clement born 1891 and Alfred Ernest born 1894.

In 1901 the family was residing in Hull, Mr John Thomas Boddy was a Chronometer Maker to the Wilson Line of steamers.

Thomas joined the army on 13 July 1905 and served at home from 1905 to 1907. He served in India from 1907 until his return home in 1913. He left the army and joined the Special Reserve, making his home at 31 Marlborough Avenue, Hornsea. He was recalled to the colours on 4 August 1914 and left for France on 7 September 1914.

The commander of the section Tom was in wrote:
"My section was sent on point duty about two hundred yards in front of our line so as to prevent surprise. Tom and I were working as a pair in the centre and I split up the others, ten men on each flank. We went along nicely until we came to the village of La Couronne, when we sighted the Germans. These we drove along in front of us

for a distance of half a mile, when we saw the enemy advancing towards us in large numbers and a long shot wounded one of my men. We then took cover behind a house and opened rapid fire to check their advance. I sent two men back immediately for reinforcements, the enemy were within four hundred yards of us so I again sent for reinforcements that never came. I made up my mind to try and get the wounded away with my remaining men and I am sorry to say that it was while Tom and I were firing to cover the rescue party that poor Tom got killed."

His death was reported in the *Hull Daily Mail* on 6 November 1914.

His photograph appeared in *Green's Almanac* in 1916.

Mr John Thomas Boddy: Born in Hull in 1852 and died in Hull in July 1913. Mrs Mary Ann Artis Boddy: Born in Hull in 1853 and died in Hull in 1899.

Thomas Boddy is commemorated on:
The War Memorial, Memorial Gardens, New Road, Hornsea.
The Ploegsteert Memorial to the Missing, Belgium.
Du Ruvigny's Roll of Honour.

Bowen. Geoffrey.
Sergeant 11/542/43981. 11th Battalion East Yorkshire Regiment, 2nd Hull Pals, 92nd Hull Brigade, 31st Pals Division.

In 1918, after the 11th Battalion was disbanded, he was transferred to the 6th Battalion Royal Dublin Fusiliers. 197th Brigade. 66th 2nd East Lancs Division, as part of the Army of Occupation.

He died of influenza on 7 March 1919, aged 23 years, and is buried in Dunkirk Town Cemetery, France.

He was born in Hull in 1896 and was the son of Joseph and Eleanor Kate Bowen of 5 Elm Avenue, Garden Village, Hull. They married in Hunslet, Leeds, in 1895 and had four other children: Eleanor Mary born Hull in 1899. Roland born in Hull in 1901. Ethelwyn Kate born in Hull in 1902 and Josephine born in Hessle, nr Hull, in 1907.

In 1901 the family resided at 146 St George's Road, Hull, and Joseph was employed as a Rope Makers Agent. In 1911 the family resided at 15 Malm Street, Hull, Joseph is not recorded on the census record.

Mr Joseph Bowen: Born in Stockton on Tees in 1869 and died in Barton upon Irwell, Lancs, 1923. Mrs Eleanor Kate Bowen: Born in Hawkshead, Lancs, in 1868 and died in Hornsea on 11 September 1931. At the time of her death her address was 2 Park Row, Hornsea.

Geoffrey Bowen is commemorated on:
The War Memorial, Memorial Gardens, New Road, Hornsea.
The brass memorial plaque in the United Reform Church, Hornsea.
The War Memorial in the Old Drill Hall, Back Southgate, Hornsea. Now the Ex-Servicemen's Club.

Bradforth. John Bertram.
Private 30951. 8th Battalion East Yorkshire Regiment. 8th Brigade, 3rd Division.
    Died of Wounds on 9 April 1917, aged 32 years. Buried in Tilloy British Cemetery, France.

John Bertram was wounded during the first day of the Battle of the Scarpe, Arras, 9–14 April 1917. He died of his wounds the same day.

He was born in Nottingham in 1884 and was the son of George and Margaret Bradforth, nee Deighton, of Masham, Yorkshire. They married in Nottingham in 1883 and had one daughter: Helen Mary born 1888.

In 1891 John Bertram was living with his grandfather, Francis Deighton, at the Market Place, Masham. In the census record his mother is recorded as Eleanor Deighton.

Mr George Bradforth died in Masham on 3 July 1893.

In 1901 the family home was at Baptist Row, Masham, and the 16 year old John Bertram was working as a Railway Clerk.

John Bertram was the husband of Evelyn Boyston Bradforth, nee Shirbon, of Back West Gate, Hornsea, in 1911, later of 28 Marlborough Avenue, Hornsea. They married at Howden parish church on 12 September 1910 and had two children: Dorothy Margaret who was born on 29 June 1911 and John S who was born 1916 and died the same year. In 1911 John and Evelyn were living at Back Westgate, Hornsea.

Before the war John Bertram worked as a Clerk at the Hornsea Bridge Railway Station and enlisted in Hull on 5 July 1915 into 5th Cyclists Battalion, East Yorkshire Regiment. He landed in France on 26 July 1916 when the Somme Battle was in full swing. On the 4 September 1916 he was attached to the 1/4th Battalion and later sent to the 8th Battalion East Yorkshire Regiment.

He was listed in a casualty list in the *Hull Daily Mail* on 9 May 1917.

Mrs Evelyn Boyston Bradforth: Born in Howden in 1887 and remarried in Hornsea in 1923 to Alfred Maleham. She died in Scalby, Scarborough, on 23 April 1966.

St Mary's Churchyard, Masham.

Mr George Bradforth: Born in Greatham, Durham, in 1859, and died in Masham on 3 July 1893. Mrs Margaret Bradforth: Born in Masham in January 1853 and died in Masham on 3 November 1919. They are buried together in St Mary's Church Yard, Masham, and their son John Bertram is commemorated on the headstone.

John Bertram Bradforth is commemorated on:
    The War Memorial, Memorial Gardens, New Road, Hornsea.
    The War Memorial in St Nicholas Church, Hornsea.
    The War Memorial in the Old Drill Hall, Back Southgate, Hornsea. Now the Ex-Servicemen's Club.
    The War Memorial, St Mary's Church Yard, Masham.
    The family headstone in St Mary's Church Yard, Masham.
    The North Eastern Railway Memorial, Station Road, York.

The North Eastern Railway Roll of Honour, Railway Museum, York.
The Druids Roll of Honour, 22 Albion Street, Hull.

Rifleman Charles Edwin Brighouse.

Brighouse. Charles Edwin.
Rifleman C/13010. 15 Platoon, D Coy, 21st Battalion King's Royal Rifle Corps. 124th Brigade, 41st Division.
Killed in Action 22 June 1916, aged 23 years. Buried in Berks Cemetery Extension, Belgium.

He was born in Hull in 1892 and was the son of Charles Davidson Brighouse, Pharmacist, and Sarah Jessie Brighouse, nee Piper, of Marine Road, Hornsea. They married in Hull in July 1890 and had moved to Hornsea by 1901. Their other children were: Doris who was born in Hull in 1891, Marjorie who was born in Hull in 1893 and Gilbert who was born in Hornsea in 1906. By 1923 the family had moved to St Ives, Hornsea Bridge.

In 1901 the family resided at Summer Leigh, The Esplanade, Hornsea. By 1911 they had moved to Wensley, Marine Road, Hornsea.

Charles Edwin emigrated to Canada in 1911 and returned to Hornsea to enlist in 1915. He swore the oath of loyalty and attested in Hornsea on 10 January 1916, giving his occupation as farmer and enlisted in Beverley on 12 January 1916. He joined his unit in France on 5 May 1916.

Charles Edwin Brighouse was featured in a Roll of Honour in the *Beverley Guardian* on 1 July 1916. A photograph of him appeared in the same publication on 15 July 1916.

A photograph of him appeared in *Green's Almanac* in 1917.

Mr Charles Davidson Brighouse died in 1919, at the time of his death his address was Book Cottage, Wath Road, Pateley Bridge.

Pateley Bridge Cemetery.

Mr Charles Davidson Brighouse: Born in Askrigg in October 1863 and died in Pateley Bridge on 13 October 1919, he is buried in Pateley Bridge Cemetery. His son Charles Edwin is commemorated on the headstone.

Mrs Sarah Jessie Brighouse: Born in Stonehouse, Devon, in July 1867 and died at 1,246 Roland Street, Bellingham, Whatcom County, USA, on 12 December 1927.

Charles Edwin Brighouse is commemorated on:
The War Memorial, Memorial Gardens, New Road, Hornsea.
The War Memorial in St Nicholas Church, Hornsea.
The War Memorial, brass plaque, in the Hornsea Wesleyan Methodist Chapel.
The War Memorial in the Old Drill Hall, Back Southgate, Hornsea. Now the Ex-Servicemen's Club.
The family headstone, Pateley Bridge Cemetery, Yorkshire.

Private Charles Frederick Brooks.

Brooks. Charles Frederick.
Private 17/1122. 17th Pioneer Battalion Northumberland Fusiliers.
Killed in Action in the Ypres Salient on 19 November 1917, aged 36 years. Buried in Bard Cottage Cemetery, Belgium.

He was born in Hull on 6 April 1879 and was the son of John and Emily Brooks, nee Rudd, of Brantingham.

He was married to Rose Brooks, nee Simpson, of 30 Southgate, Hornsea. They married in the Primitive Methodist Chapel, Hornsea, on 22 December 1904 and had eight children: Allan born on 8 July 1905, Nora born on 2 June 1907, Eric born 29 June 1908, Percy born 7 June 1910, Donald born on 12 February 1912, Eunice born on 22 March 1913, Fred born on 28 March 1915 and Muriel born on 30 April 1918. All the children were born in Hornsea.

Fred was brought up by his grandparents, Charles and Jane Rudd of Brantingham.

He worked as a Plate Layer for the North Eastern Railway Company before the war and enlisted in January 1915.

Rose Brooks received a letter from Fred's officer in late 1917: Your husband was very highly thought of by all his officers and in him we have lost one of whom it was a pleasure to have in the company.

The death of Charles Frederick Brooks was reported, with picture, in the *Beverley Guardian* on 29 December 1917, and in the *North Eastern Railway Magazine*, volume 3, January–December 1918.

Mrs Rose Brooks.

Mrs Emily Brooks: Buried in All Saints Churchyard, Brantingham.

Southgate Cemetery, Hornsea.

Rose Brooks: Born in Hornsea in 1883 and died in Hornsea on 21 May 1943. She is buried in Southgate Cemetery, Hornsea, with her daughter in law: Hilda Catherine, died 2001 and her husband Percy Brooks, died 6 January 1975. In the same plot are the ashes of Heather Heasman, born 1939, died 21 March 2013. Fred Brooks is commemorated on the family headstone.

Charles Frederick Brooks is commemorated on:
The War Memorial, Memorial Gardens, New Road, Hornsea.
The War Memorial in St Nicholas Church, Hornsea.
The War Memorial in the Old Drill Hall, Back Southgate, Hornsea. Now the Ex-Servicemen's Club.
The family headstone, Southgate Cemetery, Hornsea.
The North Eastern Railway Memorial, Station Road, York.
The North Eastern Railway Roll of Honour, Railway Museum, York.
De Ruvigny's Roll of Honour.

On 30 August 2016 I visited Colin and Joyce Brooks of Leven, Colin is the grandson of Fred. They shared their extensive family archive with me and explained some facts I was not aware of regarding the family. Their kindness and generosity was much appreciated.

The Headstone of Private George Brown. Seafield Cemetery, Leith, Edinburgh.

Brown. George.
Private 34861. 9th Battalion King's Own Yorkshire Light Infantry. 64th Brigade. 21st Division. Formerly 3215, Yorkshire Regiment.
Died of Wounds in Leith Hospital, Edinburgh, on 29 November 1916, aged 26 years. Buried in Seafield Cemetery, Leith, Edinburgh.

He was born at Billing Hill Farm, Bewholme, Nr Hornsea, on 9 November 1890 and was the son of Christopher, Farm Foreman, and Isabella Brown, nee Lazenby, of Bewholme. They married in North Dalton on 17 December 1873 and had nine other children: Mary born and died in 1874, John William born in North Dalton in 1876 died in 1882, George born in 1879 died in 1882. Sarah Ann born in 1883, Jack born in Hornsea in 1884, Tom born in 1885, Harold born in 1889, Clara born in 1893 and Elizabeth born in 1896. All the children but John William and Jack were born at Billing Hill Farm, Bewholme.

In 1901 the family resided at Nunkeeling, Yorkshire. In 1911 Mr Christopher Brown was a widower and was working as a farm labourer. He resided at Warley Cross, Brandsburton, Yorkshire.

In 1911 George was working as a wagoner on the farm of Fred and Sarah Ann Woodward of Nunkeeling, Seaton. He enlisted in Beverley in 1914 into the Yorkshire Regiment.

Southgate Cemetery, Hornsea.
Mrs Isabella Brown: Born in North Dalton on 24 March 1852 and died in Hornsea on 12 December 1906. Mr Christopher Brown: Born in Leven on 5 August 1848 and

died in Hornsea in 1925. They are buried together in an unmarked grave in Southgate Cemetery, Hornsea.

George Brown is commemorated on:
The War Memorial, Memorial Gardens, New Road, Hornsea.
The War Memorial in St Nicholas Church, Hornsea.
The War Memorial in the Old Drill Hall, Back, Southgate, Hornsea. Now the Ex-Servicemen's Club.
The Bewholme War Memorial.
A bronze memorial plaque in Leith Cemetery.
On a screen wall in Edinburgh, Seafield, Cemetery, Leith.

On 16 August 2016 I visited David Brown, relative of George, in Hornsea and we chatted and exchanged information. At one point George Brown's grave was unmarked, recently the family complained to the War Graves Commission and now he has a military headstone that marks his last resting place.

Bulson. Henry.
Lance Corporal M/305669. 717 MT Coy, Army Service Corps. Attached to 242 Brigade, 275 Siege Battery, Royal Field Artillery.
Killed in an accident on 11 June 1918, aged 26 years. Buried in Ecoivres Military Cemetery, France.

Lance Corporal Henry Bulson.

He was born in Hornsea in 1892 and was the son of David and Leith Emma Bulson, nee Russell, of 59 Southgate, Hornsea. They Married in Driffield in 1885 and had three other children: Lillian was born Aldborough in 1887, William was born in Aldborough in 1888 and Kathleen was born in Hornsea on 27 February 1895.

In 1901 the family resided at the above address. The make-up of the household was: David 40, Leith Emma 36, Lillian 14, William 13, Henry 9 and Kathleen 6. In 1911 they were at the same address but Lillian had left home by then.

Henry married Nora Anderson in Hornsea in 1915, they resided at 58 Winchester Road, Armley, Leeds.

Before the war Harry worked as a Cycle and Motor mechanic at W H Johnson's Motor Garage, enlisting in Leeds on 9 December 1915 into the Army Service Corps. He went to France on 22 May 1917. Harry was riding a motorbike when he collided with a lorry and was badly injured, he was taken to hospital but died of his wounds the same day at the 2nd Lowland Field Ambulance.

He was reported as accidentally killed while working as a Dispatch Rider in the *Hull Daily Mail* of 22 June 1918.

Mr David Bulson is named in the Wills and Probate records as the beneficiary of Henry's will and his personal effects were sent home to his father at 59 Southgate in 1919.

Mr David Bulson: Born in Hornsea in 1861 and died in Hornsea in June 1947. Mrs Leith Emma Bulson: Born in Wassand, Yorkshire, in 1865 and died in York on 29 December 1960.

Harry Bulson is commemorated on:
The War Memorial, Memorial Gardens, New Road, Hornsea.
The War Memorial in St Nicholas Church, Hornsea.
The War Memorial in the Old Drill Hall, Back Southgate, Hornsea. Now the Ex-Servicemen's Club.

Private Frederick Burgess.

Burgess. Frederick.
Private 6278. 1st Battalion East Yorkshire Regiment. 64th Brigade, 21st Division.
Killed in Action 9 August 1915, aged 32 years. He has no known grave and is commemorated on the Menin Gate Memorial to the Missing, Ypres.

In August 1915 the Germans attacked the British Line at Hooge and for the first time liquid fire was used driving the British troops from their positions. The 1st Battalion East Yorkshire Regiment counter-attacked on 9 August and in the most fierce fighting so far encountered re-took all the British positions that had been lost. Frederick lost his life in the vicious melee.

He was born in Hornsea in 1883 and was the son of John Burgess and Nancy Burgess, nee Knaggs, of the Brickyards, Hornsea. They married in Hornsea on 10 October 1874 and had 11 other children: Myra Knaggs born on 7 September 1863, Davison Knaggs born on 10 March 1871, Eliza Burgess born in September 1875, John Henry Burgess born in September 1877, Nelly/Ellen Burgess born on 29 May 1878, Lucy Burgess born on 5 May 1880, Arthur Burgess born on 16 September 1882, George Burgess born on 14 November 1884, he would perish in the Great War, John William Burgess born on 11 July 1886 and Harry Burgess born in October 1889. All the children were born in Hornsea.

John and Nancy Burgess with two of their daughters.

In 1881 the family resided at Back Westgate, Hornsea, and in 1891 at Back Southgate, Hornsea, Mr John Burgess was employed as a general labourer. In 1901 and 1911 the family lived at Brickyard House, Hornsea, and John was employed as a Foreman Bricklayer.

Frederick was the husband of Ellen Burgess, nee Smith, of 42 Beaver Road, Beverley. They married in Beverley in 1909 and had three children: Ellen, Rose and Harold.

Before the war he was a regular soldier with the 2nd Battalion East Yorkshire Regiment serving in India. Fred left the army in 1908, when war broke out he was still on the reserve and was recalled, going to France on 27 October 1914.

Frederick Burgess was reported killed in the *Hull Daily Mail* of 3 June 1916.

His photograph appeared in *Green's Almanac* in 1916 and 1917.

Southgate Cemetery, Hornsea.

Mrs Alice Burgess and Charles Henry Smith on their wedding day at Atwick Church, 1922.

Mr John Burgess: Born in Howe, Norfolk, in 1851 and died in Hornsea on 23 January 1933. Mrs Nancy Burgess: Born in Atwick on 28 November 1844 and died in Hornsea on 24 December 1927. They are buried in Southgate, Cemetery, Hornsea, with their son, David, who died on 1 March 1945.

Their daughter, Ellen Burgess, is buried in the same cemetery with George and Esther Binning, they lost their son in the war. She resided at Grainger's Yard, Southgate, Hornsea and died on 28 May 1964.

Queensgate New Cemetery, Beverley.

Mrs Ellen Burgess: Born in Beverley in 1883, she never re-married and died in Beverley on 17 January 1961. She is buried in Queensgate New Cemetery, Beverley, with her son Harold who died on 19 December 1989 and daughter Rose who died on 24 November 1983.

Frederick Burgess is commemorated on:
The War Memorial, Memorial Gardens, New Road, Hornsea.
The War Memorial in St Nicholas Church, Hornsea.
The War Memorial in the Old Drill Hall, Back Southgate. Now the Ex-Servicemen's Club.
The family headstone in Queensgate New Cemetery, Beverley.
The East Yorkshire Regimental Memorial in Beverley Minster.
The Great War Memorial, Hengate, Beverley.
The Druids Roll of Honour, 22 Albion Street, Hull.

Burgess. George. Brother of the above.
Corporal S/8198. 8th Battalion Seaforth Highlanders.
Killed in Action at Loos on 25 September 1915, aged 31 years. He has no known grave and is commemorated on the Loos Memorial to the Missing.

George Burgess was born in Hornsea on 14 November 1884.

He was the husband of Alice Burgess, nee Burgess, of Southgate, Hornsea. They married in Glanford, Brigg, Lincs, in 1906 and had three children: Francis Alice born in 1907, Florence Lucy born in 1908 and Winifred Olive born in 1912. All the children were born in Hornsea.

Corporal George Burgess.

George Burgess joined up on 26 April 1915 in Beverley and was sent to Draycott Camp for training.

He was listed as a casualty in the *Hull Daily Mail* on 26 November 1915.

Mrs Alice Burgess: Born in North Coates, Lincs, on 17 November 1882, she remarried after her husband's death to Charles Henry Smith in Atwick Church in June 1922. She died in Hornsea at the Cottage Hospital on 14 February 1969. Mr Charles Henry Smith was born in Atwick in 1888 and died in August 1962.

Alice Burgess was able to borrow some money and set herself up in a bakery shop on the corner of Atwick Road and Eastgate, she baked bread for the troops and was successful enough to pay back the loan. Her girls helped with the deliveries from time to time and the business thrived.

George Burgess is commemorated on:
The War Memorial, Memorial Gardens, New Road, Hornsea.
The War Memorial in St Nicholas Church, Hornsea.
The War Memorial in the Old Hornsea Drill Hall, Back Southgate. Now the Ex-Servicemen's Club.
The hand written Roll of Honour in the Hornsea Wesleyan Methodist Chapel.
The Loos Memorial to the Missing.

On 5 September 2016 I visited Mrs Brenda Coneyworth of Leven, she is the daughter of Florence Lucy Burgess and was kind enough to let me copy photographs from her family archives. The family anecdote she gave me is recorded in the 1915 chapter.

Cannell. Walter Cecil.
Sergeant 13/54 13th Battalion East Yorkshire Regiment. 92nd Hull Brigade, 31st Pals Division.
Sergeant 60319 22nd Battalion Northumberland Fusiliers. 3rd Tyneside Scottish. 48th Brigade, 16th Division.
Sergeant 13/54. 1st Battalion East Yorkshire Regiment. 64th Brigade. 21st Division.
Killed in Action 10 September 1918 with the 1st Battalion East Yorkshire Regiment, during the Battle of the Hindenburg Line, aged 27 years. He has no known grave and is commemorated on the Vis-en-Artois Memorial to the Missing, France.

He was born in Hull in 1891 and was the son of Robert Holmes Cannell and Eleanor Cannell, nee Seddon, of 9 Clifford Street, Hornsea. They married in Hull in 1889 and had one other son: Roland Seddon Cannell who was born in Hull in 1890.

Roland Seddon Cannell served in the Machine-Gun Corps in the Great War.

In 1891 Robert Holmes Cannell, his wife Eleanor and their new born son, Roland Seddon Cannell, resided at Grafton Street, Park Villas, Hull.

In 1901 Walter Cecil Cannell was living at his grandmother's house, Ellen Seddon, in the St Paul's District, Hull, with his mother and brother Roland. No mention is made of his father. I can find no record of the family in the 1911 census.

Walter Cecil worked as a Furnisher's Assistant before the war and enlisted at the Hull City Hall on 16 November 1914 into the 4th Hull Pals Battalion of the East Yorkshire Regiment. They went to Egypt in 1915 and to France in March 1916 to take part in the Battle of the Somme. In 1917 his battalion took part in the Battle of Arras and was in action on 3 May 1917 at Oppy Wood, on 7 May Walter seriously sprained his ankle while in the Line, an enquiry was held into this but it was found to be accidental and not a self-inflicted wound, he was sent to the Australian General Hospital at Rouen on 9 May. He returned to the 13th Battalion on 22 February 1918, they were then disbanded and he was sent to the 22nd Battalion Northumberland Fusiliers on 29 March 1918, while he was serving with them they were constantly in action during the German offensive and lost most of their compliment, only a cadre remaining. He was then sent to the 1st Battalion East Yorkshire Regiment who were also constantly in action and suffered horrendous casualties, experienced senior NCOs like Robert were in short supply as the German Offensive continued to roll forward. The final allied advance began in August 1918 and as the 1st Battalion attacked the Hindenburg Line Walter was killed.

In 1919 his father, Robert Holmes Cannell, and his brother, Roland Cannell, received Walter Cecil's personal effects.

His death was reported in the *Hull Daily Mail* in late 1918. He was listed as missing in the same publication on 16 January and 3 June 1919.

Mr Robert Holmes Cannell: Born in the West Indies in 1864, death unknown.

Southgate Cemetery, Hornsea. Mrs Eleanor Cannell; Born in Hull on 13 December 1863 and died in Hornsea on 5 June 1944. She is buried in Southgate Cemetery, Hornsea, with her son: Roland Seddon Cannell, born on 11 June 1890 and died on 5 September 1963, and his wife: Edna Jessie Cannell, born 14 May 1892 and died in Hornsea on 18 November 1949.

Walter Cecil Cannell is commemorated on:

The War Memorial, Memorial Gardens, New Road, Hornsea.

The War Memorial, brass plaque, in the Hornsea Wesleyan Methodist Chapel.

The Vis-en-Artois Memorial to the Missing France.

Carr. Henry/Harry.
Private 20. 1st Battalion Northumberland Fusiliers. 9th Brigade, 3rd Division.

Killed in Action in the Ypres Salient on 1 November 1914, aged 29 years. He was the first Hornsea man to die in the war and has no known grave, his name is recorded on the Menin Gate Memorial to the Missing, Ypres, Belgium.

Harry was born in Hornsea in 1884 and was the son of Louisa Carr, nee White, of Wades House, Hornsea. She had two other children: Eliza was born in Hornsea in 1878 and Ethel was born in Hornsea in 1882. I can find no record of Louisa marrying.

Private Harry Carr.

He was the husband of Edith Mary Carr, nee Andrew, of 4 Welbourne Terrace, Hornsea. They married in Hull in January 1914 and had one child, Harry, born in Hull in 1914. Edith Mary was the sister of John William Andrew from Hornsea who was killed in 1918.

The first husband of Jane Carr, William, died before 1876 and in 1891 Mrs Louisa Carr was living at her parent's house, Edward White, stepfather, and Jane White, nee Carr, with her children, Eliza, Ethel and Harry, at Southgate, Hornsea. Edward White and Jane Carr married in Beverley in October 1878, Edward was employed as a fisherman and Louisa as a charwoman.

In 1901 Harry was working as a barman in Hull and before his enlistment was employed as a bricklayer. He enlisted in Hull on 10 November 1903 into the 1st Battalion Northumberland Fusiliers and in 1911 he was on his way to India.

He was featured in a Roll of Honour in the *Beverley Guardian* on 4 November 1916.

His photograph appeared in *Green's Almanac* in 1916.

Harry was listed 'In Memoriam' in the *Beverley Guardian*, from his mother, sister and son Harry, on 15 May 1920.

Mrs Louisa Carr: Born in Hornsea in 1860, death unknown.

Mrs Edith Mary Carr: Born in Sigglesthorne in 1892, death unknown.

Harry Carr is commemorated on:
The War Memorial, Memorial Gardens, New Road, Hornsea.
The War Memorial in St Nicholas Church, Hornsea.
The hand written Roll of honour in the Wesleyan Methodist Chapel, Hornsea.
The War Memorial in the Old Drill Hall, Back Southgate, Hornsea. Now the Ex-Servicemen's Club.
The Druids Roll of Honour, 22 Albion Street, Hull.
The Menin Gate Memorial to the Missing, Ypres, Belgium.

Lieutenant William Holmes Collinson.

Collinson. William Holmes.
2nd Lieutenant 6th Battalion Northumberland Fusiliers.
Killed in Action at Hill 60 on 5 January 1916, aged 26 years. Buried in Railway Dugouts Burial Ground, Transport Farm, Belgium.

He was born in Edmonton, Middlesex, in 1890 and was the son of William Rowley Field Collinson, Insurance Manager, and Sarah Haslewood Collinson, nee Holmes, of Fairfield, Cliff Road, Hornsea. They married in Wharfedale on 9 May 1889 and had a daughter: Ethel Mary Haslewood Collinson, born in Enfield, Middlesex in 1892.

In 1901 and 1911 the family resided at Fairfield, Hornsea.

In 1911 William was living with his grandmother, Harriet Ann Collinson, 69, of The Knoll, Beckenham. He was employed as a Printer's Representative.

William attended Aldenham School, Herts, from September 1903 to December 1906 and Clare House School, Beckenham, Kent, and Aidenham School, Herts. Before the war he was employed at Messrs Waterlow and sons, EC. In 1914 he joined the Honourable Artillery Company as a Private and went to France on 18 September 1914, he was later commissioned into the 6th Battalion Northumberland Fusiliers on 21 April 1915 and was ordered to go home to receive his commission. Before he could leave the trenches another order arrived telling him to join his new regiment near Ypres, which he did on 26 April and was appointed Machine-gun officer. They had suffered badly at the Battle of St Julian and officers were badly needed.

In the Wills and Probate records of 1916 his address in Hornsea is confirmed.

He was listed in a Local Roll of Honour, with obituary, in the *Beverley Guardian* on 15 January 1916. His death was reported in the *Hull Daily Mail* on 11 January, 1916 and his obituary appeared in the same publication on 15 January 1916.

On 1 May 1916 Mr William Rowley Field Collinson was granted permission by the Hornsea Council to erect a stone seat in Eastgate, north side, to the memory of his beloved only son. By 2002 the now forgotten seat was in a sorry state and an Eastgate resident, Mr Ian Barrett, decided it was time it was restored to its former glory and approached Reg Anderson of Hornsea Council who got council funding for the project. Two local men worked on the project, Jack Pearson and Brian Massey, they undertook to replace the woodwork and to their credit did not charge for their time. They only asked that the council make a donation to the Hornsea Cottage Hospital. This was done and the seat was re-dedicated on 11 May 2003.

Mr William Rowley Frederick Collinson: Born in Brixton, London, in 1864 and died at Park Wall Cottage, Cranham Village, Stroud, Gloucestershire, on 12 May 1937.

Mrs Sarah Haslewood Collinson: Born in Hull in 1865 and died at Park Wall Cottage, Cranham Village, Stroud, Gloucestershire, on 21 August 1956.

William Holmes Collinson is commemorated on:
The War Memorial, Memorial Gardens, New Road, Hornsea.
The War Memorial in St Nicholas Church, Hornsea.
A stained glass memorial Screen in St George's Drill Hall, Northumberland Road, Newcastle.
The War Memorial in the Old Drill Hall, Back Southgate, Hornsea. Now the Ex-Servicemen's Club.
A stone Memorial Seat, Eastgate, Hornsea.

Cooper. George William.
Private 24690. 1st Battalion East Yorkshire Regiment. 64th Brigade, 21st Division.
Killed in Action 4 October 1917, aged 36 years. He has no known grave and is commemorated on the Tyne Cot Memorial to the Missing, Belgium.

Private George William Cooper.

George William was killed during the Battle of Broodseinde, Passchendaele. With Polygone Wood to their rear the 64th Brigade attacked at 6:00 a.m. on 4 October into a storm of fire but reached and held their objectives, losing many men in the process.

He was born in Hull in 1881 and was the son of Benjamin, Master Fisherman, and Phoebe Cooper, nee Woolas, of 9 Cleveland Terrace, Walcott Street, Hull. They married in Hull, in 1874, and had three children: Gertrude born in Hull in 1877, George William born in Hull in 1881 and Hetty born in Hull in 1882.

In 1881 the family resided at 9 Cleveland Terrace, Walcott Street, Hull.

Mrs Phoebe Cooper died in Hull in 1885.

Benjamin re-married in 1886 to Mary Selina Cooper, nee Milner, of 18 Division Road, Hessle Road, Hull, they had four children: Sarah born in Hull in 1887, Benjamin born in Hull in 1893, Thomas Martin born in Hull in 1896 and Matilda Annie born in Hull in 1900

In 1891 the family resided at 5 Eastbourne Street, Hull.

George William married Mary Jane Chapman in Hornsea in October 1909. In 1911 the newly wed couple lived at 1 Bank Street, Hornsea. Later moving to 49 Southgate, Hornsea, and had a son called Thomas Richard who was born in Hornsea on 15 March 1912.

George William was a farm labourer before the war, he attested on 6 December 1915 at Hornsea and was posted to the 7th Battalion East Yorkshire Regiment in France on 11 December 1916. He was posted to the 1st Battalion on 25 December 1916.

George William was reported as missing, later killed in action, in the *Hull Daily Mail* on 9 November 1917.

Mr Benjamin Cooper: Born in Middlesex in 1853 and died in Hull in 1922. Mrs Mary Selina Cooper: Born in Hull in 1859 and died in Hull in 1919. Mrs Phoebe Cooper: Born in Hull in 1854 and died in Hull in 1885.

Mrs Mary Jane Cooper: Born in Hornsea in July 1885, she never re-married and died in Hull in 1968.

George William Cooper is commemorated on:
The War Memorial, Memorial Gardens, New Road, Hornsea.
The War Memorial in St Nicholas Church, Hornsea.
The War Memorial in the Old Drill Hall, Back Southgate, Hornsea. Initials T R. Now the Ex-Servicemen's Club.
The Druids Roll of Honour, 22 Albion Street, Hull.
The Tyne Cot Memorial to the Missing.

Curtin. Alexander. [also known as Allan]
Private 4100. 27th Battalion. Australian Infantry Force. 5th Australian Division.
Killed in Action on 9 August 1918, aged 25 years. Buried in Heath Cemetery, France.

He was born on 16 August 1893 in Norwood, South Australia, and was the son of Frederick Faulding Curtin and

Private Alexander Curtin.

Margaret Curtin, nee Willison, of Glyde Street, Norwood, South Australia. They married in Adelaide on 2 July 1887 and had three other sons: Frank Norman born 1888, Edgar Catley born 1890 and Bernard Joseph born 1892.

Francis Catley Curtin, Alexander's grandfather, was born in Hull and emigrated with his family to Australia in 1855.

In Southgate Cemetery, Hornsea, are buried Mr Richard Curtin, died on 20 April 1905, aged 44 years and his wife Alberta Mary Curtin who died on 12 July 1928, aged 67 years. Their son Harry, who was lost at sea on 31 January 1909, aged 23 years, is commemorated on the headstone. Buried in the same plot is Mary Walker of 87 Newcomen St Hull, who died on 20 August 1944, aged 55 years. I assume that in her grief Alberta Mary put Alexander's name forward in the early twenties to be featured on the Hornsea War Memorials even though he never lived in Hornsea.

Alexander was the husband of Esther Jane Curtin, nee Johnson. They married in Holy Trinity Church, Adelaide in 1912 and resided at 2 Bowden Lane, off Gillies Street, Adelaide. They had two children: Edna May born 1913 and Allan Edward Frederick born 1916.

He enlisted in Adelaide on 20 November 1915 and embarked for France on 9 March 1916.

His family commemorated him in the *Adelaide Advertiser* on 9 August 1919 and in the *Adelaide Chronicle* on 16 August 1919.

Private 465 Frank Norman Curtin, 32nd Battalion, Australian Infantry Force was Killed in Action on 20 July 1916 at Fromelles, he is buried/commemorated in VC Corner Australian Memorial, Fromelles, France.

Lieutenant Edgar Catley Curtin, 59th Battalion, Australian Infantry Force, served in the Gallipoli Campaign and was later badly gassed in France, he returned to Australia on 21 May 1919 and died in 1969.

Mr Frederick Faulding Curtin: Born in South Australia on 19 September 1860 and died in Adelaide on 19 October 1918. Mrs Margaret Curtin: Born in Tree Gully, South Australia, on 29 March 1861 and died in Norwood, South Australia, on 15 June 1895.

Alexander Curtin is commemorated on:
The War Memorial, Memorial Gardens, New Road, Hornsea.
The War Memorial in St Nicholas Church, Hornsea.
The War Memorial in the Old Drill Hall, Back Southgate, Hornsea. Now the Ex-Servicemen's Club.
The Australian War Memorial, Treloar Crescent, Campbell, Australia.

Dawson. Richard Douglas.
Sergeant B/3439. 7th Battalion the Rifle Brigade. 41st Brigade, 14th Light Division.
Killed in Action 24 July 1915, aged 36 years. He has no known grave and is commemorated on the Menin Gate Memorial to the Missing, Ypres, Belgium.

He was born in Hull in 1879 and was the son of Edward, Hemp Merchant, and Clara Jane Dawson, nee Brown, of 6 Suffolk Terrace, Hornsea. They married in Hull in 1871 and had four other children: Arthur born in Hull in 1873, Alice born in Hull in 1874, Reginald born in Hull in 1877 and Bertha born in Hull in 1884.

In 1881 and 1891 the family resided at 63 Albany Street, Hull. By 1901 they had made the move to Suffolk Terrace, Hornsea.

In 1901 Richard Douglas was a boarder at 68 Clyde Road, Croydon, Surrey, in the house of Henry and Minnie Gent, he was employed as a clerk in the oil trade. In 1911 he was a boarder at 82 Grove Lane, Camberwell, in the house of William and Minnie Taylor and worked as a Stock Exchange Commission Agent.

On 7 November 1914 he married Maud Helen Hodsall at St Mathews, Croydon, Surrey. Maud moved to Hornsea and stayed with her in-laws before she got her own house at Burton Lodge, Hornsea in 1916, she was still at this address in 1919.

Richard Douglas had served in the 1st Volunteer Battalion East Yorkshire Regiment for three years from 1900 to 1903. He joined the 8th Service Battalion the Rifle Corps on 1 September 1914 at Winchester and was promoted sergeant on 29 September and posted to the 7th Battalion, they embarked to France in May 1915 and were posted to the infamous Ypres Salient. While in France he was admitted to a field hospital with measles on 30 June 1915 and discharged on 20 July. Richard Douglas was killed four days later.

In 1919 his service papers tell us his sister Alice Mary Douglas was living at 3 Suffolk Terrace, Hornsea. His brother Reginald Douglas was living at Worthing Street, Hull and his sister Bertha Wilson, nee Dawson, was living at Portman Mansions, London.

The death of Richard Douglas Dawson was reported in the *Beverley Guardian* on 14 August 1915.

Southgate Cemetery, Hornsea.

Mr Edward Dawson: Born in Hull in 1847 and died in Hornsea on 29 December 1929. Mrs Clara Jane Dawson: Born in Hull in 1851 and died in Hornsea on 20 February 1914. They lie together in Southgate Cemetery, Hornsea. Their son Richard Douglas is commemorated on the family headstone.

Maud Helen Dawson: Re-married in Kent in 1921 to Clive Aubrey Hastings Sutton, Stockbroker, she was born in Croydon, Surrey, in 1887 and died in the War Memorial Cottage Hospital, Hornsea, on 5 April 1956. Clive Aubrey Hastings Sutton: Born in Hull in 1885 and served as a 2nd lieutenant in the Lancashire Fusiliers in the Great War. He died at Heronsmere, Seaton Road, Hornsea, on 18 April 1958.

Richard Douglas Dawson is commemorated on:

The War Memorial, Memorial Gardens, New Road, Hornsea.

The War Memorial in St Nicholas Church, Hornsea.

The War Memorial in the Old Drill Hall, Back Southgate, Hornsea. Now the Ex-Servicemen's Club.

The Family headstone, Southgate Cemetery, Hornsea.

The Menin Gate Memorial to the Missing, Belgium.

Lance Corporal Richard Alma Dry.

Dry. Richard Alma.
Lance Corporal 23252. 13th [Bantam] Battalion the Yorkshire Regiment. 121st Brigade, 40th Division.

Died of Wounds received at Bourlon Wood on 24 November 1917, aged 29 years, his body was lost to the battle-field. On 2 June 1923 Rose Ellen Dry was informed that her brother's remains had been recovered near Graincourt and he was reinterred at Anneux British Cemetery, France.

He was born at Burton Agnes on 11 August 1888 and was the son of Annie Elizabeth Dry, nee Brooks, and James Thomas Dry, Railway Porter, of Newbegin, Hornsea. They married at St Jude's, Hull, on 27 November 1875 and had 10 other children: Joseph born in Hull in April 1876, Florence Ann born in Hull in July 1877, James Farrand born in Hull on 21 March 1881, Samuel born in Hull in 1882, William Albert born in Winestead on 28 July 1883, Rose Ellen born in Hornsea on 29 August 1891, Sydney born in Hornsea in 1896, Emma Alice born in Hornsea in July 1897, Elsie May born in Hornsea on 27 October 1900 and Hilda Jane born in Hornsea in April 1902.

In 1881 the family resided at 19 Glasshouse Row, Stoneferry, Hull, James Thomas was employed as a stonemason's labourer. By 1891 they had moved to Newbegin, Hornsea, and James Thomas was working as a railway porter, a job he did all his life. In 1901 and 1911 they were at the same address.

In 1911 Richard was working as a servant at the Commercial Hotel, Withernsea. He enlisted in July 1915

Richard was the husband of Sarah Ellen Dry, nee Collins, of 8 Rose Terrace, Barnsley Street, Holderness Road, Hull. They married in Hull in April 1915 and had a son: Ernest, who was born in Hull in 1916 and died in Hull in 1917.

Mr James Thomas Dry: Born in Hull in 1854 and died in Hornsea on 16 March 1914. Mrs Annie Elizabeth Dry. Born in Whitedale, Yorkshire in 1857 and died in Hornsea on 29 January 1928.

Mrs Sarah Ellen Dry: Born in Hull in 1889, she re-married in 1919 to Walter Hardy in Hull and died in Hull in December 1960.

Mrs Annie Elizabeth Dry.

Richard Alma Dry is commemorated on:
The War Memorial, Memorial Gardens, New Road, Hornsea.
The War Memorial in St Nicholas Church, Hornsea.
The War Memorial, brass plaque, in the Wesleyan Methodist Chapel, Hornsea.
The War Memorial in the Old Drill Hall, Back Southgate, Hornsea. Now the Ex-Servicemen's Club.

Lance Corporal George Herbert Dunn.

Dunn. George Herbert.
Lance Corporal 13484. 1st Battalion Coldstream Guards. 1st Guards Brigade, Guards Division.
Killed in Action 16 September 1916, aged 26 years.

He has no known grave and is commemorated on the Thiepval Memorial to the Missing of the Somme, France.

The 1st Guards Brigade was in the Line in September 1916 with Guillemont to their rear and Flers to their front left. George Herbert was killed in the Battle of Flers/Courcelette, 15–22 September. At 1:30 p.m. the Guards attacked without artillery support into a storm of machine-gun fire and were stopped 250 yards short of their objective when they dug in. A badly depleted brigade was relieved that night in the pouring rain.

A pre-war patriotic parade in Hornsea, Mr James Thomas Dry is on the left of the picture wearing his North Eastern Railway uniform.

George Herbert was born in Hornsea in 1889 and was the son of George, Gardener and Florist, and Isabella Dunn, nee Atkinson, of 6 Headland View, Hornsea and Church Lane, Withernwick. They married in 1877 and had five other children: Charlotte Mary born 1877, Annie Maria born 1879, Peter Allen born 1884, Juliana Isabella born 1885, died in 1914 and Archibald Grenville born 1886. All the children were born in Hornsea.

In 1891 and 1901 the family resided in Hornsea. By 1911 the children had left home and George and Isabella lived at Lawn Terrace, Withernwick. In that year George Herbert was a boarder at the Woolpack Hotel, Wakefield, he worked as a Clerk for the West Riding County Council.

George Herbert's brother, Private Peter Allen Dunn, served in the Yorkshire Regiment and was a regular soldier of 15 years' service. He went to France on 18 April 1915 and was reported as wounded in the *Hull Times*, with picture, on 21 October 1916. A picture of him was featured in *Green's Almanac* in 1916 and he died in the East Riding in September 1961.

Archibald Grenville Dunn served in the war and when he came home lived at 6 Stanley Avenue, Hornsea. He married Edith Annie Dunn and died in Hornsea on 18 February 1950. Edith Annie Dunn died in Hornsea on 5 June 1950. They now lie together in Southgate Cemetery, Hornsea.

He enlisted in Hull and went to France on 15 August 1915. Gorge Herbert Dunn was listed in a Roll of Honour in the *Beverley Guardian* on 21 October 1916. A photograph of him appeared in the same publication on 28 October 1916. His death was reported in the *Hull Daily Mail* on 20 October 1916.

St Alban's Churchyard, Withernwick.

Mr George Dunn: Born in Thorngumbald, Yorkshire, in 1849 and died in Withernwick on 23 January 1921. Mrs Isabella Dunn: Born in Skeffling, Yorkshire, in 1842 and died in Withernwick on 4 November 1944. They are buried together in St Alban's Churchyard, Withernwick. George Herbert Dunn is commemorated on the family headstone.

George Herbert Dunn is commemorated on:

The War Memorial, Memorial Gardens, New Road, Hornsea.

The War Memorial in St Nicholas Church, Hornsea.

The War Memorial, brass plaque, in the Wesleyan Methodist Chapel, Hornsea.

The War Memorial in the Old Drill Hall, Back Southgate, Hornsea. Now the Ex-Servicemen's Club.

The War Memorial, Withernwick.

The family headstone in St Alban's Churchyard, Withernwick.

A Roll of Honour in St Alban's Church, Withernwick.

The Thiepval Memorial to the Missing of the Somme, France.

Private George Mathew Evans.

Evans. George Mathew.
Private 33395. 7th Battalion East Yorkshire Regiment. 50th Brigade. 17th Northern Division.
Killed in Action during the Advance to Victory at the Battle of Amiens on 12 August 1918, aged 32 years.

Buried in Heath Cemetery, Harbonnieres, France.

He was born in Hornsea on 2 November 1886 and was the son of George Henry, plumber, and Lucy Jane Evans, nee Daggit, of Southgate, Hornsea. They married in Beverley in 1878 and had 11 other children: Annie Lizzie born 1879, William Daggit born 1882, Robert Henry born 1883, Agnes Grace born 1884, Tom Leck born 1889, Ethel Maude born 1891, Kathleen born 1892, Frank born 1893, Ivy born 1895, Olive born 1899 and Lucy Jane born and died in 1900. All the children were born in Hornsea.

In 1891 the family resided at 1 Welburn Terrace, Hornsea, by 1901 they had moved to Southgate, Hornsea, and were still there in 1911.

George Mathew was the husband of Annie Ellen Evans, nee Hunt, of Southgate, Hornsea. They married in Hornsea in 1909 and had three children: Lilly who was born in Hornsea on 6 February 1909, Frank who was born in Hornsea in 1912 and George Kenneth who was born in Hornsea on 16 February 1916.

Before the war George Mathew worked as a chimney Sweep/labourer and enlisted in 1916. In the above portrait he is wearing the light blue uniform worn by wounded soldiers.

On 7 December 1918 the *Beverley Guardian* listed him in a Roll of Honour with the above picture. He was listed in a casualty list in the *Hull Daily Mail* in 1918.

His photograph appeared in *Green's Almanac* in 1919.

Lilly Evans.

In 1930 the daughter of George Mathew and Annie Ellen Evans, Lilly Evans, married Allen Norman whose father, John William Norman, also died in the Great War and is commemorated on the Hornsea War Memorial

Mrs Annie Ellen Evans: Born in Hull on 4 December 1884 and died in Hornsea in July 1950.

Mr George Henry Evans: Born in Seaton, Yorkshire, in 1856 and died in Hornsea in 1926. Mrs Lucy Jane Evans: Born in Beverley in 1857 and died in Hornsea in 1930.

George Mathew Evans is commemorated on:
The War Memorial, Memorial Gardens, New Road, Hornsea.
The War Memorial in St Nicholas Church, Hornsea.
The War Memorial in the Old Drill Hall, Back Southgate, Hornsea. Now the Ex-Servicemen's Club.
The Druids Roll of Honour, 22 Albion Street, Hull.

Allen Norman.

Ford. Ernest.
Private 10044. 10th Battalion East Yorkshire Regiment. Hull Commercials. 1st Hull Pals. 92nd Hull Brigade. 31st Pals Division.

Killed in Action on 27 April 1918, aged 19 years. He has no known grave and is commemorated on the Ploegsteert Memorial to the Missing, Belgium.

Ernest was killed during a trench raid on the night of 26/27 April 1918. Four officers and 125 other ranks of the 10th Battalion attacked the German trenches at La Becque, they captured 24 Germans, one machine-gun and killed over 60 other Germans.

He was born in Beverley in 1899 and was the son of John and Dinah Ford, nee Turner, of 2 Long Lane Beverley, later of Ivy Cottage, Newbegin, Hornsea. They married in Beverley in 1896 and had two other children: Winifred born in Beverley in 1897 and Cecil born in Acomb, York, in 1907.

In 1901 the family was living at Victoria Barracks, Beverley, John Ford was a sergeant in the East Yorkshire Regiment. By 1911 he had retired and the family was living at 2 Long Lane, Beverley.

Ernest Ford was listed as Missing since 27 April 1918 in the *Hull Daily Mail* of 24 February 1919.

Mr John Ford: Born in Openshaw, Lancs, in 1885, and died in Beverley in 1962.

Southgate Cemetery, Hornsea. Mrs Dinah Ford: Born in Beverley in 1875 and died in Hornsea on 19 March 1951. She is buried in Southgate Cemetery, Hornsea, with her daughter, Winifred Gertrude Ford, who died on 27 August 1986, aged 89 years.

Commemorated on vases and buried in the same plot are Clifford Aaron, died 19 January 1951, from his workmates at East Yorkshire Motor Services, and Emily Jane Perkins, died 5 November 1951.

Ernest Ford is commemorated on:
The War Memorial, Memorial Gardens, New Road, Hornsea.
The War Memorial in St Nicholas Church, Hornsea.
The War Memorial in the Old Drill Hall, Back Southgate, Hornsea. Now the Ex-Servicemen's Club.
The Great War Memorial, Hengate, Beverley.
The East Yorkshire Regimental Memorial in Beverley Minster.
The Ploegsteert Memorial to the Missing, Belgium.

Private Thomas Fowler.

Fowler. Thomas.
Private 205634.. 10th Battalion Essex Regiment. 53rd Brigade, 18th Division.
Killed in Action 2 September 1918, aged 19 years. He has no known grave and is commemorated on the Vis-en-Artois Memorial to the Missing, France.

He was born in Hornsea in 1899 and was the son of William, tailor, and Elizabeth Fowler, nee Barker, of 5 St Nicholas Mount, Hornsea, later of Southgate, Hornsea. They married in Hornsea in 1895 and had one other child: Maria born in Hornsea in 1896.

In 1901 the family resided at Newbegin, Hornsea, living with them was William Fowler's father, Thomas Fowler, a retired Inn Keeper, aged 71 years. By 1911 they had moved to 5 St Nicholas Mount, Hornsea.

Thomas was educated at Hull Grammar School and worked as a clerk at a Hull timber firm, R Wade and sons, before the war. He enlisted in the Lincolnshire Yeomanry and was later transferred to the Essex Regiment.

His photograph appeared in *Green's Almanac* in 1919.

He was listed In Memoriam in the *Hull Daily Mail* on 1 September 1919. From Olive and mother and father.

Southgate Cemetery, Hornsea.

Mr William Fowler: Born in Rise, Yorkshire, in 1868 and died in Hornsea on 20 April 1929. Mrs Elizabeth Fowler: Born in Atwick in 1868 and died in Hornsea on 15 December 1950. They lie together in Southgate Cemetery, Hornsea. Their son, Thomas, is commemorated on the family headstone.

Thomas Fowler is commemorated on:
The War Memorial, Memorial Gardens, New Road, Hornsea.
The War Memorial in St Nicholas Church, Hornsea.
The War Memorial in the Old Drill Hall, Back Southgate, Hornsea. Now the Ex-Servicemen's Club.

The family headstone, Southgate Cemetery, Hornsea.
The Hull Grammar School Roll of Honour, Bishop Alcock Road, Hull.
The Vis-en-Artois Memorial to the Missing, France.

Frankish. Leonard.
Private 32412. Yorkshire Regiment/South Staffordshire Regiment.
He died in the East Riding Asylum on 3 December 1918, aged 38 years. Buried in Southgate Cemetery, Hornsea, in an unmarked grave.

He was born in Skipsea in 1880 and was the son of Thomas, Butcher, and Betsy Jane Frankish, nee Suddaby. They married in Skirlaugh in 1872 and had four other children: Joyce born 1874, Tom born 1875, Lilly born 1876 and Leonard born and died 1878. All the children were born in Skipsea.

In 1881 Thomas Frankish was a farmer with six acres of land, the family resided at Ivy Cottage, Skipsea. I have found no record of them for 1891 but in 1901 they resided at Front Street, Skipsea, and Thomas was working as a butcher. Living with them was their granddaughter, Lilly C Hutchinson. In 1911 the children had all left home and Thomas and Betsy Jane lived at Eastgate View, Hornsea.

In 1901 Leonard was an apprentice bricklayer and lodged at the house of Annie Whittaker of 5 Harper Street, Great Driffield. In 1911 he was working as a bricklayer and was a lodger in the house of Jane Harding of 96 Somerset Street, Hull.

Leonard was the husband of Helena Frankish, nee Patrick, they married at Harley Street Registry, Hull, on 7 August 1915 and had one child: Thomas Wilfred born in Hull on 6 November 1915. They lived at 17 Poplar Avenue, Reynolds Street, Hull, later at Back Westgate, Hornsea.

Before the war Leonard was a Bricklayer/Plasterer and attested in Hull on 10 December 1915, enlisting in Beverley on 15 June 1916. He went to France on 11 July 1916, while in France he was attached to the Army Service Corps Labour Companies. He was admitted to the 2nd Canadian Stationary Hospital, Boulogne, and diagnosed as having Incontinence of Urine. On 13 August 1916 he was sent back to England and admitted to Bethnal Green Military Hospital. He was diagnosed as suffering from a pre-existing condition that had been aggravated by his military service. He was discharged from the hospital and the army on 7 September 1916, being no longer fit for war service, with a conditional pension and he was diagnosed as suffering from Locomotor Ataxia, people who have this can no longer precisely control their bodily movements.

Poor Leonard tried to play his part in the war effort but his physical disability would not get better. On his return to Hornsea he worked as a driver for a short while at the Steam Laundry on Cliff Road. His health got worse and he was admitted to the East Riding Asylum in May 1917 and was categorised as a lunatic/pauper and died on 3 December 1918.

Mr Thomas Frankish: Born in Skipsea in 1850 and died in Bridlington in 1924.
Mrs Betsy Jane Frankish: Born in Aldborough in 1851 and died in Bridlington in 1925.

Leonard Frankish is commemorated on:
The War Memorial, Memorial Gardens, New Road, Hornsea.
The War Memorial in St Nicholas Church, Hornsea.
The War Memorial in the Old Drill Hall, Back Southgate, Hornsea. Now the Ex-Servicemen's Club.
The Skipsea War Memorial.
A Roll of Honour inside All Saints Church, Skipsea.

Fridlington. John Francis.
Private 11216. 7th Battalion East Yorkshire Regiment. 50th Brigade, 17th Northern Division.
Killed in Action 8 June 1918, aged 35 years. Buried in Auchonvillers Military Cemetery, France.

A large scale trench raid was launched on the night of 8 June 1918 by the 50th Brigade, south of Beaumont Hamel, on a frontage of 500 yards. The raiding party consisted of 18 officers and 500 other ranks, many Germans were killed or captured but the casualties taken by the attacking force was severe, many as a result of their own creeping barrage that went before them.

He was born in Hull in December 1883 and was the son of William James Fridlington and Agnes Cordelia Fridlington, nee Acklam, of Hull, later of 42 Southgate, Hornsea. They married in Drypool, Hull, on 29 September 1872 and had eight other children: Lucy Ann born in Brigg, Lincoln, in 1873, Mary Agnes born in Hull in 1876, William James born Hull in 1878, George Robert born in Hull in 1880, Robert West born in Hull in 1886, Charles born in Hull in 1890, Sarah Jane born in Hull in 1892 and Elsie born in Hull in 1897 and died the same year.

In 1881 the family resided at 17 Parker's Buildings, Hull, William James worked as a general labourer. In 1891 they had moved to 3 Brighton Terrace, Hull, William James was then working as a gasworks labourer.

In 1897 Agnes Cordelia died in Hull during childbirth giving birth to Elsie who also died as she was born.

In 1901 the family was at the same address and William James was in the same occupation. In 1911 William James was living in the home of his daughter and son-in-law, Thomas and Mary Agnes Jackson, nee Fridlington, at Mill Lane, Hornsea, aged 63 years.

Before the war John Francis worked in an Oil Mill in Stoneferry, Hull. In 1911 he was staying at his brother George's house at 5 John's Place, York Street, Hull. He enlisted in 1915 and went to France on 7 October 1915.

The death of John Francis Fridlington was reported in the *Hull Daily Mail* in July 1918. He featured in a Roll of Honour, with picture, on 5 June 1919 and he was listed 'In Memoriam' in the same publication from his parents and brothers and sisters on 6 July 1919.

Mr William James Fridlington: Born in Wrawby, Lincolnshire, in March 1850 and died in Hull in 1931. Mrs Agnes Cordelia Fridlington: Born in Hornsea on 12 April 1852 and died in Hull in 1897.

John Francis Fridlington is commemorated on:
The War Memorial, Memorial Gardens, New Road, Hornsea.

**Fullam. Claude Stanley. Merchant Navy.
Apprentice. SS Okement, Sunderland.**
   Killed when the U-64 torpedoed the Collier SS Okement on 17 February 1917, 140 nautical miles south east by south of Malta, aged 17 years. His body was lost to the sea and he is commemorated on the Tower Hill Memorial, London.

Claude Stanley Fullam.

   He was born in Hornsea in January 1900 and was the son of Alfred Fullam and Mary Ann Fullam, nee Elvin, of the Elms, Chambers Lane, Hornsea. They married in Hull in 1888 and had four other children: Clifford Townley Fullam born in December 1891, Gladys Ward Fullam born in March 1893, Mervyn Kempley Fullam born in December 1895 and Maxwell Alfred Fullam born on 8 February 1896. All the children were born in Hornsea.

   In 1891 the family resided at Stanley Lodge, Westgate, Hornsea, Alfred worked as a Cabinet Maker. In 1901 they had moved to The Elms, Chambers Lane, Hornsea, Alfred was self-employed as a Livery and Stable Retailer. In 1911 they were at the same address and Mary Ann was working as a Chemist, all the children had left home.

   Claude Stanley is the youngest man and the only Merchant Seaman on the Hornsea War Memorial.

   Mr Alfred Fullam: Born in Canada in 1861 and died in Hornsea on 26 April 1912. Mrs Mary Ann Fullam: Born in Forncett, Norfolk, in 1855 and died in Hornsea on 12 November 1948.

   Southgate Cemetery, Hornsea.

   The brother of Claude Stanley, Maxwell Alfred Fullam, was born in Hornsea on 8 February 1896 and died on 9 May 1980, aged 84 years. His wife Dorothy Fullam died on 24 March 1975. They lie together in Southgate Cemetery, Hornsea

Claude Stanley Fullam is commemorated on:
The War Memorial, Memorial Gardens, New Road, Hornsea.
The Tower Hill Memorial, London.

**Grantham. Richard Arthur.
Private 38369. 8th Battalion East Yorkshire Regiment. 8th Brigade, 3rd Division.**
   Died of Wounds on 28 November 1917, aged 42 years. Buried in Achiet-le-Grand Communal Cemetery Extension, France.

Private Richard Arthur Grantham.

   The Battle of Cambrai opened on 20 November 1917 until it finished on 6 December 1917. On 20 November Bullecourt was attacked by the 16th Division and the 9th Brigade of the 3rd Division. The 8th Battalion East Yorkshire Regiment were in the support trenches waiting for the order to advance which never came. The Germans held the British at bay and on 25 November the 8th Brigade moved into the Front Line to relieve a badly mauled 9th Brigade. Richard Arthur Grantham lost his life as the 8th Brigade held the Line.

He was born in Hornsea in 1878 and was the son of George Grantham, bricklayer, and Sarah Ann Grantham, nee Duxbury, of Southgate, Hornsea. They married in Hull in 1869 and had nine other children: Frances Amelia Grantham born in 1869, William Henry Grantham Duxberry born in 1871, George Edward Grantham born in 1873, Alfred Grantham born in 1876, Helen Duxberry Grantham born in 1880, John Newlove Grantham born in 1882, Frederick Duxberry Grantham born in 1883, Hilda Jane Grantham born in 1888 and Ivy Grantham born 1890. All the children were born in Hornsea.

In 1871 George and Sarah Ann Grantham and two children were living in the house of Sarah Ann's parents in Hornsea, William and Helen Duxberry, nee Grantham. By 1881 they were living in their own house in Southgate, Hornsea. George Grantham died in Hull in 1901 and in 1911 Sarah Ann was working as a boarding house keeper at Milton House, Southgate, Hornsea. Her mother, Helen Duxbury, was living with her that year, aged 84 years.

Richard Arthur was a Bricklayer by trade and was the husband of Elizabeth Jane Grantham, nee Leighton. In 1901 they resided at Mereside, Hornsea and by 1911 had moved to Back Westgate, Hornsea. They married in Beverley on 7 January 1899 and had five children: Mabel born on 31 October 1900, Doris born on 31 October 1901, Alfred Leslie born in 1902, Gladys May born in 1904 and died in 1905 and Fred born on 6 November 1912. All the children were born in Hornsea.

Richard Arthur enlisted into the 3rd Battalion East Yorkshire Regiment on 16 May 1917 at Beverley.

He was listed 'In Memoriam' in the *Hull Daily Mail* on 27 November 1919.

Mrs Elizabeth Jane Grantham: Born in Kirton, Lincs, in 1877, she re-married after the war to Thomas Martin Vessey in Hornsea in 1924 and died in the East Riding in September 1949. Mr Thomas Martin Vessey: Born in Glanford, Brigg, Lincs, on 22 February 1880, and died in Hornsea in 1959.

Mr George Grantham: Born in Hornsea on 5 September 1849 and died at 10 Cromwell Street, Hull on 26 July 1901. Mrs Sarah Ann Grantham: Born in Benningholme, Yorkshire, in October 1849 and died in Bridlington in 1919.

Richard Arthur Grantham is commemorated on:
The War Memorial, Memorial Gardens, New Road, Hornsea.
The War Memorial in St Nicholas Church, Hornsea.
The War Memorial in the Old Drill Hall, Back Southgate, Hornsea. Now the Ex-Servicemen's Club.
The Druids Roll of Honour, 22 Albion Street, Hull.

Gresham. John Francis.
Lieutenant 1/4th Battalion East Yorkshire Regiment. 150th Brigade, 50th Northumbrian Division.

He died of influenza on 16 February 1919, aged 26 years and was buried in Janval Cemetery, Dieppe, France.

He was born in Bradford in 1893 and was the son of Frank Gresham, timber merchant, and Helena Pitchford Gresham, nee Dyson, of La Estancia, South Cliff, Bridlington. They married in West Yorkshire in 1891 and had four other sons: Gordon born in Bradford in 1893, Leonard Stanley born in Hull in 1895, Frank Howard born in Hull in 1898 and Ronald born in Hull in 1903. They would lose three sons in the war.

In 1901 the family resided at 32 Westbourne Avenue, Hull. By 1911 they were living at 63 Trinity Road, Bridlington, later moving to South Cliff, Bridlington. Before the war John Francis and his brothers, Gordon and Stanley, worked as merchant's clerks.

Two of his brothers died in the war:

2nd Lieutenant Gordon Gresham: 1/4th Battalion East Yorkshire Regiment. Killed in Action on 18 June 1916 and is buried in Bailleul Communal Cemetery Extension, France. He is commemorated on the Bridlington Cenotaph and on the Priory Church War Memorial, Bridlington.

2nd Lieutenant Leonard Stanley Gresham: 1/1st East Riding Yeomanry. Killed in Action on 7 May 1917 and is buried in Kantara War Memorial Cemetery, Egypt. He is commemorated on the Bridlington Cenotaph and on Bridlington School War Memorial. His death was reported in the *Hull Daily Mail* on 17 May 1917.

Mr Frank Gresham: Born in Hull in 1862 and died in Scarborough on 20 January 1940. Mrs Helena Pitchford Gresham: Born in Stannington, Sheffield in 1867 and died in Bridlington on 15 January 1931.

John Francis Gresham is commemorated on:

The War Memorial, Memorial Gardens, New Road, Hornsea.

The War Memorial in St Nicholas Church, Hornsea.

The War Memorial in the Old Drill Hall, Back Southgate, Hornsea. Now the Ex-Servicemen's Club.

The Bridlington Cenotaph, with his two brothers.

Griffiths. Walter Harold.
2nd Lieutenant 7th Battalion Queen's Own Royal West Kent Regiment. 55th Brigade, 18th Eastern Division.
    Killed in Action on the Somme, 30 September 1916, aged 20 years. Buried in Mill Road Cemetery, France.

He was born in Hornsea on 6 August 1896 and was the son of Walter Gould Griffiths, assistant Master at Hymers College, Hull, and Olive Hicks Griffiths, nee Hiller, of Berkley House, Burton Road, Hornsea. They married in Bristol on 14 August 1895 and had one other child: Olive Kathleen born in Hornsea in 1898.

He was killed during the Battle of Thiepval Ridge, 26–30 September 1916. The 18th Division was in the Line with Thiepval to their front. On 30th the Division was heavily involved in hand to hand fighting at the Schwaben Redoubt which they took, later resisting fierce German counter-attacks.

Walter Harold was educated at St Dunstan's College, Catford, from 1907 to 1914 and in 1914 joined Corpus Christi College, Oxford.

In 1901 the family resided at 1 Sunrise Terrace, Hornsea. In 1911, after the death of his wife, Walter Gould Griffiths was living as a lodger at the house of Edith Patience Little of Melrose Villas, Hornsea. Walter Harold and his sister Olive Kathleen were living at their aunt's house at 109 Inchmerry Road, Catford, London.

Mrs Olive Hicks Griffiths: Born in Plymouth, Devon, in 1866 and died in Bristol in 1903.

Mr Walter Gould Griffiths: Born in Clifton, Glos, in 1866 and died in Bristol, in 1937.

Walter Harold Griffiths is commemorated on:
The War Memorial, Memorial Gardens, New Road, Hornsea.
The War Memorial in St Nicholas Church, Hornsea.
The War Memorial in the Old Drill Hall, Back Southgate, Hornsea. Now the Ex-Servicemen's Club.
Corpus Christi College Roll of Honour, Oxford.
St Dunstan's First World War Memorial, Catford.

Grummitt. Hugh Cecil.
2nd Lieutenant 1/4th Battalion East Yorkshire Regiment. 150th Brigade, 50th Northumbrian Division.
Died of influenza at the Brooklands Military Hospital, Newland, Hull, 25 March 1919, aged 20 years, and is buried in Southgate Cemetery, Hornsea.

He was born in Hornsea in 1899.

His death was reported in the *Hull Daily Mail* on 26 March 1919 and his funeral was reported in the same publication on 31 March 1919.

Lieutenant Hugh Cecil Grummitt.

He was twice Mentioned in Dispatches and his medals were sold at auction by Dix, Noonan and Webb, London, on 18 September 1998.

Hugh Cecil's death was reported in the *Hull Daily Mail* on 27 March 1919.

Grummitt. Joseph Roland. Brother of the above.
Lieutenant 1/4th Battalion East Yorkshire Regiment. 150th Brigade, 50th Northumbrian Division.
Died of Pneumonia at Colchester Military Hospital on 14 November 1918. Buried in Southgate Cemetery, Hornsea.

Joseph Roland was born in Hull in 1894 and emigrated to Canada in 1911. He enlisted in a Canadian unit as a Private at Alberta, Canada, in November 1914 and was given a commission in the 1/4th Battalion East Yorkshires in 1916.

Lieutenant Joseph Roland Grummitt.

The death of Joseph Roland Grummitt was reported in the *Hull Daily Mail* on 18 November 1918. His death certificate records he died of bronchial pneumonia and that his mother was present at the end.

Both men were the sons of Hugh Joseph and Bertha Grummitt, nee Eastwood, of Elim Lodge, Cliff Road, Hornsea. They married in St Philip's Church, Sculcoates, Hull, on 4 May 1891 and had three other children: Ethel Adelaide born in Hull in 1890 and died there in 1893, Evelyn May born in Hull in 1892, and Irene Lydia born in Hornsea in 1903.

In 1901 the family resided at 1 Grosvenor Terrace, Hornsea, and Hugh Joseph is recorded as a retired corn merchant. By 1911 they had moved to Elim Lodge, Hornsea.

In 1927 Mrs Bertha Grummitt applied for her sons medals to be sent to her at Le Grand Hotel de Clarens, Montreaux, Switzerland.

Southgate Cemetery, Hornsea.

Mr Hugh Joseph Grummitt: Born in Sutton, Nr Hull, in 1869 and died in Hornsea on 9 March 1919. In the same plot is their daughter, Ethel Adelaide Grummitt, who died aged three years old on 18 September 1893 and their soldier sons Joseph Roland and Hugh Cecil Grummitt. They are buried together in Southgate Cemetery, Hornsea.

Mrs Bertha Grummitt: Born in Hull in 1871, her name is quoted on the Southgate headstone but she is not buried there. She died in Bowral, New South Wales, Australia, on 4 July 1942.

Hugh Cecil Grummitt and Joseph Roland Grummitt are commemorated on:
The War Memorial, Memorial Gardens, New Road, Hornsea.
The War Memorial in St Nicholas Church, Hornsea.
The War Memorial in the Old Drill Hall, Back Southgate, Hornsea. Now the Ex-Servicemen's Club.
Neither man has a Commonwealth War Graves headstone though others in the same cemetery have. The family plot is uncared for and dilapidated.

Hamshaw. Gordon.
Private 27236. 8th Battalion East Yorkshire Regiment. 8th Brigade, 3rd Division.
Died of Wounds at the Western General Hospital, Manchester, on 11 June 1917, aged 32 years. Buried in Gainsborough General Cemetery, Lincs.

He was born in Hull in March 1885 and was the husband of Hilda Hamshaw, nee Colver, of 158 Lea Road, Gainsborough, Lincs. They married on 1 November 1911 in Gainsborough and had one son: Robert Gordon, born on 2 May 1913.

In early 1911 Gordon was a boarder at 7 Thornton Terrace, Gainsborough, and worked in a flower Mill. He later worked as a travelling salesman with Kelsey and sons of Gainsborough before enlisting in Gainsborough on 15 December 1915. He was posted to the West Riding Brigade No1 Territorial Force Artillery Training School at Ripon and then to the 11th Hull Service Battalion East Yorkshire Regiment, 2nd Hull Pals. He went to France on 25 November 1916 and was transferred to the 8th Battalion East Yorkshire Regiment.

On 3 May 1917 the 8th were in action in the Battle for Arras, 3rd Battle of the Scarpe, 3–5 May. The 8th Battalion East Yorkshire Regiment moved into the Front Line north of Monchy-le-Preux on 1 May. The attack began at 3:45 a.m. on 3 May, as the British barrage fell on the German Lines dozens of white vary lights soared into the black night sky, a signal for their own artillery to return fire. Artillery fire from both sides was heavy and thundered to earth with ear splitting detonations. The enemy trenches were strongly held and a murderous machine-gun fire from Infantry Hill cut down many of the attacking British halting the assault. Men took shelter in shell holes and any attempt to leave them was met with a hail of bullets. On 3 May 1917 the 8th Battalion suffered 35 dead, 161 wounded and 39 missing.

Gordon Hamshaw received gun-shot wounds to the left thigh and right hand on 3 May 1917, he was evacuated to the Etaples General Hospital and then to the 2nd Western General Hospital, Manchester, where infection set in and he died at 4:30 a.m. on 11 June 1917. His body was returned to his wife at Gainsborough where he was buried with full military honours.

Gainsborough General Cemetery, Lincs.

Hilda Hamshaw: Hilda never re-married and died in Gainsborough on 18 January 1973, age 83 years, she is buried with her husband in the above grave.

Gordon Hamshaw is commemorated on:
The War Memorial, Memorial Gardens, New Road, Hornsea.
The War Memorial in St Nicholas Church, Hornsea.
The War Memorial in the Old Drill Hall, Back Southgate, Hornsea. Now the Ex-Servicemen's Club.

Hamshaw. Joseph. Brother of the above.
Private 200305. 1/4th Battalion East Yorkshire Regiment. 150th Brigade, 50th Northumbrian Division.

Killed in Action 23 April 1917, aged 35 years. He has no known grave and is commemorated on the Arras Memorial to the Missing, France.

Joseph was killed in the Second Battle of the Scarpe, 23–25 April 1917, the Battle of Arras. At 4:45 a.m. on 23rd the troops of 150th Brigade moved to the attack into a ferocious enemy bombardment, their objective being the high ground north-west of Cherisy. In the fierce fighting that raged all day the 1/4th East Yorkshires lost 10 officers and 215 other ranks.

Joseph was born in Hull on 26 May 1882. Gordon and Joseph were the sons of John Hamshaw, shipping clerk, and Elizabeth, Lilly, Briggs Hamshaw, nee Widdas, of 12 Cliff Terrace, Cliff Road, Hornsea. They married in Hull in 1881 and had one other child: Gwendoline born in 1887.

In 1891 the family resided at 117 Constable Street, Hull. By 1901 they had made the move to 11 Clifton Street, Hornsea, Elizabeth Briggs Hamshaw died in Hornsea in1901. In 1911 John Hamshaw, widower, and his daughter Gwendoline resided at 30 Clifford Street, Hornsea.

Joseph was the husband of Nellie Hamshaw, nee Hornsby Pegg. They married in Hornsea in 1905 and had one son: Jack Raymond born in Sydenham, London, in 1907. In 1911 Joseph was living at 20 Park Avenue, Bush Hill Park, Edmonton, London, and was working as an auctioneer's clerk. Nellie is not named in the census record of that year.

He went to France on 17 April 1915.

Southgate Cemetery, Hornsea.

Mr John Hamshaw: Born in Hull in 1858 and died in Knaresborough on 9 September 1936. Mrs Elizabeth, Lilly, Briggs Hamshaw: Born in Hull on 5 March 1860 and died in Hornsea on 27 July 1901. They now lie together in Southgate Cemetery, Hornsea.

Joseph Hamshaw is commemorated on:
The War Memorial, Memorial Gardens, New Road, Hornsea.
The War Memorial in St Nicholas Church, Hornsea.
The War Memorial in the Old Drill Hall, Back Southgate, Hornsea. Now the Ex-Servicemen's Club.
The Arras Memorial to the Missing.

Harker. Frederick George.
Private 2241. 3/1st Suffolk Yeomanry.
Died on 9 February 1916, aged 21 years. Buried in Southgate Cemetery, Hornsea.

He was born at White House Farm, Southgate, Hornsea, in 1895 and was the son of John Clappison Harker and Pamela Jane Harker, nee Waines, of The Whitehouse, Hornsea. They married in Hornsea in 1881 and had seven other children: Annie born 1881, Henry born 1883, Rachel Ethel born 1887, Mary Jane born 1889, Mabel Doris born 1896, Pamela Edith born 1899 and Rosamund born 1907, died 1908. All the children were born in Hornsea.

Private Frederick George Harker.

Before the war Frederick George worked as a Clerk in the London Joint Stock Bank, Holderness Road, Hull. He enlisted at Bury St Edmunds in July 1915, while training in Colchester he contracted diphtheria and spent some time in hospital before being invalided home. He was visiting Middleton on the Wolds in January and attended a service at Middleton Parish Church. His health seemed to improve but he was taken ill in February and died there.

The death of Frederick George Harker was reported in the *Hull Daily Mail* of 11 February 1916. The Hornsea Council minutes of 22 February 1916 passed on their condolences to Mr and Mrs Harper on the death of her son.

Southgate Cemetery, Hornsea.

Mr John Clappison Harker: Born in Swine on 4 May 1858 and died in Hornsea on 8 April 1925. Mrs Pamela Jane Harker: Born in Bempton in 1864 and died in Hornsea on 31 December 1932. They lie together in Southgate Cemetery, Hornsea. Lying in the same plot is their daughter Rosamund Harker, born on 25 February 1907, died 22 August 1908 and Frederick Harker, son of H and S Harker, died 1 April 1941, aged two years. Frederick George Harker is buried in the same plot.

In the same cemetery are buried the following:

The daughters of John Clappison and Pamela Jane Harker. Pamela Edith, who died on 31 August 1979 and Mabel Doris who died on 1 September 1984. Recorded on the headstone is the faithful companion of the two women, Albert Henry Taylor, who died on 19 September 1971, his ashes are interred here. They all resided at the Whitehouse, Southgate, Hornsea.

Also:

The son of John Clappison and Pamela Jane Harker. Henry, who died on 16 January 1948, aged 64 years, and his wife, Sarah Ann, who died on 13 February 1974.

Frederick George Harker is commemorated on:

The War Memorial, Memorial Gardens, New Road, Hornsea.

The War Memorial in St Nicholas Church, Hornsea.

The War Memorial in the Old Drill Hall, Back Southgate, Hornsea. Now the Ex-Servicemen's Club.

The family headstone, Southgate Cemetery, Hornsea.

On 18 April 2016 I met Carol Harker at the Hornsea Museum, her husband, Thomas Harker, was the Nephew of Frederick George Harker. We had a most interesting and useful chat about Hornsea and she gave me the names of other contacts.

Harman. James.
Private 3/7143. 7th Battalion East Yorkshire Regiment. 50th Brigade, 17th Northern Division.
Killed in Action 23 June 1916. Buried in the Citadel New Military Cemetery, Fricourt, France, aged 32 years.

Private James Harman.

In late June 1916 the 7th Battalion East Yorkshire Regiment had been attached to the 21st Division in preparation for the attack on Fricourt on 1 July. The Germans could see the large concentrations of troops moving into the area and bombarded the British positions regularly.

He was born in Rimswell, Yorkshire, in 1885 and was the son of Robinson Harman, farm labourer, and Ann Valentine Harman, nee Cook, of Rimswell and later of Marlborough Avenue, Hornsea. They married in Patrington in 1878 and had seven other children: George born in Rimswell in 1881, Sarah born in Harrogate in 1882, Maud born in Harrogate in 1887, Jane born in Patrington in 1891, Emily born in Rimswell in 1895, Ada born in Frodingham in 1897 and Dora born in Frodingham in 1902.

In 1891 the family was residing at 5 High Road, Rimswell, Yorkshire, Robinson was a farm labourer. In 1901 they had moved to South Frodingham, Yorkshire. By 1911 they had made the move to 42 Marlborough Avenue, Hornsea.

In 1901 James was working as a farm servant in Otteringham and in 1911 he was working as a Wagoner at the Manor House, Bewholme. In the portrait above he is wearing the badge and uniform of the Royal Artillery.

Howden Minster Churchyard.

Mrs Ann Valentine Harman: Born in Louth, Lincs, in 1858 and died in Howden on 11 March 1936. Mr Robinson Harman: Born in Rimswell, Yorkshire in 1857 and died in Howden on 17 January 1939. They are buried together in Howden Minster Churchyard.

James Harman is commemorated on:
The War Memorial, Memorial Gardens, New Road, Hornsea.
The War Memorial in St Nicholas Church, Hornsea.
The War Memorial in the Old Drill Hall, Back Southgate, Hornsea. Now the Ex-Servicemen's Club.

Hedley. John Ralph.
Lieutenant Colonel DSO MID 6th Battalion, Northumberland Fusiliers. Commanding 1/5th Cumberland Battalion the Border Regiment. 149th Brigade, 50th Northumbrian Division.
Died on 15 July 1917, aged 46 years. Buried in Bucquoy Road Cemetery, Ficheux, France.

John Ralph Hedley was born in Chaddleworth Woolley, Berkshire, on 21 March 1871 and was the son of John and Anne Hedley, nee Colley. They married in Castle Ward, Northumberland, in 1859 and had seven other children: Mary Isabella born in Stamfordham, Northumberland in 1860, James Frederick born in Stamfordham, Northumberland in 1861, Elizabeth Ann born in Stamfordham, Northumberland in 1863, Jane born in Stamfordham, Northumberland in 1864, Cecil born in Stamfordham, Northumberland in 1865, Annie Dora born in Chaddleworth Woolley, Berkshire in 1867 and Thomas Mason born in Chaddleworth Wooley, Berkshire in 1869.

John Ralph was the husband of Ada Marie Hedley, nee Bainbridge, of Westgate House, Westgate, Hornsea. They married in Gateshead in 1900 and had two children: Joan Violet Hudson Hedley born in Newcastle in 1902 and John Richard Percival Hedley born in Newcastle in 1903. In 1901 the family resided at Parkhead, Jesmond Dene, Newcastle.

He was educated at the Royal Grammar School, Newcastle, and in 1891 was a lodger in the house of Sarah Hildred at 27 Lincoln Street, Gateshead, working as an Auctioneer's Clerk, later he worked as an Auctioneer at Eshott Hall, Felton, Newcastle. By 1911 the family had moved to Hornsea and he was employed by the Inland Revenue as a District Valuer and was a member of the St Nicholas Church choir.

On 18 June 1898 he was initiated into the Masons, Percy Lodge, Northumberland. By 1903 he was the Worshipful Master of the Victoria Commemoration Reserve Forces Lodge, Northumberland, resigning on 30 September 1911.

He enlisted into the Northumberland Fusiliers in 1901, was a major by 1912 and was promoted to lieutenant colonel on his move to France on 11 November 1915. He was awarded Distinguished Service Order on 3 June 1916.

It was reported in the *Hull Daily Mail* of 21 July 1917 that Lieutenant Colonel John Ralph Hedley had died of a heart attack.

A window was dedicated to the memory of John Ralph Hedley in St Nicholas Church, Hornsea, on 24 April 1919.

Ada Marie Hedley: Born in Newcastle in 1874. Died in Holderness on 29 September 1961.

Jesmond Old Cemetery, Newcastle.

Mr John Hedley: Born in Eglington, Northumberland, on 20 January 1830 and died in Wantage, Berks, on 19 April 1886. Mrs Anne Hedley: Born in Northumberland in 1829 and died in Newcastle on 6 November 1896. They are buried together in Jesmond Old Cemetery, Newcastle.

John Ralph Hedley is commemorated on:
The War Memorial, Memorial Gardens, New Road, Hornsea.
The War Memorial in St Nicholas Church, Hornsea.
A Memorial Window in St Nicholas Church, Hornsea.
The War Memorial in the Old Drill Hall, Back Southgate, Hornsea. Now the Ex-Servicemen's Club.
The Masonic Roll of Honour 1914/18.
The Royal Grammar School Roll of Honour, Newcastle.
A brass plaque in the Methodist Chapel, Eshott, Newcastle.
A stained glass memorial screen in St George's Drill Hall, Northumberland Road, Newcastle.

Hetherington. Geoffrey Nevill.
Private 81279. 15th Battalion Durham Light Infantry.
Died of Wounds at Number 13 Harvard USA General Hospital, Boulogne, on 21 April 1918, aged 18 years. Buried in Boulogne Eastern Cemetery, France.

On 21 March 1918 Operation Michael was launched by General Ludendorf. On 4 April 1918 the Germans attacked towards Amiens and the 15th Battalion Durham Light Infantry took the full force of the German assault, by the end of the day they were forced to retire and were reduced from three companies to one, losing over 200 men. Geoffrey Nevill Hetherington was badly wounded and rushed to the rear and he died of his wounds 18 days later.

He was born on 29 September 1899 in Alton, Hampshire, and was the son of Walter Hudswell Hetherington and Gertrude Annie Margaret Hetherington, nee Nevill, of 20 Clifford Street, Hornsea. They married at Portsea Island, Hampshire, in 1897 and had three other children: Marjorie Alice born in Alton on 22 October 1898,

Joan born in Alton on 19 September 1901 and Richard Nevill born in Alton on 19 November 1908.

In 1901 the family was living at 52 Anstey Road, Alton, Hampshire. Walter was working as a Sanitary Engineer. By 1911 they were living at 84 Victoria Road North, Portsmouth. Walter was employed as a Traveller in printing and stationary.

Geoffrey was privately educated and acted as a Sea Scout on the East Yorkshire Coastal defences in 1915, 1916 and 1917, and was awarded three good service badges. He was called up and enlisted in Beverley into the East Yorkshire Regiment on his 18th birthday, 28 September 1917. His service papers give his occupation as school boy. In October 1917 he was sent to Rugeley Camp, Staffs, for training with the DLI. He injured his right knee and was admitted to the Military Hospital at Cannock Chase in late 1917. On 31 March 1918 he was at the Base Depot at Boulogne and was transferred to the 15th DLI on 3 April 1918. Geoffrey received gun-shot wounds to the chest which resulted in his death 18 days later.

An officer wrote home to his wife:
"He was a general favourite with the officers and men, who always speak of him in affectionate terms."

The death of Geoffrey Nevill Hetherington was reported in the *Hull Daily Mail* of 7 May 1918.

Mrs Gertrude Annie Margaret Hetherington: Born in Martyr Worthy, Hampshire, in 1876 and died in Hampstead, London, in December 1927. Mr Walter Hudswell Hetherington: Born in Alton, Hampshire, in 1867 and died in Leeds in 1942.

Geoffrey Nevill Hetherington is commemorated on:
The War Memorial, Memorial Gardens, New Road, Hornsea.
The War Memorial in St Nicholas Church, Hornsea.
The War Memorial in the Old Drill Hall, Back Southgate, Hornsea. Now the Ex-Servicemen's Club.
Du Ruvigny's Roll of Honour. 1914–18.

Jackson. Harold Willows.
Lieutenant 1/4th Battalion East Yorkshire Regiment. 150th Brigade, 50th Northumbrian Division.

He was wounded on 3 May 1917 in the Battle of Arras and Died of Wounds at the 8th Casualty Clearing Station, Duisans, on 14 May 1917, aged 20 years. Buried in Duisans British Cemetery, France.

Lieutenant Harold Willows Jackson.

In late April 1917, at the Second Battle of the Scarpe, the 1/4th Battalion East Yorkshire Regiment had suffered badly and had lost 17 officers and 352 other ranks in the hard fighting there. The 3rd Battle of the Scarpe opened on 3 May 1917 but the 1/4th East Yorkshires were not directly involved.

He was born in Hull on 26 February 1897 and was the only son of John Henry and Caroline Maud Jackson, nee Willows, of Holly Lodge, 12 Grosvenor Terrace, New Road, Hornsea. They married in Hatfield, Herts, in 1895 and had two more children:

Adele Mary Jackson born in Hull in 1900 and Nora Willows Jackson born Hornsea in 1904.

In 1901 the family resided at 93 Westbourne Avenue, Hull. John Henry is recorded as a self-employed bit manufacturer and when he died in Hornsea in 1911 the wills and probate records state he left over 16,000 pounds to his wife. That same year Caroline Maud, Adelle Mary, Nora Willows, Lillian Mary, niece, and two servants were living at Holly Lodge, 12 Grosvenor Terrace, New Road, Hornsea.

Harold was educated at the Red House School, Marston Moor, Yorkshire, and was a pupil there in 1911. He joined the 10th Battalion East Yorkshire Regiment, Hull Commercials, 1st Hull Pals, as a private and was given a commission in the 1/4th in March 1915. He went to France on 21 March 1917.

Lieutenant Harold Willows Jackson was listed under 'The Stricken Brave' in the *Beverley Guardian* on 19 May 1917. His death was reported in the *Hull Daily Mail* on 21 May 1917 and on 19 June 1917.

Southgate Cemetery, Hornsea.

Mr John Henry Jackson: Born in Hull on 3 November 1856 and died in Hornsea on 16 January 1911. Mrs Caroline Maud Jackson: Born in High Holborn, London, on 23 October 1863 and died in Hornsea on 3 January 1936. They are buried together in Southgate Cemetery, Hornsea. Their son, Harold Willows Jackson, is commemorated on the headstone.

Harold Willows Jackson is commemorated on:
The War Memorial, Memorial Gardens, New Road, Hornsea.
The War Memorial in St Nicholas Church, Hornsea.
The War Memorial in the Old Drill Hall, Back Southgate, Hornsea. Now the Ex-Servicemen's Club.
The family headstone, Southgate Cemetery, Hornsea.

Lieutenant Henry Douglas Jackson, MC.

Jackson. Henry Douglas.
2nd Lieutenant MC. 1/4th Battalion East Yorkshire Regiment. 150th Brigade, 50th Northumbrian Division.
Killed in Action on 26 October 1916, aged 22 years. Buried in Bazentin le Petit Communal Cemetery Extension, France.

He was killed by shell-fire at High Wood during operations on the Somme, the 50th Division was in the Line with Warlencourt to their front left.

Henry Douglas was born in Hull in June 1894 and was the son of Henry Ollerenshaw Jackson and Bertha Amelia Jackson, nee Smith, of 18 Leicester Street, Hull, later of 4 Clifford Street, Hornsea. They married in Southwell, Notts, in July 1890 and had three other children: Phyllis Mary born in Hull in 1892, Enid Bertha born in Hull in 1899 and Dorothy Frances born in Hornsea in 1902.

In 1891 Henry and Bertha resided at 27 Grove Street, Hull, and Henry was a self-employed Grocer. In 1901 they had moved to Cromwell House, Cliff Road, Hornsea, and Henry worked as a Butter Merchant. He worked as a Provisions Agent in 1911 and the family resided at Melsonby, Eastgate, Hornsea.

The year Henry Ollerenshaw Jackson died, 1926, he and Bertha resided at Bazantan, Carr Lane, Kirkella, he left his wife 2,500 pounds in his will.

Henry Douglas was educated at St Bede's School, Hornsea, and worked as an Oil Merchant's Clerk in Hull before enlisting in 1915.

In 1916 his battalion was in action on the Somme and Henry led a party that laid wire up to the second objective over ground swept by Machine-gun and shell-fire. He formed a signal post in a shell hole within 10 yards of the objective enabling important messages to be relayed to the rear. For his bravery and devotion to duty he was awarded the Military Cross.

Lieutenant Cecil Slack, 1/4th Battalion East Yorkshire Regiment, of Reckitt's Factory, Hull, was present when Henry Douglas Jackson was killed, he wrote:

"I had been standing talking to two officers, after long experience one can sometimes hear or sense an approaching shell. By a split fraction of a second I dived down flat, when it was over we could not find the two officers I had been talking to. Then we came across a head and shoulders and trailing guts, all that was left of Lieutenant Cranswick. The other body, that of young Henry Douglas Jackson, a nephew of Major H B Jackson, was found some thirty yards away from where we had been standing."

Mr Henry Ollerenshaw Jackson: Born in Hull in 1862 and died in Kirkella, Nr Hull, on 20 March 1926. Mrs Bertha Amelia Jackson: Born in Cromwell, Notts, in 1866 and died in Willerby, Nr Hull, on 29 October 1938.

Henry Douglas Jackson is commemorated on:
The War Memorial, Memorial Gardens, New Road, Hornsea.
The War Memorial in St Nicholas Church, Hornsea.
The War Memorial in the Old Drill Hall, Back Southgate, Hornsea. Now the Ex-Servicemen's Club.

Keith. John.
Private 17086. 3rd Battalion West Yorkshire Regiment.
Died in Armstrong College Hospital, Newcastle, on 30 December 1914, aged 44 years. Buried in Newcastle upon Tyne, St Andrew's and Jesmond, Cemetery.

He was born in Watton, Yorkshire, on 7 January 1871 and was the son of George and Ellen Keith, nee Walker, of Newbegin, later of Mere Side, Hornsea. They married in Driffield in October 1870 and had seven other children: Emma born in Hull in 1875, Henry born in Hornsea in 1877, Frank born in Hornsea in 1879, Fred A born in Hornsea in 1882, Annie born in Hornsea in 1884, George A born in Hornsea in 1886 and Alfred born in Hornsea in 1888.

In 1871 George, Ellen and their son John were lodgers in the house of John Walker, farm labourer and widower, of Watton, Yorkshire. By 1881 they were in Hornsea at 2 Ocean Terrace, George worked as a farm labourer. In 1891 and 1901 they lived at

Southgate, Hornsea, and in 1911 they moved to Newbegin, Hornsea. George was working as a caretaker in his later years.

John Keith served as an Able Seaman in the Royal Navy on HMS *Pembroke* and numerous other vessels from 10 January 1890 to 11 September 1911. After which he was released on a pension. Before his service in the navy his profession is given as a butcher.

John was a general labourer at the Hornsea Brickyard before the war and was the husband of Elizabeth Keith, nee Green, of 32 Southgate, Hornsea. They married in Hull in 1903 and resided at the above address in 1911.

His death certificate records he died of cardiac failure due to bronchial pneumonia and that J R Moffatt was present at the end.

Southgate Cemetery, Hornsea.

Elizabeth Keith: Born in Chester on 10 April 1866. She never re-married and died in Hornsea on 5 April 1961. She lies in the Griffin family plot, Southgate Cemetery.

Mr George Keith: Born in Hatfield, Yorkshire, in 1849 and died in Hornsea in March 1927. Place of burial unknown. Mrs Ellen Keith: Born in Watton, Yorkshire, in 1847 and died in the East Riding in 1938. Place of burial unknown.

John Keith is commemorated on:

The War Memorial, Memorial Gardens, New Road, Hornsea.

The War Memorial in St Nicholas Church, Hornsea.

The War Memorial in the Old Drill Hall, Back Southgate, Hornsea. Now the Ex-Servicemen's Club.

Private Frederick Keith.

Keith. Frederick.
Private 13294. 2nd Battalion Coldstream Guards. 1st Guards Brigade, Guards Division.
Killed in Action 9 October 1917. Buried in Artillery Wood Cemetery, Belgium.

He was killed at the Battle of Poelcapelle, Passchendaele. The Guards Division attacked at 5:20 a.m. and made good progress taking all three objectives but paid a terrible price in lives lost.

He was born in Hornsea on 2 July 1882 and was the son of Robert, farm labourer, and Mary Keith, nee Smith, of Hornsea. They married in Hull on 23 May 1864 and had 10 other children: Amelia born in Garton on the Wolds on 11 July 1864, Maria born in Seaton on 29 July 1866, George born in Garton on the Wolds on 11 December 1867, Thomas born in Garton on the Wolds in January in 1869, Annie born in Garton on the Wolds in 1871, Clara born in Garton on the Wolds on 2 August 1874, William born in Hornsea on 3 September 1876, Emily born in Hornsea on 3 February 1878, Sarah born in Hornsea on 5 October 1879 and Harry born in Hornsea on 2 July 1883.

In 1871 Robert and Mary resided in Goxhill, Yorkshire, and by 1881 had moved to Mereside, Hornsea, where they lived all their lives. Robert died in Hornsea in 1891 and in 1901 the only family members living at their Mereside home were Mary and her son William.

In 1911 Mary had brought into her home her daughter's family: Marmaduke and Anne Medley, nee Keith, and their son Fred, aged four years. Marmaduke died in 1911 and Annie re-married in 1913 to John Andrew of Hornsea, John lost his son, John William, in the Great War. He is recorded on the Hornsea War Memorial.

Fred Keith was the husband of Beatrice Keith, nee Rodgerson, of 6 York Avenue, St Mark's Street, Hull, later of Mereside, Hornsea. They married in Hull in 1906 and had five children: George Robert born on 5 December 1906, Beatrice born 1908, Lilly born 1910 and died in 1911, Fred born 1912 and died 1913 and Fred born on 13 April 1914. All the children were born in Hull.

Before the war he had served with the Hornsea Artillery Volunteers, disbanded in 1908. In 1901 he was working as a servant on the farm of Frederick and Ann Ellen Towse of Atwick. Later he worked for the North Eastern Railway.

His photograph appeared in *Green's Almanac* in 1918.

The death of Fred Keith was reported in the *Beverley Guardian*, with picture, on 3 November 1917.

Mrs Beatrice Keith: Born in Hull in 1885, she never re-married and died in Hull in September 1950.

Mr Robert Keith: Born in Hatfield, Yorkshire, on 5 March 1847. Died in Hornsea on 24 April 1891.

Mrs Mary Keith: Born at Garton on the Wolds March 1844. Died at Hornsea in September 1925.

Frederick Keith is commemorated on:

The War Memorial, Memorial Gardens, New Road, Hornsea.
The War Memorial in St Nicholas Church, Hornsea.
The War Memorial in the Old Drill Hall, Back Southgate, Hornsea. Initials J K. Now the Ex-Servicemen's Club.
The handwritten Roll of Honour in the Wesleyan Methodist Chapel, Hornsea.
St Mark's Street Roll of Honour, Hull.
The North Eastern Railway memorial, Station Road, York.
The North Eastern Railway Roll of Honour in the Railway Museum, York.

Keith. J K. This name is inscribed on the War Memorial in the Memorial Gardens, New Road, Hornsea, but after searching civilian and military records for quite some time I have to agree with Michael Sewell, that this man does not exist. I have discovered two other men from Hornsea who were killed with the surname of Keith that are not recorded on the war memorial but neither of them has the initial J K.

Lieutenant Frank Kemp.

Kemp. Frank.
2nd Lieutenant 11th Battalion King's Own Yorkshire Light Infantry, attached to 56th Battalion Machine Gun Corps. 56th Brigade, 19th Western Division.

Killed in Action 22 July 1916, aged 24 years. He has no known grave and is commemorated on the Thiepval Memorial to the Missing of the Somme, France.

On the night of the 22 July 1916 the 19th Division attacked at Bazentin le Petit with Mametz Wood to their rear. The assault was held up by heavy machine-gun fire, after numerous attempts to advance they were withdrawn in the early hours of the 23rd after suffering heavy casualties.

He was born in Hull in 1892 and was the son of William, flour miller's clerk, and Ada Ellen Kemp, nee Coulson, of Rockleigh, Wilton Road, Hornsea. They married in Hull in 1888 and had four other children: Arthur Roland born in Hull in 1890, William born in Hull in 1893, John Harold born in Hull in 1894 and Leslie Stephenson born in Hull in 1905.

In 1891 the family resided at 43 Thomas Street, Hull. By 1901 they had made the move to 5 St Nicholas Mount, Hornsea. In 1911 Frank was an apprentice fitter at Messrs Coopers and Sons of Hull and planned to take a Board of Trade Certificate as a marine engineer. The family was living at 9 Ash Grove, Beverley Road, Hull.

He joined the 11th Service Battalion King's Own Light Infantry in April 1915.

Frank Kemp was listed in a casualty list in the *Hull Daily Mail* on 28 July 1916, and in a Roll of Honour, with picture, in the *Beverley Guardian* and the *Hull Daily Mail* on 5 August 1916.

Southgate Cemetery, Hornsea.

Mr William Kemp: Born in Hull in 1861 and died in Hornsea on 20 May 1938. Mrs Ada Ellen Kemp: Born in Hull in 1860 and died in Hornsea on 11 September 1945. They lie together in Southgate Cemetery, Hornsea. Their son Frank is commemorated on the headstone.

Edenfield Cemetery, Hornsea.

John Harold Kemp: Brother of Frank. Born in Hull on 22 March 1894 and died in Hornsea on 3 May 1982.

Edith Lois Kemp: John Harold's wife. Born on 10 December 1893 and died in Hornsea on 16 June 1984.

Frank Kemp is commemorated on:
The War Memorial, Memorial Gardens, New Road, Hornsea.
The War Memorial in St Nicholas Church, Hornsea.
The War Memorial in the Old Drill Hall, Back Southgate, Hornsea. Now the Ex-Servicemen's Club.
The War Memorial, brass plaque, in the Wesleyan Methodist Chapel, Hornsea.

The family headstone, Southgate Cemetery, Hornsea.
The Thiepval Memorial to the Missing of the Somme, France.

Lieutenant Kenneth Loftus.

Loftus. Kenneth.
2nd Lieutenant 107370. Royal Field Artillery.
Died of wounds at the Royal Free Hospital, London, on 9 November 1918, aged 26 years. Buried in Brookwood Military Cemetery, Pirbright, Surrey.

He was born in Leeds on 16 December 1892 and was the son of Alfred and Isabella Loftus, nee Seward, of Leeds. They married in Hull in 1876 and had four other children: Ernest Alfred born in Hull in 1877 and died in Leeds in 1895, Douglas Seward born in Hull in 1880 and died in Hull on 23 January 1905, Barbara Isabel born Leeds in 1888 and Marjorie Caroline born in Leeds in 1895.

In 1901 the family resided at Headingly, Leeds. In 1911, after the death of his parents in 1902, Kenneth was living with his aunt, Mary English, at 1 Alexandra Terrace, Railway Street, Hornsea, and worked as an accountant's clerk. He left England in 1911 and landed in St John, Brunswick, Canada. The Wills and Probate records give his address at the time of his death as Balamaine, Newland Park, Hull. This address is that of his sister Mrs Barbara Isabel Massey, nee Loftus.

Kenneth landed in France on 22 September 1915 with the Canadian contingent and was commissioned into the Royal Field Artillery in 1917.

Mr Alfred Loftus: Born in Nantwich, Cheshire, in 1851 and died in Leeds in 1902.
Mrs Isabella Loftus: Born in Hull in 1858 and died in Leeds in 1902.

Kenneth Loftus is commemorated on:
The War Memorial, Memorial Gardens, New Road, Hornsea.
The War Memorial in St Nicholas Church, Hornsea.
The War Memorial in the Old Drill Hall, Back Southgate, Hornsea. Now the Ex-Servicemen's Club.
The Books of Remembrance in the peace Tower, Parliament Hill, Canada.

Lord. John Frederick Wilson.
2nd Lieutenant 1/5th Battalion King's Own Yorkshire Light Infantry. 148th Brigade, 49th West Riding Division.
Killed in Action during the Battle of Arras 9 April 1917, aged 34 years. Buried in London Cemetery, Neuville Vitasse, France.

He was born in Hull on 10 October 1883 and was the son of Frederick, Estate Agent, and Jane Lord, nee Wilson, of Belvedere, 37 the Esplanade, Hornsea. They married in Scarborough in July 1881. Their other children were: William Ronald Lord born in Hull in 1884, Percy Wilson Lord born in Hull in 1885, Gladys Annie Lord born in Hull on 27 November 1887, Beatrice Mary Lord born in Hull on 9 June 1889, Dorothy Elizabeth Marguarite Lord born in Hull on 13 June 1890 and died 1893,

Elsie Elvina Lord born in Hull in 1892 and died 1910 and Hilda Beeforth Lord born in Hull on 19 November 1893 and died 1895.

In 1891 the family was living at 52 Kingston Villas, Witham, Hull, Mr Frederick Lord was self-employed as a Coal Merchant. By 1901 they were living at Belvedere, 37 the Esplanade, Hornsea, and Mr Frederick Lord was employed as a Land and Estate Agent. In 1911 the family resided at the same address and John Frederick Wilson Lord was an Architect by trade.

John Frederick Wilson Lord was a volunteer in the East Riding Yorkshire Yeomanry on their formation pre-1914. When war broke out he was granted a commission and went to France on 22 September 1915. His brother, William Ronald Lord, was commissioned into the Machine-Gun Corps and survived the war.

In May 1917 the *Hull and East Riding Times* reported a memorial service that was held in St Nicholas Church, Hornsea, for John Frederick Wilson Lord, the vicar gave his condolences to Mr and Mrs Lord and the family.

He was featured in a Roll of Honour in the *Hull Daily Mail* on 23 and 24 April 1917.

Southgate Cemetery, Hornsea.

Mr Frederick Lord: Born Scarborough in 1859 and died in Hornsea on 12 September 1937. Mrs Jane Lord: Born in Scarborough in 1861 and died in Hornsea on 30 June 1932. They are buried in Southgate Cemetery, Hornsea. Their son, John Frederick Wilson Lord, is commemorated on the headstone. Three of their children are buried in the same plot: Beatrice Mary Lord was born on 9 June 1889 and died on 26 December 1981. Elsie Elvina Lord was born on 15 August 1891and died on 27 December 1910. Gladys Annie Lord was born on 27 November 1887 and died on 23 April 1955.

Dorothy Elizabeth Marguerite Lord was born on 13 June 1890 and died on 6 November 1893 of pneumonia. Hilda Beeforth Lord was born on 19 November 1893 and died on 26 January 1895 of convulsions. Both are commemorated on the family headstone but are interred in Hedon Road Cemetery, Hull.

Ruth Gillam Lord was the wife of William Ronald Lord, she died in Hornsea on 17 August 1939, aged 48 years, and is buried in Southgate Cemetery, Hornsea. William Ronald died in Bridlington in 1953.

John Frederick Wilson Lord is commemorated on:

The War Memorial, Memorial Gardens, New Road, Hornsea.

The War Memorial in St Nicholas Church, Hornsea.

The War Memorial in the Old Drill Hall, Back Southgate, Hornsea. Now the Ex-Servicemen's Club.

The family headstone, Southgate Cemetery, Hornsea.

Lyon. Arthur Stanton.
Private B/19490. 26th Battalion Royal Fusiliers. 124th Brigade, 41st Division.
Killed in Action between 4 and 10 October 1916. Aged 34 years. He has no known grave and is commemorated on the Thiepval Memorial to the Missing of the Somme, France.

Arthur Stanton was killed during the Battle of the Ancre Heights, the Somme, 1–11 October 1916. In October the 41st Division was in the Line with Flers to their rear, facing them was the 21st Bavarian Regiment.

He was born in Hornsea in 1882 and was the son of Charles Edward Augustus, Ships Insurance Broker, and Betsie Milicah Rafton Lyon, nee Chew, of Victoria Avenue, Hornsea. They married in Hull in 1876 and had five other children: Dora born in Hull in 1878, Alice born in Hull in 1880, Elsie born in Hornsea in 1886, Mary born in Hornsea on 18 September 1889 and Agnes born in Hornsea in 1892.

In 1891 the family resided at New Road, Hornsea. By 1901 they had moved to The Lair, Eastgate, Hornsea, and in 1911 only Charles and Betsy were in the family home at Eastgate.

Before the war Arthur was educated at Hymers College, Hull. In 1911 he was a boarder in the house of Emma Cox of 32 West Street, Wisbech, and worked as a Bank Clerk. He later worked at the Birmingham Branch of the National Provincial Bank, his home address at that time was 58 Beaufort Road, Birmingham. He enlisted in 1915 into the 26th Battalion, Royal Fusiliers. This was a Pals Battalion known as the Bankers, made up mainly of Bank Clerks and Accountants.

His death was reported in the *Hull Times* on 21 October 1916, and in the *Hull Daily Mail* on 19 October 1916.

Southgate Cemetery, Hornsea.

Mrs Betsy Milicah Rafton Lyon: Born in Hull in 1850 and died in Hornsea on 11 September 1917. Mr Charles Edward Augustus Lyon: Born in Hull in 1850 and died in Hornsea on 5 September 1931. They are buried in Southgate Cemetery, Hornsea. Arthur Stanton Lyon is commemorated on the headstone. In the same plot are two of their daughters: Dora Lyon, died 19 February 1962 and Mary Lyon, died 4 September 1967.

Arthur Stanton Lyon is commemorated on:
The War Memorial, Memorial Gardens, New Road, Hornsea.
The War Memorial in St Nicholas Church, Hornsea.
The War Memorial in the Old Drill Hall, Back Southgate, Hornsea. Now the Ex-Servicemen's Club.
The Memorial Window in St Nicholas Church, Hornsea.
The family headstone, Southgate Cemetery, Hornsea.
The Hymers College Roll of Honour, Hymers Avenue, Hull.
The Thiepval Memorial to the Missing of the Somme, France.

Lieutenant George Stanley Mansfield.

Mansfield. George Stanley.
2nd Lieutenant 1/4th Battalion East Yorkshire Regiment, attached to 1st Battalion East Yorkshire Regiment.

Killed in Action on 22 March 1918 during the Battle of St Quentin, on the second day of the Great German offensive, aged 22 years. He has no known grave and is commemorated on the Pozieres Memorial to the Missing, France.

The 1/4th Battalion East Yorkshire Regiment had suffered badly in 1917 and was moved to a supposed quiet part of the Line at Harbonnieres. They had no way of knowing that this area would be the main thrust of General Ludendorf's Great Offensive on 21 March, 1918. They were moved by rail to Brie and took up positions at Bernes on the 22nd. The grey avalanche broke over them and they fell back before the violence of the assault, fighting from village to village until they could fight no more. As the German infantry advanced low flying aircraft straffed the retreating British, Lieutenant Mansfield was hit through the leg by an aeroplane bullet and quickly bled to death. By the 31 March the 1/4th had lost the biggest part of its complement, only three officers and 36 other ranks still remaining. The news of his death distressed his father and mother so that Mr Mansfield died shortly after.

He was born in Hull in 1896 and was the son of George, Clerk, and Emily Mansfield, nee Best, of 5 Grosvenor Terrace, Hornsea. They married at the New Jerusalem Church, Spring Bank, Hull, on 23 May 1889 and had four other children: Henry born in Hull in 1891, Edgar Arthur born in Hull in 1892, Douglas born in Hull in 1893, died 1909 and George F born in Hull in 1896.

In 1901 the family resided at 17 Berkeley Street, Hull. By 1911 they were living at 5 Grosvenor Terrace, Hornsea.

George Stanley was educated at Hull Grammar School and at Brampton House, Hornsea. He enlisted as a ranker into the 1st Hull, Pals, Service Battalion, Hull Commercials, at the Hull City Hall in 1914, regimental number 10/496, later to be the 10th Battalion East Yorkshire Regiment. He was later commissioned into the 1/4th Battalion East Yorkshire Regiment and went to France on 26 December 1917.

His brother Henry served in the war as a 2nd lieutenant and survived.

George Stanley Mansfield was reported Killed in Action in the *Beverley Guardian* in April 1918. The *Hull Daily Mail* recorded his death on 5 and 12 April 1918.

Southgate Cemetery, Hornsea.

Mr George Mansfield: Born in Hull in 1858 and died in Hornsea on 7 April 1918, aged 60 years. Mrs Emily Mansfield: Born in Hull in 1866 and died in Hornsea on 19 March 1928, aged 62 years. They lie together in Southgate Cemetery, Hornsea. Their son, George Stanley, is commemorated on the family headstone.

In the same cemetery are the graves of the parents of George Mansfield, John Overton Mansfield who died on 19 October 1905, aged 72 years, and Hannah Mansfield who died on 14 January 1908, aged 74 years. In the same plot are the remains of Douglas Mansfield, son of George and Emily, who died on 9 April 1909, aged 16 years.

George Stanley Mansfield is commemorated on:
The War Memorial, Memorial Gardens, New Road, Hornsea.
The brass memorial plaque in the United Reform Church, Hornsea.
The War Memorial in St Nicholas Church, Hornsea.
The War Memorial in the Old Drill Hall, Back Southgate, Hornsea. Now the Ex-Servicemen's Club.
The family headstone, Southgate Cemetery, Hornsea.
The Hull Grammar School Roll of Honour, Bishop Alcock Road, Hull.
The Pozieres Memorial to the Missing, France.

The grave of Lieutenant Hugh Stewart McDowall. Southgate Cemetery, Hornsea.

McDowall. Hugh Stewart.
2nd Lieutenant Royal Air Force. 62nd Training Squadron.
Died in an aircraft accident at Hounslow Heath Aerodrome, Middlesex, London, on 28 June 1918, aged 19 years, and is buried in Southgate Cemetery, Hornsea.

On 29 June 1918 the Hounslow Chronicle reported: Yet another flying officer killed: Yesterday morning as Lieutenant Hugh Stewart McDowall was flying over the district his machine got out of control and in falling crashed into one of the buildings of a local gun-powder factory. Both building and machine were wrecked, and the young officer was taken out of the debris dead. His terrible injuries included a broken back, arms and legs. Fortunately the petrol did not ignite or the consequences might have been more disastrous, as large numbers of hands were working in the vicinity at the time.

A service with full military honours was held at Hounslow Aerodrome before his body was returned to his parents for burial.

He was born on 28 November 1898 in Castleford and was the only son of Robert Moffat McDowall, Architect and Engineer, and Helen Murdock McDowall, nee Murdock, of Victoria Street, Hornsea. They had two other children: Ethelwyne born in Castleford in 1897 and Sheila Helen born in Castleford in 1910.

Hugh was educated at the Wakefield Grammar School from 1908 to 1913. In 1901 and 1911 the family resided at Ferry Bridge Road, Glasshoughton, Castleford. They came to Hornsea in 1913.

The death of Hugh Stewart McDowall was reported in the *Hull Daily Mail* on 4 July 1918.

Before the war Hugh worked in Hornsea and in 1915 became a Ship's Officer for the Ellerman Line in Hull. He suffered a serious illness on one long voyage home and was discharged. He made a full recovery and in 1917 enlisted in the Royal Flying Corps, this became the Royal Air Force in 1918. He trained other pilots in the use of a variety of aircraft.

His sister, Ethelwyn Stewart McDowall, attended the Leeds Girls High School, where she gained a music scholarship, and in 1918 she had a poem about her brother published in the school magazine, issue 61, the opening lines read:

The Last Homecoming: So you are dead, are dead my little brother, and forever sleeping under a marble stone. So you have winged your way like many another, down into the mystic silence and dark alone.

Southgate Cemetery, Hornsea.

Robert Moffatt McDowall: Born in Pontefract, Yorkshire, on 19 April 1853 and died in Hornsea on 31 May 1940. Helen Murdock McDowall: Born in Scotland on 19 January 1869 and died in Hornsea on 31 May 1946. They are buried with their son in Southgate Cemetery, Hornsea.

Hugh Stewart McDowall is commemorated on:
The War Memorial, Memorial Gardens, New Road, Hornsea.
The War Memorial in St Nicholas Church, Hornsea.
The brass memorial plaque in the United Reform Church, Hornsea.
The War Memorial in the Old Drill Hall, Back Southgate, Hornsea. Now the Ex-Servicemen's Club.
The Wakefield Grammar School War Memorial.

Miller. Richard.
A/Sergeant 10/493. 10th Battalion East Yorkshire Regiment. 1st Hull Pals, Hull Commercials. 92nd Hull Brigade, 31st, Pals, Division.
Killed in Action 29 June 1917, aged 24 years. Buried in Albuera Cemetery, France.

On 3 May 1917 the Hull 92nd Brigade attacked Oppy Wood and suffered heavy casualties in a failed assault. On 28 June 1917 the wood was to be attacked again by the 94th Brigade of the 31st Pals Division. In this new attack the 92nd Brigade would support the assault troops by making trench raids into the enemy lines. The 10th Battalion East Yorkshire Regiment was in reserve, machine-gun fire and the enemy barrage took its toll on the Yorkshire men and it was here that Sergeant Richard Miller lost his life. Oppy Wood was taken.

He was born in Kroonstad, Orange River Colony, South Africa in 1895 and was the son of the late Richard and Sarah Miller of Lynton Cottage, Burton Road, Hornsea. Sarah had another child: Edith Ann born in South Africa in 1893.

They came to Britain in 1905 aboard the SS Kenilworth Castle. In 1911 they were residing at Burton Road, Hornsea. Sarah was recorded as a widow. I assume Mr Richard Miller died in South Africa.

Richard joined up at the Hull City Hall in 1914 into the 1st Hull Service Battalion, 1st Hull Pals or Hull Commercials. Later to be the 10th Battalion East Yorkshire Regiment. He went to Egypt on 22 December 1915 and then moved to France in March 1916 to take part in the Battle of the Somme. He was killed in the Battle of Arras and his personal effects were sent home to his mother in Hornsea in 1919.

Mrs Sarah Miller: Born in Kilham in 1861, she died in Hornsea in December 1943.

Edith Ann Miller: Born in Kroonstad, Orange River Colony, South Africa, in 1893, she never married and died in Hornsea in 1974.

Richard Miller is commemorated on:
The War Memorial, Memorial Gardens, New Road, Hornsea.
The War Memorial in St Nicholas Church, Hornsea.
The War Memorial in the Old Drill Hall, Back Southgate, Hornsea. Now the Ex-Servicemen's Club.

Leading Seaman Thomas Herbert Myers.

Myers. Thomas Herbert.
Leading Seaman. 150682. Royal Navy. HMS *Defence*.
Killed in Action at Jutland, 31 May 1916, aged 41 years. He has no known grave and is commemorated on the Plymouth Naval Memorial.

HMS *Defence* was sunk while under heavy fire from the big guns of the German battleship Friedrich der Grosse, all of her compliment of 904 men were lost in this action.

He was born in Hornsea on 25 July 1874 and was the son of James, agricultural labourer and gardener, and Anne Myers, nee Milner, of Hornsea. They married in Hornsea in December 1860 and had six other children: William Milner born in Atwick in 1858, Martha Myers born in Atwick in 1861, George Myers born in Hornsea in 1864, Mary Jane Myers born in Hornsea in 1866, Joseph Henry Myers born in Hornsea in 1876 and Francis Arthur Myers born in Hornsea in 1879.

In 1861 and 1871 the family resided in Atwick. By 1881 they had moved to Southgate, Hornsea.

Thomas Herbert was a member of the Ancient Order of Druids, Victoria Perseverance Lodge, Hornsea. He joined the Royal Navy on 23 September 1889 for a term of 12 years, this term expired on 10 August 1902 but he chose to stay in the Navy. The first ship he served on was HMS *Impregnable*, in his career he served on a number of vessels moving from ship to ship on a regular basis.

He was the husband of Elizabeth Myers, nee Wetherston. They married in 1909 and lived at 14 Marlborough Avenue, Hornsea. In 1911 Thomas Herbert was at sea, calling at ports in Australia and South Africa.

Thomas Herbert Myers was listed in a Roll of Honour in the *Beverley Guardian* on 17 and 24 June 1916, with a picture in the latter.

His death was reported in the *Hull Daily Mail* on 12 June 1916.

His picture was featured in *Green's Almanac* in 1917.

Southgate Cemetery, Hornsea.

Mr James Myers: Born in Atwick in 1836 and died in Hornsea on 23 June 1915, aged 79. Mrs Anne Myers: Born in Atwick in 1842 and died in Hornsea on 29 November 1925, aged 84. They are buried in Southgate Cemetery, Hornsea. Thomas Herbert Myers is commemorated on the family headstone.

Elizabeth Myers: Born in Hednesford, Staffs, in 1883 and died in 1947.

Thomas Herbert Myers is commemorated on:
The War Memorial, Memorial Gardens, New Road, Hornsea.
The hand written Roll of Honour in the Wesleyan Methodist Chapel, Hornsea.
The War Memorial in St Nicholas Church, Hornsea.
The War Memorial in the Old Drill Hall, Back Southgate, Hornsea. Now the Ex-Servicemen's Club.
A stained glass window in the Primitive Methodist Chapel, Hornsea.
The Druids Roll of Honour, 22 Albion Street, Hull.
The family headstone, Southgate Cemetery, Hornsea.
The Plymouth Naval Memorial.

Norman. John William.
Private 12/1495. 8th Battalion East Yorkshire Regiment. 8th Brigade. 3rd Division.
Killed in Action 3 November 1917, aged 31 years. Buried in Favreuil British Cemetery, France.

His regimental number shows he originally joined up at the Hull City Hall into the 3rd Hull Pals Service Battalion, 12th Battalion East Yorkshire Regiment. Transferring to the 8th Battalion later. He went to Egypt in 1915 with the 12th Battalion and moved to France in March 1916 to take part in the Battle of the Somme.

On 3 November 1917 the 8th Battalion East Yorkshire Regiment was in the Front Line, a patrol was sent out into no-man's land led by 2nd Lieutenant A B Ward. A German patrol was encountered and in the ensuing fight John William Norman was seriously injured. He was carried back to his own lines but died of his wounds.

He was born in Hornsea in 1887 and was the son of John William, bricklayer's labourer, and Ada Elizabeth Norman, nee Barr, of Southgate, Hornsea. They married in 1886 and had 10 other children: Elsie born in 1888, Wilkinson born in 1890, Lester born 1892, Harry born 1895, Ruth born 1897, May born 1899, Sidney born 1901, Bertha born 1902, Harold born 1904 and Gladys May born and died 1905. All the children were born in Hornsea.

In 1891 and 1901 the family resided at 11 Brickyard Cottages, Hornsea.

John William Jnr was the husband of Florence Ellen Norman, nee Wells, of 10 Belle Vue Terrace, Alexander Street, Hull. They married in Hornsea in 1905 and had three children: Herbert William Norman born in Hornsea in 1907, Allan Norman born in Hornsea on 18 April 1909 and Annie Wells Norman born in Hornsea on 27 March 1910. John William worked as a market gardener and by 1911 the family had moved to 5 Hillerby Lane, Hornsea.

His death was recorded in the *Hull Daily Mail* on 13 and 14 November 1917 and on 5 December 1917.

Southgate Cemetery, Hornsea.

Mr John William Norman: Born in Wetwang on 11 August 1863 and died in Hornsea on 8 June 1906. Mrs Ada Elizabeth Norman: Born in Aldborough in July 1865 and died in Hornsea on 22 July 1908. Gladys May Norman: Died on 15 July 1905, six weeks old. The three lie together in Southgate Cemetery, Hornsea.

Florence Ellen Norman. Born in Hull in 1884, she never re-married and died in Hull in March 1966.

John William Norman is commemorated on:
The War Memorial, Memorial Gardens, New Road, Hornsea.
The War Memorial in St Nicholas Church, Hornsea.
The War Memorial in the Old Drill Hall, Back Southgate, Hornsea. Now the Ex-Servicemen's Club.

Parrott. Robert.
Gunner 184937. Royal Field Artillery. 64th Battery, 5th Brigade.
Killed in Action on 22 October 1918, aged 30 years. Buried in Highland Cemetery, France.

He was born in Paull in 1888 and was the son of James, fisherman, and Jane Parrott, nee Barley, of Main Street, Paull. They married in Hull in 1874 and had six other children: Lillian M born 1875, Francis born 1878, Gertrude born 1881, William born 1883, James born 1885 and Thomas H born 1891 died 1895. All the children were born in Paull.

In 1891 the family resided at Paull Main Street, James worked as a fisherman. By 1901 only Robert and Francis, mariner, were at home with their parents and in 1911 only Robert was at home.

Robert, labourer, was the husband of Sarah Jane Parrott, nee Smith, they married in Patrington in 1915 and resided at Lighthouse Road, Paull. They had one son: Thomas Arthur born 1916.

Sarah Jane Parrott: Re-married to Dudley Hulme in Patrington in 1919. He was a widower, whose wife had died in 1918, leaving a daughter, Ena, born in 1910. They had one child together: Dudley, who was born in 1920. Sarah Jane was born in Paull in 1894 and died in Hull in 1987. Dudley Hulme was born in Chatham, Kent, in 1886, and died in Hull in 1980.

Mr James Parrott: Born in Paull in 1850 and died in Hull in 1923. Mrs Jane Parrott: Born in Broughton, Lincs, in 1849 and died in Paull in 1921.

Robert Parrott is commemorated on:
The War Memorial, Memorial Gardens, New Road, Hornsea.
The War Memorial in St Nicholas Church, Hornsea.
The War Memorial in the Old Drill Hall, Back Southgate, Hornsea. Now the Ex-Servicemen's Club.
The Paull War Memorial.

Peers. George Stanley.
Rifleman C/12955. 21st Battalion King's Royal Rifle Corps. 124th Brigade, 41st Division.
Died of Wounds 7 October 1916, aged 25 years. He has no known grave and is commemorated on the Thiepval Memorial to the Missing of the Somme, France.

George Stanley Peers was killed in the Battle of the Transloy Ridges which began on 7 October. With Flers to their rear the 124th Brigade attacked the 21st Bavarian Regiment. They were met with a hail of heavy machine-gun fire and were unable to reach their objective. After the battle the 124th Brigade mustered less than battalion strength, so great were their losses.

He was born in Hornsea in 1891 and was the son of George Henry Peers and Jane Peers, nee Davey, of 9 Atwick Road, Hornsea. They married in Hull in 1880 and had four other Children: William Henry born in Hornsea in 1882, Maud born in Hornsea in 1883, Hilda Jane born in Hornsea in 1885 and Mabel Ann born in Hornsea in 1893.

In 1891 the family resided at 3 Headland View, Hornsea, and George Henry worked as a Grocer's Porter. In 1901they were at the same address and George Henry was working as a labourer on the North Eastern Railway. 1911 saw a change of address to 9 Atwick Road, Hornsea, Jane had died in 1908 and George Henry was employed as a Gardener's Labourer. George Stanley was a Draper's Apprentice, Hilda Jane was a Dressmaker and Mabel Ann was a Dress Maker's Apprentice.

Before the war George Stanley worked as a Draper's Assistant at Harry Stephenson's shop in Newbegin, Hornsea, and enlisted in Hull on 13 November 1915. He went to France on 5 May 1916 and was reported as wounded and missing between the dates of 5/10 October 1916.

His death was reported in the *Hull Daily Mail* on 24 February 1917.

In 1919 William Henry Peers, brother of George Stanley, was living with his wife Rose May and children, Gertrude and Mabel, at 37 Brecon Street, Holderness Road, Hull. George Stanley's sisters, Maud, Hilda and Mabel Ann, were living with their father at 9 Atwick Road, Hornsea in 1919.

Southgate Cemetery, Hornsea.

Mrs Jane Peers: Born in Spilsby, Lincs, 1851 and died in Hornsea on 22 February 1908. Mr George Henry Peers: Born in Hornsea in 1856 and died in Hornsea on 7 June 1925. Maude Peers, daughter of the above: Born in Hornsea in 1883, died in Hornsea on 16 January 1945. The three lie together in Southgate Cemetery Hornsea. Their son George Stanley Peers is commemorated on the headstone.

In the same cemetery are buried:

William Henry Peers, brother of George Stanley, who died on 2 July 1948, and his wife Rose May Peers who died on 6 September 1954.

Also:

Two of the sisters of George Stanley Peers: Hilda Jane Peers of 9 Mount Pleasant, Hornsea, who died on 27 October 1965, and Mabel Ann Peers of The Laurels, Edenfield Estate, Hornsea, ashes, who died in Cottingham on 7 January 1980.

George Stanley Peers is commemorated on:

The War Memorial, Memorial Gardens, New Road, Hornsea.

The War Memorial in St Nicholas Church, Hornsea.

The War Memorial, brass plaque, in the Wesleyan Chapel, Hornsea.

The War Memorial in the Old Drill Hall, Back Southgate, Hornsea. Now the Ex-Servicemen's Club.
The family headstone, Southgate Cemetery, Hornsea.
The Thiepval Memorial to the Missing of the Somme, France.

Private Arthur Pooley.

Pooley. Arthur.
Private 25660. 12th Battalion East Yorkshire Regiment. 3rd Hull Pals, 92nd Hull Brigade, 31st Pals Division.

He was originally in the 1st Battalion East Yorkshire Regiment, later moved to 12th Battalion, and was taken prisoner at Oppy Wood during the Battle for Arras on 3 May 1917. He was a Prisoner of War at Limberg Camp, Germany, and died of influenza on 31 December 1918, aged 24 years, aboard the SS La Cour, as he was about to be returned home. Arthur is buried in Copenhagen Western Cemetery, Denmark.

He was born in Hornsea in 1894 and was the son of Jane Marlow Pooley of 34 Southgate, Hornsea. She never married and had seven other children: Ethel born in Goxhill in 1883, John born in Goxhill in 1888, Emily born in Goxhill in 1889, Laura Anne born in Hornsea in 1891, Frank born in Hornsea in 1900, Doris born in Hornsea in 1903 and Eric born in Hornsea in 1911.

The parents of Jane Marlow Pooley, William and Jane Ann Pooley, resided at the Railway Gatehouse, Goxhill, Holderness, in 1881. Jane Ann Pooley died in Goxhill on 4 December 1890 and by 1891 William had made the move to 10 Southgate, Hornsea.

In 1901 the family was living with Jane's father, William Pooley, at 34 Southgate, Hornsea, he was aged 56 years old and employed as a platelayer for the North Eastern Railway. In 1911 they were at the same address.

Arthur was the husband of Cecilia Agnes Pooley, nee Sutton, and resided at 1 Fern Avenue, Middleburg Street, Hull. They married at St Nicholas Church, Hornsea, on 14 December 1915, and had one child: Cecilia Agnes Pooley, born in Hornsea on 8 February 1916. Her mother died giving berth and Cecilia Agnes was brought up by her grandmother, Jane Marlow Pooley.

For a time before the war Arthur Pooley worked at the Hornsea Steam Laundry and later, at the time of his enlistment, was working as a Mill Hand at the British Oil and Cake Mills, Stoneferry, Hull. He worked in the plant that was pressing gun-cotton for the Navy and in March 1916 was listed as working in a reserved occupation.

Arthur enlisted and was posted to the 1st Battalion East Yorkshire Regiment on 11 December 1916, moved to the 12 Battalion on 28 December 1916 and was posted as missing in action on 3 May 1917 at Oppy Wood.

Mrs Cecilia Agnes Pooley: Born in Hull on 18 January 1895 and died in Hornsea on 8 February 1916. Her daughter of the same name married Richard Harsley in Hull in 1940 and died in Hull on 15 January 1967.

In 1919 Cecilia Agnes Jnr, was living with her grandmother at 34 Southgate, Hornsea. There is a touching letter in Arthur Pooley's military records from Jane Marlow Pooley to the authorities that states she had never married, she was worried her army widows' pension would be stopped, but she got her pension.

The death of Arthur Pooley was reported in the *Hull Daily Mail* on 10 January 1919 and he was listed 'In Memoriam' in the same publication on 30 December 1919. He was recorded in a Roll of Honour in the *Beverley Guardian* on 1 March 1919.

His photograph appeared in *Green's Almanac* in 1919.

Southgate Cemetery, Hornsea.

Mrs Jane Marlow Pooley: Daughter of William and Jane Ann Pooley, nee Sowden, of Goxhill and later Hornsea. She was born in Sutton, Nr Hull, in 1873, and died in Hornsea on 5 November 1960.

William Pooley. Father of Jane Marlow Pooley, Born in Shibden, Norfolk in 1843 and died in Hornsea on 5 May 1935, the son of Jane Marlow Pooley, Eric Pooley, born 1911, and died in Hornsea on 9 April 1958, are buried in the same plot. They lie together in Southgate Cemetery, Hornsea.

In the same cemetery are buried the remains of Frank Pooley, son of Jane Marlow Pooley, he died in Hornsea on 20 March 1990, and his wife Edith Mildred who died in Hornsea on 12 June 2002.

Arthur Pooley is commemorated on:

The War Memorial, Memorial Gardens, New Road, Hornsea.

The hand written Roll of Honour in the Wesleyan Methodist Chapel, Hornsea.

The War Memorial in the Old Drill Hall, Back Southgate, Hornsea. Now the Ex-Servicemen's Club.

A memorial obelisk in Copenhagen Western Cemetery.

Preston. James Routledge.
Private 13/923. 13th Battalion East Yorkshire Regiment. 4th Hull Pals. 92nd Hull Brigade. 31st Pals Division.

Killed in Action 25 May 1916. Buried in Sucrerie Military Cemetery, Colincamps, France.

In April and May 1916 the battalions of the 31st Division were being move into the Front Line for short periods to get them used to the rigours of trench warfare.

He was born in Hornsea in 1880 and was the son of Walker Routledge Preston, agricultural labourer, and Margaret Routledge Preston, nee Dandy, of Welbourne Terrace, Back Southgate, Hornsea. They married in Hornsea in 1867 and had five other children: Elizabeth born in Hornsea in 1870, George Arthur born in Hornsea in 1872, Sarah born in Hornsea in 1875, William born in Hornsea in 1878 and Margaret Routledge Preston born in Hornsea in 1885. They also brought up their grandson, Arthur, born in Hornsea in 1890.

Private James Routledge Preston.

In 1881, 1891 and 1901 the family resided at 6 Back Southgate, Hornsea.

In 1901 James was living with his brother George Arthur and his wife Harriet in Sutton, Nr Hull.

He was the husband of Mary Preston, nee Jackson. They married in St Nicholas Church, Hornsea, on 16 November 1901and had three children: James Arthur born in Hornsea on 29 September 1902, Doris Routledge born in Hornsea on 10 December 1904 and Elizabeth Ellen born in Hornsea on 16 July 1906.

In 1914 the family resided at 9 Beaconsfield Avenue, Cornwall Street, Hull, by 1914 his wife had died and his children were in the care of his sister, Mrs Sarah Cardell, nee Preston, of Devon Avenue, St Paul Street, Hull, who became their Guardian. She was awarded a pension of 15 shillings a week to care for the children.

James enlisted at the Hull City Hall on 30 Novemeber1914 and joined the 4th Hull Service Battalion, later to be the 13th Battalion East Yorkshire Regiment. His service record gives his sisters address as his home: 9 Beaconsfield Avenue, Cornwall Street, Hull.

The 31st Pals Division went to Egypt in 1915 and to France in March 1916 to take part in the Battle of the Somme.

James Routledge Preston was listed in a Roll of Honour in the *Beverley Guardian*, with picture, on 24 June 1916, and in the *Hull Daily Mail* in May and June 1916.

Mr Walker Routledge Preston: Born in Withernwick in 1841 and died in Hornsea in 1922. Mrs Margaret Routledge Preston: Born in Sigglesthorne in 1842 and died in Hull in 1922.

James Routledge Preston is Commemorated on:
The War Memorial, Memorial Gardens, New Road, Hornsea.
The War Memorial in St Nicholas Church, Hornsea.
The war memorial in the Old Drill Hall, back Southgate, Hornsea. Now the Ex-Servicemen's Club.

Trooper James William Redman.

Redman. James William.
Trooper 3170. 1st Household Battalion, Household Cavalry.
10th Brigade, 4th Division.
   Killed in Action on 14 December 1917, aged 32 years.
Buried in Monchy British Cemetery, France.

He was born in Hebden Bridge in October 1885 and was the son of Richard and Sarah Redman, nee Taylor, of 40 Pleasant Villas, Hebden Bridge. They had four other children: Claude Stansfield born in Hebden Bridge in 1883 and died in 1917, Nelly born in Hebden Bridge in 1890, Edith Mary born Hebden Bridge in 1892 and Frank Stansfield born in Hebden Bridge in 1894.

In 1891, 1901 and 1911 the family resided at 40 Pleasant Villas, Hebden Bridge, Richard Preston's occupation is described as a Wholesale Clothier. In 1911 James William was employed in his father's clothing business.

Claude Stansfield Redman.
Brother of James William. Killed in Action at the 2nd Battle of Passchendaele on 30 October 1917, serving with the 1/28th London Regiment, Artists Rifles, 190th Brigade, 63rd Division. Claude has no known grave and is commemorated on the Tyne Cot Memorial to the Missing.

He was born in Hebden Bridge in 1883 and was the husband of Bertha Redman, they resided at Dittling, Hebden Bridge.

Mr Richard Redman was the founder of the Hornsea Sanitary Steam Laundry, Cliff Road.

On 3 December 1913 James William married Annie Redman, nee Head, in St James and St John Church, Hebden Bridge and had one daughter, Jean, born in Hornsea in 1916.

Heptonstall Slack Baptist Church, Mount Zion, Cemetery.

Mr Richard Redman: Born in Hebden Bridge in 1857 and died in Mytholmroyde Village, Hebden Bridge on 1 June 1941. Mrs Sarah Redman: Born in Hebden Bridge in 1857, died at 40 Pleasant Villas, Hebden Bridge on 13 January 1934.

They are buried together in Heptonstall Cemetery, Nr Leeds, and their sons, John William and Claude Stansfield, are commemorated on the headstone with the inscription: Who went to the Great War and returned not again. Buried in the same plot is Richard's second wife, Miriam Redman, nee Hoyle, who died on 31 October 1945, aged 79 years.

James William Redman is commemorated on:
The War Memorial, Memorial Gardens, New Road, Hornsea.
The War Memorial in St Nicholas Church, Hornsea.
The War Memorial, brass plaque, in the Wesleyan Methodist Chapel, Hornsea
The War Memorial in the Old Drill Hall, Back Southgate, Hornsea. Now the Ex-Servicemen's Club.
The family headstone, Heptonstall Slack Baptist Church, Mount Zion, Cemetery.

Rendell. James.
Sergeant 23022. 16th Battalion Lancashire Fusiliers. 2nd Salford Pals. 96th Brigade, 32nd Division.
Died of gas poisoning in Liverpool Hospital on 22 October 1918, aged 24 years. Buried in Southgate Cemetery, Hornsea.

Sergeant James Rendell.

He was born in Hornsea in 1894 and was the son of George William, Gardener, and Annie Rendell, nee Taylor, of 6 Clifton Street, Hornsea. They married in Hornsea in 1880 and had four other children: Clara born in Hornsea in 1881, William George born in Hornsea in 1882, Florence born in Hornsea in 1886 and Kate born in Hornsea in 1891. Four other children died in infancy.

In 1891 the family resided at Cliff Cottage, Hornsea. By 1901 they had moved to Eastgate and were still there in 1911, that year James was the only sibling living with his parents and employed as a Groom.

James enlisted in Hull and was severely gassed in France. He was invalided home only to catch Pneumonia which led to his death.

Southgate Cemetery, Hornsea.

Mr George William Rendell: Born in Newton Abbot in 1856 and died in Hornsea on 8 February 1935. Mrs Annie Rendell: Born in Seaton in 1857 and died in Hornsea on 15 November 1949. They lie with their son James in Southgate Cemetery, Hornsea.

James Rendell is commemorated on:
The War Memorial, Memorial Gardens, New Road, Hornsea.
The War Memorial in St Nicholas Church, Hornsea.
The War Memorial in the Old Drill Hall, Back Southgate, Hornsea. Now the Ex-Servicemen's Club.

Reynolds. Roland.
Lieutenant, Royal Navy. HM Drifter Catspaw.
Drowned on 31 December 1919, aged 21 years. Buried in Kviberg Cemetery, Sweden.

He was born in Hornsea in 1898 and was the son of Robert and Eva Agnes Reynolds, nee Belk, of Railway Street, Hornsea. They married in Middlesbrough in 1892 and had two other children: Eva Mary born in Jersey on 24 September 1894 and Helen Agnes born in Hornsea in 1897.

Mr Robert Reynolds was the founder and Principal of Brampton House School for Boys, Railway Street, Hornsea. Later he took over St Bede's School, Atwick Road, Hornsea.

Roland was educated at Brampton House School, Hornsea, his father was the Head Teacher. He was a naval pupil cadet from 1911 to 1913 on the training ship HMS *Conway* and had risen to the rank of lieutenant by September 1919. He was Mentioned in Dispatches on 8 January 1918 for action against a U-Boat while serving on the minesweeper HMS *Cyclamen*. In 1919 he was serving aboard HM Drifter Catspaw on coastal patrol in the Baltic during the Russian War of Intervention of 1919/20. His ship was returning to Copenhagen on 31 December and ran into bad weather and thick ice, the Catspaw sank in heavy seas with the loss of all 14 crew members.

Mr Robert Reynolds: Born in the Isle of Man in 1860. Death unknown. Mrs Eva Agnes Reynolds: Born in Hartlepool in 1862. Death unknown.

Roland Reynolds sister, Eva Mary Reynolds, married 2nd Lieutenant Ralph Noel Heathcote in St Nicholas Church on 18 December 1915. He served with the 12th Battalion East Yorkshire Regiment, 3rd Hull Pals, and took part in the attack on Serre on 13 November 1916. Ralph Noel was wounded badly and died from his wounds at the Advanced Operating Theatre, Athie, France, on 17 November, aged 30 years. He is buried in Cuin British Cemetery, France. Eva Mary lived with her husband at 143 Barlow Moor Road, West Didsbury, Manchester. He was the son of Ralph George and Emily V J Heathcote of Manchester. Eva Mary never re-married and died in Scarborough in 1979.

Roland Reynolds is commemorated on:
The War Memorial, Memorial Gardens, New Road, Hornsea.
The War Memorial in St Nicholas Church, Hornsea.
The War Memorial in the Old Drill Hall, Back Southgate, Hornsea. Now the Ex-Servicemen's Club.

Richmond. Wilfred Norburn.
Private 43129. 10th Battalion the West Yorkshire Regiment. 50th Brigade, 17th Division. Formerly 790 East Yorkshire Regiment.
Killed in Action on 7 November 1916, aged 19 years. He has no known grave and is commemorated on the Thiepval Memorial to the Missing of the Somme, France.

Private Wilfred Norburn Richmond.

He was born in Hull in 1897 and was the son of Walter, Butter Merchant, and Eva Richmond, nee Wells, of Eastbourne Road, Hornsea. They married in Louth in 1896. Their other children were: Dorothy Eva born in Hornsea in 1903, Clive born in Hornsea in 1905, Enid born Hull in 1906, Beatrice born in Hull in 1909 and George Edward born in Hornsea in 1910.

In 1901 Wilfred was living with his grandparents, Elizabeth and Thomas Richmond, at Wilton Street, Dansom Lane, Hull. His parents were living at Cliff Road, Hornsea, that year. In 1911 the whole family was residing at Seacroft, North Cliff, Hornsea.

Wilfred married Florence May Richmond, nee Harper, in Hornsea in the summer of 1916. An officer wrote home to Florence May: "His death was instantaneous, the result of a bullet wound while we were entering the trenches for a second period."

After her husband's death Florence May re-married to Thomas Jones in 1919 and moved to 34 Henry Street, Scunthorpe, Lincolnshire.

His death was reported, with picture, in the *Hull Times* on 2 December 1916.

Mr Walter Richmond: Born in Hull in 1872 and died in East Yorkshire in March 1957. Mrs Eva Richmond: Born in Withernsea in 1872 and died in Hornsea in 1915.

Wilfred Norburn Richmond is commemorated on:
The War Memorial, Memorial Gardens, New Road, Hornsea.
The War Memorial in St Nicholas Church, Hornsea.
The War Memorial in the Old Drill Hall, Back Southgate, Hornsea. Now the Ex-Servicemen's Club.
The Thiepval Memorial to the Missing of the Somme, France.

Robinson. John William.
Private 41510. 2nd Battalion Royal Inniskilling Fusiliers. 109th Brigade, 36th Ulster Division.
Formerly 522921 Training Reserve Battalion.

Mr Walter Richmond and his wife Mrs Eva Richmond.

Died of Wounds on the 15 October 1918, aged 26 years. Buried in Dadizeele, now Dadizele, New British Cemetery. It is an extension of the Communal Cemetery, Belgium.

The village of Dadizeele was in German hands for most of the war, until it was reached by 36th Ulster Division on 29 September 1918. It was taken by the 9th Scottish Division and heavy fighting followed at Hill 41, a little south of the village. In the fighting here John William was wounded, dying of his wounds on 15 October. Many of his comrades also died there.

He was born in Hornsea in 1892 and was the son of William, General Carrier, and Ann Elizabeth Robinson, nee Kearry, of Southgate, Hornsea. They married in Hornsea in 1891 and had three other children: Ada May born in Cowden in 1896, Beatrice Annie born in Hornsea in 1897 and Phillis June born in Hornsea in 1903.

In 1901 and 1911 the family resided at Southgate, Hornsea. In the latter John William was employed as a General Carrier with his father. In the 1901 census Annie Elizabeth is recorded, in 1911 William is recorded as a widower.

John William was the husband of Beatrice Robinson, nee Gullan, of Long Riston. They married in Hornsea in 1914 and had a daughter: Edith A, born 1916.

Mr William Robinson: Born in Middle Rasen, Lincs, on 27 July 1867, and died in Hornsea on 6 April 1949. Mrs Ann Elizabeth Robinson: Born in Withernwick in 1868, and died in Hornsea between 1901 and 1911.

John William Robinson is commemorated on:
The War Memorial, Memorial Gardens, New Road, Hornsea.
The War Memorial in St Nicholas Church, Hornsea.
The War Memorial in the Old Drill Hall, Back Southgate, Hornsea. Now the Ex-Servicemen's Club.
The hand written Roll of Honour in the Wesleyan Methodist Chapel, Hornsea.
The Druids Roll of Honour, 22 Albion Street, Hull.
Ireland's Memorial Records. 1914–1918.

Sedman. Llewellyn Frank.
Private 425299. 1st Battalion Canadian Mounted Rifles. 8th Canadian Brigade. 3rd Canadian Division.

Killed in Action 20 December 1916, aged 33 years. He has no known grave and is commemorated on the Vimy Ridge Memorial, France.

He was born in Hornsea on 16 December 1882 and was the son of John, Councillor, and Emma Sedman, nee Apted, of Lynton Villas, Burton Road, Hornsea. They married in Whitby on 24 June 1865 and had eight other children: Francis Prowd Sedman born in Whitby in 1866, Sarah Willis Sedman born in Whitby in 1868, Francis F Sedman born in Whitby in 1870, Emma Maria Sedman born in Whitby in 1874, Augusta Mary Sedman born in Hornsea in 1877, Alfred John Sedman born in Hornsea in 1879 and Ralph Prowd Sedman born in Snitterfield, Warwickshire, in 1883.

Llewellyn Frank Sedman left the shores of England from Liverpool for Canada on 22 August 1905 and arrived in Quebec in September that year. He worked as a Store Clerk and enlisted in Manitoba in August 1915.

In 1871 the family resided at 4 Spring Vale, Whitby. In 1881 they were in Newbegin Hornsea, John Sedman was recorded as a land and property owner. In 1891 they had moved to 1 Lynton Villas, Hornsea. In 1901 only Llewellyn was living at home with his parents and he was employed as a grocer's assistant. In 1911 only Augusta Mary was living at Lynton Villas with her parents.

Southgate Cemetery, Hornsea.

Emma Maria Sedman.

Albert Nelson Train.

Emma Maria Sedman married Albert Nelson Train, whose nephew, Albert Train, was killed in the war, he died of wounds on 7 January 1916 and is commemorated on the Hornsea War Memorial. Emma Maria Train (nee Sedman) died on 4 July 1958, her husband, Albert Nelson Train, died on 1 October 1949. They are buried together in Southgate Cemetery, Hornsea with other members of the Train family.

Llewellyn Frank Sedman was recorded in a casualty list as being killed in action in the *Hull Daily Mail* on 5 January 1917.

Southgate Cemetery, Hornsea.

Mr John Sedman: Born in Burneston, North Yorkshire, in 1835, and died in Hornsea on 29 October 1919. Mrs Emma Sedman: Born at Seamer Street, Bryanston, London, in 1836, and died in Hornsea on 6 April 1927. They lie together in Southgate Cemetery, Hornsea.

The following family members are buried in the same plot in Southgate Cemetery, Hornsea: Francis Proud Sedman, drowned at Yarmouth on 18 January 1881, Aged 15 years. Alfred John Sedman, died 25 December 1897, aged 20 years. John Thomas Sedman, died in infancy 1875. Ralph Prowd Sedman, died 19 February 1909, aged 27 years and Albert Sedman Train, died in infancy. Llewellyn Frank Sedman is commemorated on the family headstone.

Llewellyn Frank Sedman is commemorated on:

The War Memorial, Memorial Gardens, New Road, Hornsea.

The War Memorial in St Nicholas Church, Hornsea.

The War Memorial in the Old Drill Hall, Back Southgate, Hornsea. Now the Ex-Servicemen's Club.

The family Headstone, Southgate Cemetery, Hornsea.

The Vimy Canadian Memorial, France.

The Books of Remembrance in the Memorial Chamber of the Peace Tower, Parliament Hill, Canada.

Shaw. Cyril Trevor.
Cpt. 122nd Rajputana Infantry. Attached to the 120th.
Killed in Action 22 November 1915, aged 32 years. Buried in Al Basra Memorial Cemetery, Iraq.

He was born in Maradabad, India, on 20 December 1882, educated at Bedford School and was the youngest son of Henry James, Consular Official, and Helen Marcia Shaw, nee Huntley, of Middleton Lodge, Eastbourne Road, Hornsea. They married on 1 January 1874 in Bareilly, Uttar Pradesh, India, and had five other children: Maria Shaw born in Aligarh, India in 1876, Herbert Huntley Shaw born in Maradabad, India in1878, Muriel Helen Shaw born in Maradabad, India, in 1880, Dora Shaw born in Maradabad, India in 1882 and Stella Sybil born on 8 January 1886 in Almora, Uttaranchal, India.

The family left India before 1891 leaving Mr Henry James Shaw in India to complete his work. In 1891 the family was living at 46 Coham Road, Croydon. In 1901 Cyril was a boarder at The Shanty, Tothill, Isle of Wight, and was a 2nd lieutenant in the Sligo Artillery Militia. He moved to the York and Lancs on 29 January 1902 and became a Full lieutenant on 29 April 1904. Two years later he was sent to the 122nd Rajputana Infantry and was promoted to captain because of his good work on the North West Frontier. When war broke out in 1914 he requested to be sent to a regiment on active service and was transferred to the 120th Rajputana Infantry, then moved back to the 122nd then in Iraq.

The death of Cyril Trevor Shaw was reported in the *Newcastle Journal* on 4 December 1915 and in the Times that same year.

He was listed in the *Hull Daily Mail* casualty list of 12 December 1915.

Southgate Cemetery, Hornsea.

Mr Henry James Shaw: Born in Raypintina, India, in 1848 and died in Hornsea on 25 June 1921. Mrs Helen Marcia Shaw: Born on 11 August 1856 in Islington, London and died in Hornsea on 22 February 1927. Muriel Helen Shaw, daughter: Born in India in 1880 and died in Hornsea on 6 April 1956. They are buried together in Southgate Cemetery, Hornsea. Their son, Cyril Trevor, is commemorated on the headstone.

Cyril Trevor Shaw is commemorated on:
The War Memorial, Memorial Gardens, New Road, Hornsea.
The War Memorial in St Nicholas Church, Hornsea.
The War Memorial in the Old Drill Hall, Back Southgate, Hornsea. Now the Ex-Servicemen's Club.
The family headstone, Southgate Cemetery, Hornsea.

Simpson. Herbert Edward.
Private M2/223562. Army Service Corps. Attached to 84th Heavy Artillery Group.
Killed in Action on 11 July 1917, aged 37 years. Buried in Brandhoek Military Cemetery, Belgium.

He was born in Hull in 1880 and was the son of Robert and Jane Elizabeth Simpson, nee Rounding. They married in Hull at St Paul's Church on 29 December 1862 and had eight other children: John Rounding Simpson born in Barton on Humber in 1861, William James Simpson born in Barton on Humber in 1863, Arthur Rounding Simpson born in Hull in 1865, George Taylor Simpson born in Hull in 1868, Ernest

Edwin Simpson born in Hull in 1870, Edith Mary Simpson born in Hull in 1872, Alice Mary Simpson born in Hull in 1875 and Herbert Edward Simpson born in Hull in 1880.

In the 1871, 1881 and 1891 census records the family is recorded as residing at Kent Street, Hull. Robert Simpson was a self-employed Corn Dealer and retailer. George Taylor worked with his father in the corn business, Edith Mary was an assistant school teacher and Arthur Rounding was a clerk.

Mr Robert Simpson died on 1 August 1891, his address at that time was 83 Holderness Road, Hull. He left his wife the substantial sum of 664 pounds.

In 1901 Jane Elizabeth Simpson was living by her own means at 88 Durham Street, Hull. Herbert Edward was employed as a carpenter. By 1911 Jane Elizabeth was 73 and living in the house of William Henry and Lucy Clappison of Meadow Lea, Great Hatfield, Withernwick, living with her was her daughter Alice Mary Sykes, nee Simpson, her husband Harry Sykes, who worked as a waiter and their two children: Alice Muriel and Arthur Kenneth Sykes.

Jane Elizabeth had been careful with her money and died in 1924, leaving Alice Mary Sykes and Arthur Rounding Simpson a total of 4,775 pounds.

Herbert Edward Simpson was the husband of Frances Annie Simpson, nee Coe, of Sandringham House, New Road, Hornsea, and worked as a postman before the war. They married in Hull in 1902 and had one child: Herbert Lancelot, born in Hull on 7 August 1903, Herbert Lancelot married Lilly Goodson in Hull in 1928 and served in the Merchant Navy during Second World War and died in Hull in 1973.

At the time of Herbert Edward's death the family resided at 31 Montrose Street, Dansom Lane, Hull.

Herbert Edward's death was reported in the *Hull Daily Mail* on 17 July 1917.

Mr Robert Simpson: Born in Wold Newton, Lincoln, in 1838 and died at 2 Kent Street, Hull, on 1 August 1891. Mrs Jane Elizabeth Simpson: Born at Union Square, New George Street, Hull on 19 December 1837 and died at Meadow Lea, Great Hatfield, Withernwick, on 23 April 1924.

Herbert Edward Simpson is commemorated on:
The War Memorial, Memorial Gardens, New Road, Hornsea.
The War Memorial in St Nicholas Church, Hornsea.
The War Memorial in the Old Drill Hall, Back Southgate, Hornsea. Now the Ex-Servicemen's Club.

Smith. Bertram.
Private 20663. 10th Battalion, Canadian Infantry, Alberta Regiment. 2nd Canadian Brigade, 1st Canadian Division.

Killed in Action on 22 April 1915, aged 24 years. He has no known grave and is commemorated on the Menin Gate Memorial to the Missing, Ypres, Belgium.

He was born in Wisbech, Cambs, in 1893 and was the son of William, coal merchant, and Harriet Smith of Coal Wharf, Elm Road, Wisbech, Cambs. They had seven other children: Rose Hannah Smith, born in Dowsdale, Lincs, in 1866. Annie Smith born in Dowsdale, Lincs, in 1871. William Smith born in Wimblington, Cambs, in 1878. Sarah Elizabeth Smith born in Gedney Hill, Lincs, in 1879. Thomas Smith born in Sywell, Norfolk, in 1881. Charles F Smith born in Wisbech, Cambs, in 1883 and Harry Smith born in Wisbech, Cambs, in 1886.

In 1871 the family resided in Whaplode, Lincs, William was working as a labourer and Rose Hannah, Sarah Elizabeth and Annie lived at home. In 1881 the now expanded family lived at Honey Hill, Wimblington, Cambs, William was employed as a farm bailiff. In 1891 and 1901 the family lived at Elm Road, Wisbech, Cambs, and William was a self-employed Coal Merchant.

Mrs Harriet Smith died in Whittlesey, Cambs in 1901.

In 1911 Bertie was living with his father and step mother, Mary Jane, at Cemetery Lodge, Southgate Cemetery, Hornsea. William and Mary Jane, nee Branton, married in Hornsea in 1908. William was employed as the cemetery keeper. Living with them was Harry Branton, 14, son of Mary Jane, he was born in Aldborough.

In July that year Bertie emigrated to Canada where he worked as a transfer agent and enlisted in September 1914 into the 10th Battalion Canadian Infantry, which recruited in the Winnipeg and Calgary area. His unit arrived in the dreaded Ypres Salient on 15 February 1915 in time to take part in the Battle of Hooge. Poison gas was used for the first time here and the British and Indian troops were totally unprepared for this new horror, they fell back and holes appeared in the line. The Canadians were rushed to the Front to plug the gaps and became involved in a desperate fight for survival as the Germans pushed forward in great numbers. The attacks continued in April and May and the 10th Canadian Battalion was reduced to one fifth of its original strength. In this perfect hell upon earth Bertie Smith lost his life.

Mrs Harriet Smith: Born in Dowedale, Lincs in 1839, she died in Whittlesey, Cambs, in 1901.

Southgate Cemetery, Hornsea.

Mr William Smith: Born in Whaplode Drove, Lincs, in 1843, and died in Hornsea on 11 March 1911. Mary Jane Smith: Born in Burton Pidsey in 1871 and died in Hornsea on 24 June 1902.

William and Mary Jane are buried in Southgate Cemetery, Hornsea. In the same plot is their daughter Maria Whatling, died 16 August 1905, aged 25 years.

Bertram Smith is commemorated on:
The War Memorial, Memorial Gardens, New Road, Hornsea.
The War Memorial in St Nicholas Church, Hornsea.
The War Memorial in the Old Drill Hall, Back Southgate, Hornsea. Now the Ex-Serviceman's Club.
The Menin Gate Memorial to the Missing, Belgium.
The Books of Remembrance in the Memorial Chamber of the Peace Tower, Parliament Hill, Canada.

Snowdon. Ralph.
2nd Lieutenant 1/4th Battalion East Yorkshire Regiment. 150th Brigade, 50th Northumbrian Division.
Killed in Action on 2 October 1917, aged 36 years. Buried in Wancourt British Cemetery, France.

He was born in Stockton-on-Tees in 1881 and was the son of William and Charlotte Snowdon, nee Stewardson, of 1 Clifton Terrace, Hornsea. They married in Leeds on 21 April 1872 and had five other children: Frank born in Stockton-on-Tees in 1872, William born York in 1876, Kate born in York in 1877, Louise born in York in 1879 and Leonard born in Hull in 1885.

Lieutenant Ralph Snowdon.

In 1891 the family resided at 55 De Grey Street, Hull, Mr William Snowden worked as a Merchant's Clerk. In 1901 the family was living at 182 Park Avenue, Hull, Mr William Snowden was employed as an Ironmonger's Clerk. By 1911 they had moved to 1 Clifton Terrace, Hornsea, Ralph worked as a Savings Bank Clerk, Frank was an Engineer's Clerk and William was an Engineer's Book-keeper.

Before the war Ralph worked as the Manager of the Hull Savings Bank and enlisted into the Hull Commercials, 1st Hull Pals, later to be the 10th Battalion East Yorkshire Regiment, in September 1914 at the Hull City Hall, regimental number 10/1070. He served in Egypt in 1915 and in France in 1916 on the Somme and was gassed. He was commissioned into the 1/4th Battalion East Yorkshire Regiment on 26 June 1917.

The death of 2nd Lieutenant Ralph Snowdon was reported in the *Beverley Guardian*, with picture, on 20 October 1917.

His picture was featured in *Green's Almanac* in 1918.

Southgate Cemetery, Hornsea.

Mr William Snowdon: Born in Slingsby, North Yorkshire, on 19 August 1848 and died in Hornsea on 30 December 1913, aged 65 years. Mrs Charlotte Snowdon: Born in Snainton, North Yorkshire, in 1849 and died in Hornsea on 10 July 1912, aged 62 years. They are buried in Southgate Cemetery, Hornsea. Buried in the same plot are their sons: Leonard, born 1 August 1884, died on 1 January 1910, and Frank, died 18 April 1951, aged 78 years. 2nd Lieutenant Ralph Snowdon is commemorated on the family headstone.

Ralph Snowdon is commemorated on:
The War Memorial, Memorial Gardens, New Road, Hornsea.
The War Memorial in St Nicholas Church, Hornsea.
The War Memorial in the Old Drill Hall, Back Southgate, Hornsea. Now the Ex-Servicemen's Club.
The Family headstone, Southgate Cemetery, Hornsea.

Stephenson. Charles Waudby.
Gunner 765546. Royal Field Artillery, A Battery, 223rd Home Counties Brigade. 63rd Royal Naval Division.
Died of Wounds 6 May 1917, during the Battle of Arras, aged 20 years. Buried in Etaples Military Cemetery, France.

Gunner Charles Waudby Stephenson.

He was born in Hornsea in 1897 and was the son of Joseph Samuel, joiner, and Ada Rachel Stephenson, nee Waudby, of 3 Rise Terrace, Hornsea. They married on 3 October 1886 and had eight other children: Arthur born in 1888, Ernest born in 1889 and died on 26 March 1912, Ida born in 1891, Kathleen born in 1893, Dorothy born in 1894, Joseph born in 1896, Elsie born on 21 November 1902 and Edith born on 31 May 1907. One child died in Infancy. All the children were born in Hornsea.

In 1891 the family resided in Southgate, Hornsea, Joseph Samuel was working as a joiner. By 1901 they had moved to 3 Rise Terrace, Hornsea, and in 1911 they were at the same address.

Charles was a Draper by trade and worked at Harry Stephenson's store in Newbegin, Hornsea. He enlisted into the Royal Field Artillery in 1915, was wounded on 22 April 1917 at Arras and died of his wounds on 6 May in a Base hospital at Etaples, France.

The death of Charles Waudby Stephenson was reported in the *Hull Daily Mail* in June 1917. He was listed in the *Beverley Guardian* under the title of 'Hornsea soldiers killed and missing' on 2 June 1917 and in the same publication, with picture, in a Local Roll of Honour on 9 June 1917.

His picture was featured in *Green's Almanac* in 1918.

Southgate Cemetery, Hornsea.

Mr Joseph Samuel Stephenson: Born in Cherry Burton on 24 September 1863 and died in Hornsea on 3 January 1937, aged 73 years. Mrs Ada Rachel Stephenson: Born in Hull in 1864 and died in Hornsea on 12 July 1913, aged 49 years. They are buried in Southgate, Cemetery, Hornsea. Ernest Stephenson, their son, died on 26 March 1912, aged 23 years, and is buried in the same plot. Charles Waudby Stephenson is commemorated on the headstone.

Charles Waudby Stephenson is commemorated on:
The War Memorial, Memorial Gardens, New Road, Hornsea.
The War Memorial in St Nicholas Church, Hornsea.
The War Memorial in the Old Drill Hall, Back Southgate, Hornsea. Now the Ex-Servicemen's Club.
The War Memorial, brass plaque, in the Wesleyan Methodist Chapel, Hornsea.
The family headstone, Southgate Cemetery, Hornsea.

Sutherby. Albert.
Private 201474/4423. 1/4th Battalion East Yorkshire Regiment. 150th Brigade, 50th Northumbrian Division.
Killed in Action 23 April 1917, aged 23 years. He has no known grave and is commemorated on the Arras Memorial to the Missing, France.

Private Albert Sutherby.

On the night of 23 April 1917 the 1/4th Battalion East Yorkshire Regiment was in position at their jumping off positions astride the Wancourt/Cherisy Road. The creeping barrage opened up at 4:45 a.m. with a thundering crash and the waiting troops stood up and advanced behind it. The German artillery lay down a heavy fire on the advancing

Tommies and the British barrage moved too slowly, the men were caught in their own barrage causing severe casualties. Machine-gun fire played along the advancing line and it was not long before nearly every officer was killed or wounded. The German infantry counter-attacked and drove the 1/4th back, capturing many men in the process. In this confused and fruitless attack the battalion lost 17 officers and 350 men.

Albert was born in Hornsea in 1894 and was the son of Edwin Sutherby and Esther Ann Sutherby, nee Taylor, of Mereside, Hornsea. They married in Beverley in 1890 and had three other children: Ethel born in Market Weighton in 1892, Walter born in Hornsea in 1896 and Mabel born in Hornsea in 1900.

In 1891, a year after they were married, Edwin and Esther Ann resided in Market Weighton and Edwin was employed as an agricultural labourer. In 1901 they were living at Mereside, Hornsea, and Edwin was working as a grocer's porter. I cannot find the family in the 1911 census.

In 1911, at the age of 17, Albert was working at Great Cowden, Hatfield, on the farm of M W Thompson and Hannah Thompson, as a Farm Servant/Waggoner. He enlisted in 1915.

Albert Sutherby was listed under the title of 'Hornsea soldiers killed and missing' in the *Beverley Guardian* on 2nd and 23 June 1917.

Southgate Cemetery, Hornsea.

Mr Edwin Sutherby: Born in Market Weighton in 1866 and died in Hornsea on 10 December 1937. Mrs Esther Ann Sutherby: Born in South Cave in 1871 and died in Hornsea on 9 August 1945. Buried in the same plot in Southgate Cemetery, Hornsea, are: Stanley Sutherby, died on 9 August 1968, aged 66 years, and Ethel Sutherby, died on 11 January 1977, aged 84 years. Albert Sutherby is commemorated on the family headstone.

Albert Sutherby is commemorated on:
The War Memorial, Memorial Gardens, New Road, Hornsea.
The War Memorial in St Nicholas Church, Hornsea.
The War Memorial in the Old Drill Hall, Back Southgate, Hornsea. Now the Ex-Servicemen's Club.
The hand written Roll of Honour in Wesleyan Methodist Chapel, Hornsea.
The family headstone, Southgate Cemetery, Hornsea.
The Arras Memorial to the Missing, France.

Sergeant Herbert William Thom.

Thom. Herbert William.
Sergeant 4905. 1/4th Battalion East Yorkshire Regiment. 150th Brigade, 50th Northumbrian Division.
Killed in Action 22 July 1916, aged 28 years. Buried in La Laiterie Military Cemetery, Belgium.

In late July 1916 the 50th Division was stationed in the Wytschaete Sector, Ypres, they took part in no major attacks but were very active with raids and counter raids. Aggressive patrols were constantly out in no-man's land seeking to take prisoners and gain intelligence on the enemy dispositions. Artillery fire was a constant hazard and snipers were active on both sides.

He was born in Hull in July 1889 and was the son of William Edmund and Fanny Thom, nee Dorsey, of New Road, Hornsea. They married in Hull on 28 November 1883 and had two other children: Arthur Ernest born in Hull in 1885 and Charles Frederick born in Hornsea in 1895.

In 1891 the family resided at 70 Alexandra Road, Hornsea, and William Edmund was a self-employed carver and gilder. In 1901 they lived at Newbegin, Hornsea and by 1911 they had moved to New Road, Hornsea.

He was the husband of Annie Thom, nee Chatterton, of 5 Alexandra Road, Hornsea. They married in Hornsea in April 1914 and had one son: Douglas Peter, born 1916. In Herbert William's will all his personal effects were left to his wife Annie.

Herbert William was a Coal Merchant's Clerk before the war and had served 13 years as a Volunteer and a Territorial.

The death of Herbert William Thom was reported in the *Hull Daily Mail* on 5 August 1916, the same publication listed him in a casualty list on 22 and 26 August 1916. He was recorded with others in a Roll of Honour in the *Beverley Guardian* on 5 August 1916.

Southgate Cemetery, Hornsea.

1st headstone:

Mr William Edmund Thom: Born in Hull in 1855 and died in Hornsea on 22 January 1934, aged 78. Mrs Fanny Thom: Born in Hull in 1860 and died in Hornsea on 12 June 1949, aged 89 years. They are buried in Southgate Cemetery, Hornsea. Their son, Herbert William, is commemorated on the headstone.

2nd headstone: Annie Thom: Born in Hull in 1885 and died in Hornsea on 20 March 1962. Douglas Peter Thom, her son: Born Hornsea 1916 and died in Hornsea on 28 April 1967, aged 51 years. Herbert William Thom is commemorated on the family headstone.

Herbert William Thom is commemorated on:
The War Memorial, Memorial Gardens, New Road, Hornsea.
The War Memorial in St Nicholas Church, Hornsea.
The War Memorial in the Old Drill Hall, Back Southgate, Hornsea. Now the Ex-Servicemen's Club.
The brass memorial plaque in the United Reform Church, Hornsea.
Two family headstones in Southgate Cemetery, Hornsea.

Train. Albert.
Corporal 12085. 7th Battalion King's Own Yorkshire Light Infantry. 61st Brigade, 20th Division.
Died of Gun-shot Wounds to the thigh at No 7 Casualty Clearing Station, Merville, on 7 January 1916, aged 22 years. Buried in Merville Communal Cemetery, France.

Corporal Albert Train.

He was born in Hornsea in 1894 and was the son of George Edward, Coal Merchant, and Mary Jane Train, nee Kitchen, of 1 St Nicholas Mount, Newbigin, Hornsea. They married in Hull in December 1886 and had 15: Emily Train born in Hull in 1887, Arthur Edward Train born 1888, Hubert Train born 1890, Mabel Train born 1891, Mary Elizabeth Train born 1895 and died same year, Violet Train born 1897, Elizabeth Train born 1898, Lucy Kitchen Train born 1899 and died 1900, George William Train born 1900, Lilly Train born 1902, Kenneth Kitchen Train born 1903 and died 1905, Mary Train born 1904, Thomas born 1905, Beatrice Train born 1907 and Ethel Train born 1908. All the children but Emily were born in Hornsea.

In 1891 the family resided at Southgate, Hornsea, and George Edward was employed as a coal dealer. In 1901 and 1911 they resided at St Nichols Mount, Newbegin, Hornsea. Albert worked as a grocer's assistant, Hubert was a labourer and Arthur Edward was a painter.

Albert Nelson Train, brother of George Edward Train and uncle of Albert and Hubert, married Emma Maria Sedman in Hull in 1897. Emma Maria's brother, Llewellyn Frank Sedman, had emigrated to Canada in 1905 and joined up at the outbreak of war. He died of wounds received in action on 20 December 1916 while serving with the Canadian Rifles. He is commemorated on the Hornsea War Memorial.

Trooper Hubert Train.

Hubert Train, brother of Albert, served in the 9th Lancers and survived the war. Albert landed in France on 22 July 1915.

Albert Train was listed in a Roll of Honour in the *Beverley Guardian* on 19 February 1916.

Letter to Mr George Edward Train:

"We were with a party working on the parapet of the firing trench when the German snipers peppered us. A bullet went through the forearm of the man on my left, missed me and struck Corporal Train in the thigh. We had gone through thick and thin together and Albert was one of the finest lads that ever donned khaki."

Southgate Cemetery, Hornsea.

Mr George Edward Train: Born in Burton Constable in 1868 and died in Hornsea on 7 November 1930. Mrs Mary Jane Train: Born in Hull in 1868 and died in Hornsea on 22 January 1938. Hubert Train: Born in Hornsea in 1890 and died in Hornsea on 15 November 1934.

They are buried together in Southgate Cemetery, Hornsea.

Albert Train is commemorated\on the family headstone.

Buried in the same cemetery are:

Arthur Edward Train: Brother of Albert. Born in Hornsea in 1888 and Died on 18 December 1945.

Rose Ann Train His wife: Died on 9 February 1970, and their son Donald, died on 6 December 1966, ashes.

Also:

Albert Nelson Train: Born in Burton Constable in 1869 and died in Hornsea at 8 Wilton Road on 1 October 1949.

Emma Maria Train: His wife. Born in Whitby in 1874 and died in Hornsea on 4 July 1958. Other members of the Train family are buried in this plot.

Edenfield Cemetery, Hornsea.

George William Train: Brother of Albert. Born in Hornsea in 1900 and died in Hornsea on 3 September 1959.

Isabel Train, nee Maxwell: His wife. Died in Hornsea on 10 March 1974.

Albert Train is commemorated on:
The War Memorial, Memorial Gardens, New Road, Hornsea.
The War Memorial in St Nicholas Church, Hornsea.
The War Memorial in the Old Drill Hall, Back Southgate, Hornsea. Now the Ex-Servicemen's Club.

Tungate. Robert.
Corporal 16062. 4th Pioneer Battalion Coldstream Guards. Guards Division.
Died of Wounds 3 August 1917, aged 26 years. Buried in Canada Farm Cemetery, Belgium.

Robert was mortally wounded during the Battle of Pilkem Ridge, 31 July–2 August 1917. The cemetery takes its name from a farm house that was used as a dressing station during 3rd Ypres or Passchendaele.

He was born in Rise, near Skirlaugh, in 1891 and was the son of Charles, agricultural labourer, and Eliza Tungate, nee Thorley, of 13 Brickyard Cottages, Hornsea. They married in Hornsea on 22 March 1880 and had seven other children: George Henry born in Hornsea in 1880, Sarah Jane born in Sigglesthorne in 1882, James born in Sigglesthorne in 1883, Florence Mary born in Sigglesthorne in 1885, Charles W born in Rise in 1887, Rose Ellen born in Rise in 1889 and Daniel John born and died in Hornsea in 1893.

Corporal Robert Tungate.

In 1891 the whole family was living in Rise. In 1901, after the death of Mrs Eliza Tungate in 1893, the family had moved to 13 Brickyard Cottages, Hornsea, Mr Charles Tungate was employed as a farm labourer and only Rose Ellen and Robert were still living in the family home.

In 1911 Mr Charles Tungate was still working as a farm labourer and living alone at 48 Marlborough Avenue, Hornsea. That same year Robert was living at his brother's house, George Henry and his wife Annie, at 29 Berkshire Street, Hull. Robert and George Henry both worked as shunters for the local railway company.

Robert was the husband of Nancy Tungate, nee Webster, of Hornsea, later of Beverley. They married in Beverley in 1914 and had one son: Charles, born 1915. Robert was a police constable for four years in Beverley before enlisting and went to

France on 15 December 1915. After her husband's death Nancy re-married in Hull to Alfred Purr in 1919 and moved to Badsworth, near Pontefract.

An officer wrote home to Nancy Tungate in September 1917: "Allow me to offer my sincere sympathies for the loss of your husband, Corporal Tungate, who died from wounds received in action on 3rd. He was a section commander in my platoon, a most hard working, brave and well disciplined soldier. A splendid example to his men who loved him. I cannot express the sorrow I feel for you."

His picture was featured in the *Beverley Guardian* when his death was reported on 18 August 1917. On 1 December 1917 his name was featured in a list of the Fallen from Beverley Cricket Club in the *Beverley Guardian*.

His picture was featured in *Green's Almanac* in 1918.

He was recorded in a casualty list in the *Hull Daily Mail* on 3 September 1917.

Mrs Eliza Tungate: Born in Hornsea on 2 March 1859 and died in Hornsea in March 1893. Mr Charles Tungate: Born in Runham, Norfolk, on 27 June1856 and died in Hornsea on 31 July 1943.

Robert Tungate is commemorated on:
The War Memorial, Memorial Gardens, New Road, Hornsea.
The War Memorial in St Nicholas Church, Hornsea.
The War Memorial in the Old Drill Hall, Back Southgate, Hornsea. Now the Ex-Servicemen's Club.
The Great War Memorial, Hengate, Beverley.
The Oddfellows Roll of Honour, the Memorial Hall, Lairgate, Beverley.
The Norwood Street Shrine, Beverley.
The Cricket Club Roll of Honour, Norwood, Beverley.
St Mary's Church Roll of Honour, Hengate, Beverley.
The East Riding Memorial, Beverley Minster.

West. George Christopher.
Private R/16385. 21st Service Battalion King's Royal Rifle Corps. 64th Brigade. 21st Division.
Killed in Action on 16 September 1916, aged 20 years. He has no known grave and is commemorated on the Thiepval Memorial to the Missing of the Somme.

On 16 September 1916 the 21st Division was in reserve as the Battle of Flers/Courcelette began on 15 September. They were moved into the Front Line on 23 September to take part in the Battle of Morval which began on the 15th.

He was born in Hornsea in 1896 and was the son of Frederick Augustus West and Mary Rachel West, nee Davison, of 52 Horsforth Avenue, Bridlington. They married in New Clee, Lincs, at St John's Church on 20 September 1892 and had two other children: Robert Henry West born in Grimsby on 7 October 1893, he died in Holderness in June 1973, and Walter Davison West born in Hornsea on 20 November 1900, he died in Bridlington in 1995.

In 1901 the family resided at Back Southgate, Hornsea. Frederick Augustus worked as a fisherman. In 1911 they resided at Mary Cottage, Newbegin, Hornsea, Frederick

Augustus was still a self-employed fisherman, Robert Henry was a clerk, George Christopher was a grocer's errand boy and Walter was still at school.

George Christopher's service record tells us that in 1915 he was living at 3 Eastgate View, Hornsea, at the age of 19, and enlisted on 28 October that year. His occupation is given as grocer.

In March 1917 George Augustus and Mary Rachel West resided at 52 Horsforth Avenue, Bridlington.

Mr Frederick Augustus West: Born in Sherringham, Norfolk, on 20 February 1868 and died in Bridlington on 1 November 1947. Mrs Mary Rachel West: Born in Withernsea in December 1864 and died in Bridlington on 22 January 1958.

George Christopher West is commemorated on:
The War Memorial, Memorial Gardens, New Road, Hornsea.
The War Memorial in St Nicholas Church, Hornsea.
The War Memorial in the Old Drill Hall, Back Southgate, Hornsea. Now the Ex-Servicemen's Club.
The War Memorial, brass plaque, in the Wesleyan Methodist Chapel, Hornsea.
The Druids Roll of Honour, 22 Albion Street, Hull.
The Thiepval Memorial to the Missing of the Somme.

Wiles. Thomas William.
Private 28858. 6th Battalion Leicester Regiment. 110th Brigade, 21st Division.
Killed in Action on 18 September 1918, aged 42 years.
Buried in Unicorn Cemetery, Aisne, France.
He was born in Nafferton in 1876 and was the son of William and Sarah Ann Wiles, nee Hocknell, of Village Street, Bewholme, Nr Hornsea. They married in Beverley in 1870 and had five other children: George born in Bewholme in 1871, Mary born in Bainton in 1872, Fred born in Nafferton in 1874, Catherine born in Bewholme in 1878 and Walter born in Bewholme in 1880.

Private Thomas William Wiles.

In 1871 and 1881 the family resided in Bewholme, four miles from Hornsea. Mr William West worked as an agricultural labourer. In 1901, after her husband's death, Sarah Ann Wiles lived in Bewholme and worked as a char woman.

Thomas William worked as a general labourer and was the husband of Mary Elizabeth Wiles, nee Beilby, of 10 Ocean Terrace, Hornsea. After her husband's death Mary Elizabeth lived at 46 Southgate, Hornsea. They married in Hornsea in 1901 and resided at 10 Ocean Terrace, Hornsea, they had three children: John William born in Hornsea in 1902, Gertrude Mary born in Hornsea in 1905, Gladys Muriel born in Hornsea in 1906.

Thomas William Wiles was a member of the Victoria Perseverance Lodge, United Ancient Order of Druids. He enlisted in 1916 and his death was reported in the *Hull Daily Mail* of 10 October 1918.

Mr William Wiles: Born in Welburn, Yorkshire, in 1841 and died in Bridlington in December 1882. Mrs Sarah Ann Wiles: Born in Broughton, Lincs, in 1842 and died in Hornsea in December 1925.

Southgate Cemetery, Hornsea.

Mrs Mary Elizabeth Wiles: Born in Hornsea in 1878, she never re-married and died in Hornsea on 7 August 1955. She is buried in Southgate Cemetery, Hornsea, with three of her children: John William Died on 9 March 1929, aged 27 years. Gladys Muriel died on 15 May 1986, aged 80 years and Gertrude Mary died on 23 October 1989, aged 82 years. Thomas William Wiles is commemorated on the headstone.

Thomas William Wiles is commemorated on:

The War Memorial, Memorial Gardens. New Road, Hornsea.

The War Memorial in St Nicholas Church, Hornsea.

The War Memorial in the Old Drill Hall, Back Southgate, Hornsea. Now the Ex-Serviceman's Club.

The hand written Roll of Honour in the Wesleyan Methodist Chapel, Hornsea.

The family headstone, Southgate Cemetery, Hornsea.

The Druids Roll of Honour, 22 Albion Street, Hull.

8

The Persistence of Memory: Great War Memorials in Hornsea

The Hornsea War Memorial. The Memorial Gardens, New Road, Hornsea. Made of black granite with gold lettering this memorial records the names of 77 men who were killed in action, died of wounds or died of other causes during the Great War. No formal public war memorial was erected in Hornsea after the war and it was not until 26 October 2008 that the town finally got one, when this tribute to the men of Hornsea who died was dedicated.

St Nicholas Church. Newbegin, Hornsea. The Parish Church Memorial bells. The new Peal of Bells was dedicated by the Reverend Francis Gurdon at a special service on 8 December 1919. Included as part of the memorial was the chimes and clock face, this was installed in 1921. To commemorate the dedication a memorial tablet was unveiled on 7 December 1920 and was fixed to the north wall of the tower.

The Hornsea Urban District Council Memorial. A Bronze Plaque with 68 names. It was originally intended that this plaque was to record the names of all Hornsea men who had served in the war, when it was realised that approximately 450 men from Hornsea had served the plan was amended to include only the names of the Fallen. 68 names are recorded on the plaque and it was unveiled in St Nicholas Church on 7 December 1920.

The Hedley Memorial Window. This window was dedicated on 24 April 1919 in the Lady Chapel of the Hornsea Parish Church, St Nicholas, at a special service. It commemorates Lieutenant Colonel John Ralph Hedley, DSO, who died in 1917.

The Lyon Memorial Window. This window commemorates Mrs Betsy Lyon, died 11 September 1917, and her son Private Arthur Stanton Lyon who died on 7 October 1916.

The Methodist Chapel. Formerly the Wesleyan Methodist Chapel, Newbegin, Hornsea. Brass Memorial Tablet with nine names. This was unveiled on 18 September 1921 by Lieutenant Arthur J Lonsdale of Hornsea, Indian Army. It records nine men who attended the church and died in the war.

The Market Place Church. Formerly the Primitive Methodist Chapel. Three stained glass memorial windows. These are situated at the top of the chapel steps. The Myers Memorial Window. This was unveiled on 25 February 1922 along with seven other windows that commemorated members of the chapel congregation. The Myers

Memorial Window commemorates Mr James Myers and his son Seaman Herbert Myers who was killed at Jutland on 31 May 1916.

The Primitive Methodist Chapel, hand written Roll of Honour. Now located in the Methodist Chapel, Newbegin. This memorial lists Hornsea men who served as well as the names of 20 soldiers who died in the war.

The United Reform Church. Formerly the Congregational Church. New Road, Hornsea.

Brass Memorial Tablet. This memorial was unveiled on 21 December 1919 and commemorates four church members who died in the war.

The Mansfield Memorial Tablet. This memorial is dedicated to Mr George Mansfield, Deacon and Secretary to the church, who died on 7 April 1918 and Douglas Mansfield who died aged 17 years on 9 April 1909. Lieutenant George Stanley Mansfield, who was killed in action on 22 March 1918, aged 22 years, is also commemorated here.

The Hornsea Ex-Servicemen's Club. The Old Drill Hall. Back Southgate, Hornsea. The Drill Hall was built in 1884 for the Artillery Volunteers. From 1908 it was used by the 5th Cyclists Battalion East Yorkshire Regiment, Territorial Force. After the Great War the hall became redundant, it was then used as an Ex-Servicemen's Club from 22 December 1920. The club bought the hall in 1927. The Ex-Service Men's Club Roll of Honour was unveiled on 9 April 1922. The memorial was unveiled by Mrs Ada Hedley, widow of Lieutenant Colonel Hedley, DSO, who died on Active Service in 1917.

The Hornsea and District War Memorial Cottage Hospital. Eastgate.

Rather than erect a cenotaph or other public memorial it was decided by the War Memorial Committee that a cottage hospital would be built, not only to commemorate the war dead of Hornsea but to leave something that would be of use to future generations. Mr William Collinson, who had lost a son in the war, was elected to head this committee. The Hornsea Memorial Fund was inaugurated and a total of 520 pounds pledged at its first meeting. The appeal for funds was launched and money flowed in. The two largest donations came from Mr Christopher Pickering who generously donated 10,000 pounds and the Freemasons. The foundation stone was laid on 19 October 1922, and the Hornsea and District War Memorial Hospital was opened on 8 December 1923. Since its opening numerous extensions have been added virtually blotting out the original structure.

The Hornsea and District War Memorial Cottage Hospital, Eastgate, 1923.

The United Order of Druids Roll of Honour. Lodge 478. The War Memorial Hall, 22 Albion Street, Hull. This memorial records the names of 385 members who died in the war, including the men from Hornsea Perseverance Lodge.

The Collinson Memorial Seat. Eastgate. This seat was erected by Mr William Collinson in memory of his only son, Lieutenant William Holmes Collinson, who was killed serving with the

Northumberland Fusiliers on 5 January 1916. It was dedicated on 6 August 1916. The seat was refurbished and re-dedicated on 11 May 2003.

The unnamed Seat in Seaton Road, Hornsea. It is speculated that this seat might also be a war memorial as it is identical in design and materials to the Collinson Seat, however the inscription gives no clue as to its origins. John Ralph Hedley who died in 1917 lived nearby at Westgate House.

9

Other First World War Graves in Hornsea: Men from other Counties

Private 200889. William Henry Mellish. 4th Battalion the Yorkshire Regiment. Died of pneumonia at the VAD hospital, Cliff Road, Hornsea, on 25 November 1918, aged 28 years. Buried in Southgate Cemetery, Hornsea.

He shares a grave with a soldier from the East Yorkshire Regiment. William Henry served in France from 2 September 1915 and was wounded in early 1916 on the Somme. He came home and recovered, was sent to a reserve battalion in Hornsea and caught pneumonia in the influenza epidemic of 1918 and died at the VAD hospital, Cliff Road, Hornsea.

William Henry Mellish was born on 3 January 1889 at St John the Divine, Richmond, Surrey, and was the son of John James Mellish, coachman, and Eleanor Catherine Mellish, nee Ogden, of 27 Gould Road, Twickenham, Middlesex. They married at St Peter and All Saints, Petersham, Surrey, on 23 September 1877 and resided at 5 Paradise Road, Paradise Cottage, Richmond, Surrey.

William Henry Mellish went to France in September 1915 and was wounded in early 1916.

Mr John James Mellish: Born in Surrey in 1849 and died in Richmond, Surrey, in 1892.

In 1901 William Henry was in the Felixstowe Workhouse, his mother, Eleanor Catherine, was working as a laundress in the Union Workhouse, Richmond.

Eleanor Catherine Mellish: Born in Kew, Surrey, in 1855 and died in Brentford, Middlesex, in 1932.

William Henry Mellish is commemorated on: A memorial plaque in St Leonard's Church, Loftus. The Loftus War Memorial.

Private 205179. Conrad Clarke Fletcher. 1/4th Battalion East Yorkshire Regiment. Died of sickness at the VAD hospital, Hornsea, on 27 September 1917, aged 32 years. Buried in Southgate Cemetery, Hornsea.

Conrad shares a grave with the above soldier of the Yorkshire Regiment. He was born in Castle Ashby, Northamptonshire, on 28 August 1885 and was the son of Thomas, butcher, and Emma Fletcher of 391 New Chester Road, Tranmere, Birkenhead, Cheshire.

In 1911 the family resides at Battersea Park, London, and Emma, widow, is the head of the house living on private means, at home with her is Conrad who worked as a clerk/book keeper and his sister Rita who was a typist.

At the age of 28 years misfortune befell Conrad and he was admitted to the Strood Union Workhouse, Shorne, Gravesend, Kent, on 4 April 1914 and was an inmate until 1916 when he joined the army.

In the *Soldiers Died* series and in the *Soldiers Effects* records his first name is given as Charles. But in the 1891 and 1911 census and in the workhouse records it is recorded clearly as Conrad.

His Next of Kin is given as his sister, Miss R Fletcher of 19 Marney Road, Lavender Hill, London.

186873 CH. Able Seamen William John Rodgers. Royal Naval Mine Clearance Service. HMS *Holderness*. Drowned accidentally on 16 August 1919, aged 39 years. Buried in Southgate Cemetery, Hornsea.

He was born in Tartaraghan, Armagh, Ireland, on 14 February 1880 and was the son of William James and Mary Rodgers of Cloncarrish, Tartaraghan, County Armagh, Ireland, and the husband of Mary Elizabeth Rodgers, nee Trueman.

In 1911 Mrs Mary Rodgers was living with her mother, Mrs Teresa Trueman. That same year William John Rodgers was recorded as a widower.

He joined the Navy on 9 January 1896 and his first ship was HMS *Caledonian*. In 1919 HMS *Holderness* was part of a mine clearance flotilla working in the North Sea after the Great War. His seaman's service record states that he was last seen alive on 16 August 1919 and that his body was washed ashore at Hornsea on 5 September that year.

Bugler 18/1590. Wilfred Boagey. 21st Battalion Durham Light Infantry. Died of a self-inflicted gunshot wound to the chest on 16 May 1916. He was buried in Southgate Cemetery, Hornsea, by a military Chaplin. His headstone gives his age as 18, his service records give his age as 20 as does the Southgate Cemetery register.

He was born in Hartlepool in 1894 and was the son of James and Jane Ann Boagey, nee Wilford, of Church Road, West Hartlepool, County Durham. They married in St Hilda's Church, Hartlepool on 26 October 1879.

Mr James Boagey: Born in Stockton, Durham, in 1859 and died in Hartlepool in 1900.

Mrs Jane Ann Boagey: Born in Hartlepool in 1861 and died in Hartlepool in 1915.

He enlisted in West Hartlepool on 4 June 1915 and had been in trouble on numerous occasions for returning late from leave. A note found on Wilfred read: 'I am too much of a coward to face my punishment'.

Regimental Sergeant Major Richard Lax stated: The diseased was a bugler in my battalion and was 20 years of age. He had been in the battalion for about 12 months and had shown no signs of mental deficiency as far as I know. He was an efficient soldier and was on the sick list with a skin disease about a month ago. He went on weekend leave on Saturday 14th. He should have been back at 11:00 p.m. and only returned between 5 and 6 last evening. I did not see him when he came in but there is a witness who did. The deceased was put under open arrest, being confined to camp but not to his tent. I heard the report of a rifle and went to see what was the matter. The deceased had been taken from the tent and was laid on the ground dying from a gun-shot wound to the left breast. He died almost at once and was shot with a service rifle, there was one round in the breach. He was in uniform and his punishment for being late back from leave would have been a mere nothing. He was very moody and had lost his mother some time ago.

Bugler Edward John Johnson said in his statement: I was in the same tent as the deceased with 12 others and saw him when he came back, he told me he was sick of life. We all gave money to the deceased for savings purposes, I came to the conclusion he must have spent it when only two pennies were found on him. I saw him sitting in the tent with his rifle on his knee, we all left him and by the time we had got to the second tent we heard the report of a rifle and a scream. We went for the sergeant and when we got to him his rifle was still on his knee, it is possible to reach the trigger in that position, he lay quite still and quiet.

Dr Henry Douglas Johns of Hornsea and Lieutenant James John Ross, RAMC, told the inquest they agreed that this was a case of suicide.

The personal effects of Wilfred Boagey were returned to his brother, Thomas William Boagey, at 15 Lily Street, East Hartlepool, Durham.

Private 6674. Thomas Doyle. 3rd Battalion Lancashire Fusiliers. Died of consumption on 3 May 1915, aged 45 years, at the VAD hospital, Cliff Road, Hornsea. Buried in Southgate Cemetery, Hornsea.

He shares a grave with a soldier of the Manchester Regiment.

The only record of this man I can find is with the Commonwealth War Graves Commission, only the basic facts are recorded and his death record, the latter gives his date of birth as 1867.

Private 6767. Robert Steward. 3rd Battalion Manchester Regiment. Died in the VAD hospital, Cliff Road, Hornsea, on 13 September 1915, aged 33 years. Buried in Southgate Cemetery, Hornsea.

Robert shares a grave with the above soldier of the Lancashire Fusiliers.

He was born in Scarborough in 1883 and was the son of Agnes and Charles Steward, wireworker, of 22 Colin Street, Hull.

Mr Charles Steward: Born in Sheffield in 1844 and died in Hull in 1900.

In 1911 the family resided at 19 Francis Street, East Hull. Agnes was working as a wardrobe dealer and Robert was a general labourer.

Mrs Agnes Steward: Born in Chatham, Kent, in 1845 and died in Hull in 1921.

Captain. John Gay. 30th Battalion Northumberland Fusiliers. Died on 29 May 1916, aged 63 years. Buried in Southgate Cemetery, Hornsea.

Captain Gay was born in Stamford, Lincs, on 8 December 1850 and was the son of William, Chelsea Pensioner, and Ann Gay of St Leonard Street, Stamford, Lincs.

He was an old soldier previously serving in the 23rd Battalion Royal Scots, Lothian Regiment, as a young man. He was admitted to the Royal Hospital for Chelsea Pensioners at the age of 39, with the rank of sergeant major, on 25 May 1888.

He was the husband of Annie Gay of The Lothians, Warbreck Drive, Blackpool, they married in 1888.

In 1911 he and his wife, Annie, lived in Blackpool and he was employed as a brewer's traveller.

Private 32/515. Montague William Potter 32nd Reserve Battalion, Northumberland Fusiliers. Died on 5 July 1916, aged 29 years. Buried in Southgate Cemetery, Hornsea.

Montague was born in Hull in 1887 and was the son of Montague, railway clerk, and Lydia Mary Potter, nee Train, of 9 Addderbury Crescent, Beverley Road, Hull. They married in Hornsea in 1885.

In 1901 he was living with his grandparents, William, gravel dealer, and Elizabeth Train of New Road, Hornsea. They were both 61 at that time and William was born in Hornsea.

He worked as a goods clerk for the North Eastern Railway and was the husband of Elsie Potter, nee Mills, of 4 Church Road, North Ferriby Nr Hull. They married in Hull in 1915.

The *Soldiers Died* series incorrectly lists his place of death as France and Flanders.

Mr Montague Potter: Born in Hornsea in 1860 and died in Hull on 27 February 1929.

Mrs Lydia Mary Potter: Born in Norton, Yorkshire in 1860 and died in Hull on 18 May 1936.

Montague William Potter is commemorated on:

The North Eastern Railway War Memorial, Station Road, York. The Memorial Book of Remembrance in the Railway Museum, York.

10

Hornsea Men who were Killed in the War but are not Listed on the Hornsea War Memorial

Captain Kenneth Philip. 1/4th Battalion East Yorkshire Regiment, attached to 11th Battalion, 2nd Hull Pals, East Yorkshire Regiment. Killed in Action 27 March 1918 aged 30 years. He has no known grave and is commemorated on the Pozieres Memorial to the Missing, France.

He was born in Hull on 17 September 1887 and was the son of Robert Harris Philip, Oil Merchant, and Jane Elizabeth Philip of 447 Beverley Road, Hull. They had six other children: Roland born 1880, Maurice born 1882, Evelyn Mary born 1884, Oswald born 1885, Eric born 1890 and Alan born 1897.

Before the war Kenneth lived with his mother and brother Alan at 7 Bank Terrace, Hornsea, and worked as a Merchant's Clerk. The Wills and Probate records confirm his address at the time of his death and Alan and Maurice are named.

Mr Robert Harris Philip: Born in Hull on 9 June 1857 and died in Hull on 13 April 1912.

Mrs Jane Elizabeth Philip: Born in Hull in 1860 and died in Hornsea on 4 January 1935. At the time of her death her address was 7 Bank Terrace, Hornsea.

On 6 April 1918 the *Beverley Guardian* reported Kenneth had been missing since 27 March 1918 under the title of: 'Hornsea officer killed'.

Private 26941 Herbert Keith. 1st Battalion East Yorkshire Regiment.
Killed in Action 9 April 1918, aged 28 years. Buried in Cojeul British Cemetery, France.

He was born in Hornsea in April 1890 and was the son of Michael and Sarah Ann Keith, nee Gibbs, of Ocean Terrace, Southgate, Hornsea. They married in Beverley in 1884 and had four other children: Arthur born in Hornsea in 1886, Walter born in Hornsea 1894, Elsie May born in Hornsea in 1901 and Mabel Annie born in Hornsea in 1907.

The Keith's had resided in Hornsea since the early nineteenth Century and were still there in the early war years. Mrs Keith, who lost her husband in 1912 and two sons in the war, moved to 79 Arundell Street, Hull, she was at this address when names were being collected by the War Graves Commission and for the Hornsea War Memorials.

In 1911 Herbert was working as a wagoner on the farm of John and Ethel Fox of Catwick. His brother Walter served in the East Yorkshire Regiment and survived the war, dying in Hull in 1966. His other brother Arthur was killed at the Front in 1917.

The death of Herbert Keith was reported in the *Hull Daily Mail* in April 1918.

Mr Michael Keith: Born in Seaton in April 1857 and died in Hornsea in January 1912.

Mrs Sarah Ann Keith: Born in Beverley on 25 August 1865 and died in Hull in 1938.

Herbert and Walter Keith are recorded on the Wesleyan Methodist Chapel Roll of Honour, brass plaque, Hornsea.

Private 24674 Arthur Keith. 7th Battalion East Yorkshire Regiment.

Killed in Action 12 October 1917, aged 31 years. He is buried in Bard Cottage Cemetery, France.

Brother of the above.

Arthur Keith was listed in a casualty list in the *Hull Daily Mail* in late 1917.

Private. 44071 Gordon Pinchon. 7th Battalion Lincolnshire Regiment. Formerly 1077 East Yorkshire Regiment.

Died of Wounds on 21 October 1918, aged 26 years. Buried in Rocquigny-Equancourt Road British Cemetery, Manancourt, France.

Gordon was born in Hull in 1893 and was the son of William Henry, captain, Merchant Navy, and Elizabeth Boston Pinchon originally of Hull and later of Ley's Cottage, Atwick Road, Hornsea. They had two other children: Donald born 1888 and Roy born 1891.

Gordon Pinchon, at the age of 17 years and 5 months, joined the 2nd Northumbrian Volunteers, Royal Field Artillery, in Hull, on 7 January 1911 as Driver 873. At this time he resided at 60 Park Grove, Hull. He was a farm labourer and found that his work prevented him attending drills and camps and was released with a good character on 26 July 1913. In 1914 he joined East Yorkshire Regiment and went to Egypt with them in 1915. Later he was posted to the Lincolnshire Regiment

His brother, Company Sergeant Major 10/419 Roy Pinchon, enlisted into the Hull Commercials at the Hull City Hall in 1914 and served with them throughout the war, he came home in 1919.

Southgate Cemetery, Hornsea.

William Henry Pinchon: Born in Hull in 1853 and died in Hornsea on 31 January 1927. Elizabeth Boston Pinchon: Born in Hull in 1853 and died in Hornsea on 27 March 1943. They are buried together in Southgate Cemetery, Hornsea.

Lieutenant Thomas Morris Day. Royal Naval Reserve. HMS *President*. Died of pneumonia at Home Hospital, 16 Fitzroy Square, London, on 7 August 1921, aged 38 years. Buried in Hull Western Cemetery.

Thomas was born in Hull in 1883 and was the son of Caroline Lambert Day and Charles Wilson Day of 36 Park Street, Hull. Caroline Lambert Day died in Hull on 13 January 1917. Charles Wilson Day died in Hull on 19 October 1920.

Thomas Morris Day gained his mates certificate in 1904 and was married to Gertrude Wilson Day who was recorded as living at 3 Carlton Avenue, Hornsea, at the time of her husband's death.

His death certificate gives his cause of death as bronchitis which he suffered from for three years, he was operated on and caught pneumonia and died. He is recorded as a pensioned Naval Reserve Officer and his address in Hornsea is confirmed.

He is recorded by the Commonwealth War Graves as a war casualty.

11

Men who Died in the Great War and had a Link to Hornsea but had no Right to be Included on the Hornsea War Memorial

Michael Sewell identified many men killed in the war who are not listed on the Hornsea War Memorial but have a link to Hornsea, the men listed above I have been able to verify as being entitled to be on the Hornsea War Memorial. Others are listed as residing in Hornsea because their wives or parents moved to Hornsea after the war and were there when the Commonwealth War Graves Commission was collecting information on the Fallen from families. Others lived in Hornsea at some time or were born in Hornsea but had left long before the war. The names of these men are as follows:

Private 11/472 Arthur Barton Cook. 11th Battalion East Yorkshire Regiment, 2nd Hull Pals. Died of gun-shot wounds to the abdomen on 3 May 1916, aged 32 years. Buried in Gezaincourt Communal Cemetery Extension, France.

He was born in Hull in 1884 and was the son of Arthur William and Mary Cook of Reynoldson Street, Hull. He was married to Annette Caroline Cook, they resided at 29 Gordon's Avenue, Cannon Street, Hull, in 1911. Arthur enlisted at the Hull City Hall on 8 September 1914, his service papers tell us he was a widower and that he had no children. His brother, Frederick J Cook, served in the war as a lieutenant in the West Yorkshire Regiment. His other brother, William Cook, served as a 2nd lieutenant in the same regiment. They both survived the war. By 1919 the family was living at Barton upon Humber. I can find no link to Hornsea. Arthur Barton Cook's death was reported in the *Hull Daily Mail* in May 1916.

Private 10/1028 Edgar Hyde. 10th Battalion East Yorkshire Regiment, 1st Hull Pals or Hull Commercials. Killed in action on 17 April 1916, aged 25 years. Buried in the Sucrerie Military Cemetery, France.

His parents, James Francis and Martha Radford Hiedrich, nee Fulston, lived at West Garth, The Leys, Hornsea, after the war. Edgar emigrated to South Africa in 1910 and came home in 1914 to enlist in the Hull Commercials. That same year his father changed their surname from the German sounding Hiedrich to Hyde. Edgar's grandmother, Mary Jane Fulston, is buried in Southgate Cemetery, Hornsea and he is commemorated on the headstone.

Southgate Cemetery, Hornsea.

Mary Jane Fulston, late of Hull, widow of Greaves Fulston. Died on 1 May 1924.

The death of Edgar Hyde was reported in the *Hull Daily Mail* in April 1916.

Private 10/738 George Arthur Wells. 10th Battalion East Yorkshire Regiment, 1st Hull Pals. Killed in action on 30 March 1916, aged 24 years. Buried in Auchonvillas Military Cemetery, France. George Arthur was born in Hull in 1892 and was the son of George William and Asenath Burn Wells who resided 26 Malm Street, Boulevard, Hull, in 1911. At the time of their son's death they resided at 13 Lowther Street, Albert Avenue, Hull. By 1921 they had moved to 31 Marlborough Avenue, Hornsea. George Arthur enlisted on 5 September 1914 into the 1st Hull Service Battalion at the Hull City Hall, his service papers tell us he worked as a merchant's clerk before enlistment. In February 1915 he was admitted to the Hornsea VAD Hospital on Cliff Road, with tonsillitis.

The death of George Arthur Wells was reported in the *Hull Daily Mail* on 7 April 1916.

Private 3/7735 Oswald George Precious. 2nd Battalion East Yorkshire Regiment. Killed in Action on 23 April 1915, aged 41 years. He has no known grave and is commemorated on the Menin Gate Memorial to the Missing, Belgium.

Oswald George was born in York in 1874 and was the son of William and Mary Ann Precious of 7 Arthur Street, York. In 1891he was serving as a militiaman and was stationed at Fulford Barracks, York. He married Elizabeth Kate Riley in Sheffield in 1895 and they had three children. In 1911 they lived at 115 Picton Street, Bradford, and he worked as a concrete floor layer. Elizabeth Kate re-married after her husband's death to Joseph W Bell, she and her husband lived at 27 Wood Street, White Abbey Road, Bradford. The *Soldiers Died* Series says he enlisted in Hornsea, but that is the only link to Hornsea I can find. His death was reported in the *Hull Daily Mail* in 1915.

Private 41317 John Richmond Bucktrout. 1/4th Battalion East Yorkshire Regiment. Died of wounds on 23 April 1918. Buried in Lille Southern Cemetery, France, aged 19 years. John was a boarder at Brampton House private school in Hornsea in 1911.

Robert Reynolds of Hornsea ran this establishment and would lose his own son, Roland, in 1919. John Richmond Bucktrout was born in Hull in 1899 and was the son of Edith Bucktrout of Linnaeus Street, Hull. The *Soldiers Died* Series gives his birth place as Hornsea but I can find no other links to Hornsea. He is not recorded in the 1901 census.

Deckhand FF6512 Frederick Francis Beasley. Royal Naval Reserve. H M Trawler Sir Mark Sykes, Minelayer. Died on 23 May 1915, aged 25 years and is buried in the Western Cemetery, Spring Bank, Hull.

Frederick was born in Hull on 18 September 1886 and was the son of Frederick Francis, sailor, and Isabella Beasley of Manchester Street, Hessle Road, Hull. He married in Hull in 1908 to Ellen Gill, they resided at 14 Filey Grove, Rhodesia Street, Hull. One source records him as falling overboard and drowning, the War Graves record that he died of disease. His wife re-married and became Ellen Pearce, she and her husband lived at 17 Southgate, Hornsea, after the war, later moving to 1 Mill Terrace, West Parade, Spring Bank, Hull.

The death of Frederick Francis Beasley was reported in the *Hull Daily Mail* in June 1915.

Private 20199 Samuel Teesdale. 2nd Battalion Coldstream Guards. Died of wounds on 31 July 1917, aged 26 years. Buried in Bleuet Farm Cemetery, Belgium.
He was born in Hornsea in 1891 and was the son of James and Sarah Teesdale of 137 Finkle Street, Cottingham. In 1916 Samuel was living at 6 Carlton Villas, Grovehill Road, Beverley, that year he married Florence Sumpner. Samuel's family had left Hornsea some years before the Great War.

The death of Samuel Teesdale was reported in the *Hull Daily Mail* on 3 and 5 September 1917. The report stated his brother had also been killed.

Samuel Teesdale is commemorated on:
The Beverley War Memorial. Hengate. The Cottingham War Memorial, St Mary's Churchyard. The family headstone, Eppleworth Road Cemetery, Cottingham The Primitive Methodist Chapel Roll of Honour in Hornsea. A memorial plaque fixed to the gates of the Memorial Gardens, Cottingham.

Private Albert Teesdale. 3rd Battalion Coldstream Guards. Killed in action on 9 September 1914. Brother of the above.
Albert Teesdale is commemorated on:
The Cottingham War. Memorial, St Mary's Churchyard. A memorial plaque fixed to the gates of the Memorial Gardens, Cottingham. The family headstone, Eppleworth Road Cemetery, Cottingham. The Primitive Methodist Chapel Roll of Honour in Hornsea.

A/CSM 7781 Albert Willie Birt. 1st Battalion East Yorkshire Regiment. Died of wounds on 24 March 1918, aged 35 years. Buried in Abbeville Communal Cemetery Extension, France.
Albert was born in Balsall Heath, Birmingham, in 1885, and was a reservist and storekeeper before the war.

He was the son of Charles and Annie Birt of 1 Salisbury Place, Sherbourne Road, Birmingham and the husband of Alice Gertrude Birt, nee Sly, they married in King's Norton in 1909 and had three children: Willie E born King's Norton in 1911 and died in 1916, Ronald born in Aston, Glos, on 29 December 1912 and Amy born on 11 December 1916.

Alice Gertrude resided at Mereside, Hornsea, after the war.

Spare Hand Albert Henry Norton. Steam Trawler Shakespeare. Torpedoed and sank off Whitby. Killed on 7 February 1917, aged 25 years, his ship was attacked by a U-Boat. He is commemorated on the Tower Hill Memorial, London.

He was born in Hornsea on 29 June 1893 and was the son of Ralph and Jennie Norton, they resided in Hornsea from 1892 to 1899. In 1911 they were living at 19 Havelock Street, Hull, and Albert worked as a fish house labourer. He married Ellen Norton, nee O'Connell, in Hull on 4 April 1914 and had three children: Albert Henry jnr was born in Hull in 1914, James was born in Hull 1915 and died the same year and John Patrick was born in Hull in 1917, the family resided at 5 Pretoria Avenue, Flinton Street, Hull.

Ellen Norton re-married in Hull on 12 July 1919 to George Cater and had three more children. She died in Beverley in 1977. Albert Henry jnr, son of Albert Henry and Ellen Norton, born in 1914, perished in the Second World War, he was a leading seaman on Her Majesty's Trawler the Arctic Ranger and was killed in the Mediterranean on 25 September 1940 when a convoy was attacked by a U-Boat wolf pack, 12 of the 41 British ships being sunk.

His wife Elsie Norton lived in Hessle near Hull.

Albert Henry Norton is commemorated:
On the Lowerstoft Naval Memorial.
The death of Albert Henry Norton was recorded in the *Hull Daily Mail* in February 1917.

Private 25247 George William Robson. 1st Battalion East Yorkshire Regiment. Died of wounds on 3 August 1917, aged 37 years. Buried in Croisilles British Cemetery, France.
George was born in Langtoft, Yorkshire, in 1880, and was the son of Joseph Robson of Buckton, Yorkshire, and enlisted in Beverley. He and his wife Emily resided at Wold Newton, Hunmanby in 1911, and he worked as a police constable. I can find no link to Hornsea other than his wife, Emily, who lived at 5 Marlborough Avenue, Hornsea, after the war.

Private 842573 Albert Hill. 1/5th Battalion King's Own Royal Lancaster Regiment. Killed in action 9 March 1917, aged 36 years. He is buried in Vlamertinghe Military Cemetery, Belgium.
Albert was born in Hull in 1881 and was the son of Henry, grocer and shop keeper, and Sarah Ann Hill, nee Hammond, of 45 Cave Street, Beverley Road, Hull. Albert worked as a rulleyman on a farm. The only link to Hornsea I can find is that his wife, Ethel, lived at 6 Victoria Avenue, Hornsea, after the war.

Master Joseph Hill. SS Renfrew. Sunk by U-Boat action off St Ann's Head, Milford Haven, on 24 February 1918, aged 39 years. He is commemorated on the Tower Hill Memorial, London. Joseph was born in 1879 and was the son of Peter William and Elizabeth Hill of Staithes. His widow, Florence Mood Hill, resided in Hornsea, at 32 Marlborough Avenue after the war. His death was reported in the *Hull Daily Mail* on 27 March 1918.

Trimmer 5942/TS George West.
HM Trawler Chrysolite. Royal Naval Reserve.
Died 29 December 1916, aged 19 years. He is buried in Holy Trinity Cemetery, Hessle Road, Hull. The headstones in this cemetery no longer exist. His name is recorded on a memorial screen in Hull Northern Cemetery that commemorates 29 casualties that were buried in Hessle Road Cemetery but whose graves can no longer be maintained.

He was born on 11 September 1898 in Hull and was the son of Charles Henry, shipwright, and Drusilla West, nee Odell, of 8 Harold's Terrace, Scarborough Street, Hessle Road, Hull. They married in Hull in 1886.

Mr Charles Henry West: Died in Hull in 1909.

Mrs Drusilla West: Re-married in Hull in 1912 to George K Sneller and died in Hull in 1949.

The Royal Naval Graves Roll states George West died of disease.

George West is commemorated on:
The hand written Roll of Honour in the Wesleyan Methodist Chapel, Hornsea.
A memorial screen in Hull Northern Cemetery.

Private 6/1268 Cyril Chester Cookes. Canterbury Regiment. New Zealand Expeditionary Force. Killed in Action at Gallipoli on 7 August 1915, aged 34 years. He has no known grave and is commemorated on the Chunuk Bair New Zealand Memorial, Turkey.

Cyril was born in Newland, Hull, in 1879 and was the son of Thomas Stephen, clerk, and Emily Cookes, nee Thomlinson, originally from Hull where they married in 1873. In 1901 and 1911 they resided in Withernsea and had four other children: Clarice Julia born 1874, Madelein E born 1878, Louie Mildred born 1884 and Thomas Gordon born 1886.

Cyril Chester left the shores of England from Liverpool on 29 January 1898.

Southgate Cemetery, Hornsea.

Mr Thomas Stephen Cookes: Born in Brompton, London, in 1845. Died in Hornsea on 28 June 1923.

Mrs Emily Elizabeth Cookes: Born in Hull in 1855. Died in Hornsea on 5 December 1901.

They are both buried in Southgate Cemetery, Hornsea. Their son, Cyril Chester Cookes, is commemorated on the headstone.

At the time of Thomas Stephen Cookes death his address was 17 Clifford Street, Hornsea. I cannot prove when he moved to Hornsea.

Lieutenant John George Vivian Ewings. 1st Battalion King's Own Yorkshire Light Infantry. Killed in action on 3 October 1918, aged 26 years. Buried in Prospect Hill Cemetery, Aisne, France.

John was born in Islington, London, on 17 October 1892 and was the son of George T and Sarah J Ewings of 21 Russel Road, Holloway, London.

In 1901 they resided at Hornsey, Middlesex. In 1911 John George Vivian was a private in the 2nd Battalion Lancashire Fusiliers and was stationed at Assaye Military Barracks, South Tidworth, Hants, he rose to the rank of colour sergeant, regimental number 33963, until his promotion to lieutenant in 1916.

He married Enid Thwaites Ewings in Camarthen, Wales, in 1916. His wife was residing at Waverley, Cliff Road, Hornsea, after the war. Enid re-married in Scarborough in 1922 to Sydney H Jones.

Private 34693 Percy Seddon. 10th Battalion King's Own Yorkshire Light Infantry. Formerly 4053, East Yorkshire Regiment. Killed in action on 25 September 1916. He has no known grave and is commemorated on the Thiepval Memorial to the Missing of the Somme.

Percy was born in Hull in 1900, enlisted in Hull and was the son of Walter, millright, and Susan Elizabeth Seddon, nee Swaby, of 16 Melbourne Avenue, Hull. They married in Hull in 1893 and had one other son, Walter Bernard, who was born in Hull in 1894. After the war they resided at The Poplars, Edenfield Estate, Hornsea, and are buried in Southgate Cemetery, Hornsea.

The death of Percy Seddon was reported in a casualty list in the *Hull Daily Mail* on 16 December 1916.

Southgate Cemetery, Hornsea.

Mr Susan Elizabeth Seddon: Born in Lincoln in 1875 and died in Hornsea on 23 April 1946, aged 71 years. Mr Walter Seddon: Born in Hull in 1969 and died in Hornsea on 20 November 1952, aged 83 years.

Private 25284/58625 Alfred Denis Ream. 52nd Coy Machine Gun Corps. Killed in action on 8 February 1917, aged 26 years. He is buried in Serre Road Cemetery No 1, France.

Alfred was born in Doncaster in 1892 and was the son of Charles Alfred and Ethel Maud Ream, nee Ray, of 49 Hall Gate, Doncaster. He married Emma Gelsthorpe in Mansfield in 1912. After the war Emma resided at Suncroft, Eastbourne Road, Hornsea, but I cannot find any record of them living at Hornsea before or during the war. The relative of Alfred Denis, Joe Gelsthorpe, lives in Mereside, Hornsea.

Sergeant 73883 Herbert James Fell. 37th Battalion Machine Gun Corps. Killed in action on 6 May 1918, aged 28 years. Formerly 10th Battalion East Yorkshire Regiment. Buried in Couin British Cemetery, France.

Herbert James was the son of James and Selina Fell, nee Norton, of 20 Broadfield Road, Moss Side, Manchester and Hull. He was born in Hull on 10 April 1889, was employed at the Produce Brokers' Company, Hull, and enlisted into the Hull Commercials, 1st Hull Pals, at the Hull City Hall, on 5 September 1914. On 11 September 1915 he married Lilian Warden Moore at Christ's Church, Hull, and resided at 15 Peel Street, Spring Bank, Hull. He was transferred to the 8th Battalion East Yorkshire Regiment and then to the Machine Gun Corps.

Herbert James Fell is commemorated in Du Ruvigny's Roll of Honour.

Master George Bertram Williams. M.V. Tycho. Registered in Hull. Sunk by U-Boat action off Beachy Head on 20 May 1917, aged 47 years. He is commemorated on the Tower Hill Memorial, London.
George was born in Louth, Lincs, in 1869. On 29 September 1888 he was awarded his 2nd Mates Certificate in Hull. On 14 August 1893 he was awarded his Mates Certificate in Hull, and on 20 December 1897 he was awarded his Masters Certificate in Hull.

George Bertram married Gertrude Elma Cawcutt in Hull in 1916. After her husband's death she re-married and became Gertrude Elma Denton, residing at Oriel House, Grosvenor Terrace, Hornsea, after the war. She died in Hull in 1931.

Lieutenant Robert Henry Brown. 1/5th Battalion Duke of Wellington's West Riding Regiment. Killed in action on 16 January 1917, aged 24 years. Buried in Warlincourt Halt British Cemetery.
Robert was born in Hull in 1893 and was the son of Alfred Thomas, grocer, and Annie Kezia Brown, in 1901 the family resided at Queen Street, Withernsea. By 1911 the family had moved to 32 the Promenade, Withernsea. Alfred Thomas and Annie Kezia Brown lived at Aysgarth, Withernsea, after the Great War.

Alfred Thomas was born in Masham in 1854 and died in Thorngumbald on 26 December 1946. Annie Kezia was born in Hull in 1855 and died in Withernsea on 22 March 1931. In one record their address after the Great War has been recorded as Aysgarth, Hornsea, which is incorrect.

Private 12/1241 Harold Bourner. 12th Battalion East Yorkshire Regiment. 3rd Hull Pals. Killed in action on the Somme on 19 July 1916, aged 28 years. Buried in Rue-du-Bacquerot No. 1 Military Cemetery, Laventie, France.
He was born in Driffield in 1888 and was the son of David Edward, oil miller, and Mary Ann Bourner.

In 1891 the family resided at 11 George Street, Driffield. Mr David Edward Bourner died in Driffield in 1899. By 1901 the family had moved to 41 Brook Street, Driffield. In 1911 the whole family had moved to Hull and resided at 55 Stanley Street, Spring Bank, Hull, Mrs Mary Ann Bourner earned her living as a dressmaker and Harold Bourner was a boot maker.

Harold married Mary Hopton Loughton in Stepney Chapel, Hull, on 31 August 1912, they resided at 9 Albert Terrace, Terry Street, Hull, and had one child: Millicent Edith, born in Grimsby on 14 June 1913. In 1920 Mary Hopton Bourner was residing at 11 Chestnut Grove, Hull.

Harold enlisted at the Hull City Hall on 22 December 1914 into the 3rd Hull Service Battalion, 3rd Hull Pals, serving with them in Egypt in 1915, in March 1916 they moved to France to take part in the Battle of the Somme.

His mother, Mary Ann Bourner, moved to Hornsea after the Great War and died there on 27 January 1977, she is buried in Edenfield Cemetery, Hornsea, and her son is commemorated on the headstone.

Private 241589 Cyril Pexton Pitchford. 8th Battalion the Border Regiment. Killed in action on 10 April 1918, aged 21 years. Commemorated on the Ploegsteert Memorial to the Missing, Belgium.

He was born in Blyth, Northumberland, in 1896 and was the son of the Reverend John Pitchford, Minister of the United Free Church, and Ada Fanny Pitchford. They married in Beverley in 1884 and had one other son: Donald M Pitchford, born in Blackhill, Durham in 1894.

Southgate Cemetery, Hornsea.

The Reverend John Pitchford. Born in Dawley, Shropshire, in 1857 and died in Hornsea on 9 February 1935. Ada Fanny Pitchford. Born in Beverley in 1863 and died in Hornsea on 5 February 1943. Their son Cyril Pexton Pitchford is commemorated on the family headstone.

Corporal 019134 John Arthur Hall. 4th Canadian Mounted Riffles, 2nd Central Ontario Regiment. Killed in action on 2 June 1916, aged 21 years. Commemorated on the Menin Gate Memorial to the Missing, Ypres, Belgium.

He was born in Hull on 2 March 1892 and was the son of George, Master Mariner, and Sarah Ann Hall, nee Coward, of 109 Linneaus, Hull. They Married in Christ Church, East Knottingly, Yorkshire, on 27 April 1880 and had eight children.

The brother of John Arthur, Lieutenant George Hall, Royal Naval Reserve, was killed at sea on 1 May 1918, aged 29 years, serving on HMS *Blackmore Vale*, Minesweeper. She struck a mine in the North Sea off Tod Head and sank.

George and Sarah Ann Hall are buried in Southgate Cemetery, Hornsea, but I can find no evidence of the year they moved to Hornsea.

Southgate Cemetery, Hornsea.

George Hall, Master Mariner, died on 21 July 1918, aged 64 years. Sarah Ann Hall died on 28 January 1939, aged 76 years. In the same plot are their daughters Elma died 1978, Hilda died 1968 and Florence Amy Hall, ashes, died 1964, plus a Sarah Ann Hall who was 100 years old when she died. Corporal John Arthur Hall is commemorated on the family headstone, as is his brother, Lieutenant George Hall, Royal Naval Reserve, lost at sea on 1 May 1918.

Sources

Kelly's Directory 1913. The North and East Ridings of Yorkshire.
The Treasure House, Beverley.
Beverley Guardian, 1914–1919. Microfiche.
Trustees Meeting Minutes Book, Hornsea Trinity Church. MRH/2/3/2.
Hornsea Council Minutes. UDHO/1/1/3.
Postcard of Rose Carr. DDX/1321/13/6.
Diary of Margaret Strickland Constable. DDST/1/8/2.
Diary of Margaret Strickland Constable. DDST/1/8/2/3.
Notebooks of Margaret Strickland Constable. DDST/1/8/3.
Hornsea Conservative Association records. 1880–1924. DDX/1729.
Letters from Rosa Brown. DDBB/2/4/2.
Strickland Constable family scrap-book. DDST/1/8/4/7.
News cuttings. 1914. DDST/1/8/4/2.
News cuttings. DDST/1/8/4/5.
Royal Naval Air Service log book. DDX/473/2.
Report by Lieutenant Hyams on flight to Bridlington, Flamborough and Scarborough. DDX/473/4.
Hornsea Museum archive.
The Hornsea and Goxhill Parish Magazine. January 1919.
Research notes and papers of Michael Sewell.
East Yorkshire Family History Society. *Monumental Inscriptions*.
Southgate Cemetery, Hornsea.
North Cave Cemetery.
St Alban's Churchyard, Withernwick.
Queensgate New Cemetery, Beverley.
Minster Churchyard, Howden.
Other cemetery registers.
St Mary's Churchyard, Masham.
Pateley Bridge Cemetery.
Jesmond Old Cemetery, Newcastle.
Newcastle upon Tyne, St Andrew's and Jesmond, Cemetery.
Edenfield Cemetery, Hornsea.
Gainsborough General Cemetery, Lincolnshire.
Heptonstall Slack Baptist Church, Mount Zion, Cemetery, Hebden Bridge.

Bibliography

Ascoli, David, *The Mons Star* (London: Harrap, 1981).
Dinsdale, Simon, *The First Gun Shots of the Great War* (Cleckheaton: Simon Dinsdale, 2015).
Emden, Richard Van and Humphries Steve, *All Quiet on the Home Front* (London: Headline, 2003).
Gelsthorpe, Joe, *The Royal Naval Air Service at Hornsea Mere and Killingholme* (Hornsea: Lulu Enterprises, 2014).
Harrison, Stephen, *A History of Hornsea* (London: Blackthorne Press, 2005)
Hornsea and District U3A, *Hornsea Remembers* (Hornsea 2015).
Marsay, Mark, *The Day the East Coast Bled* (Scarborough: Great Northern Publishing, 2000).
McCarthy, Chris, *The Somme* (London: Arms and Armour Press, 1993).
McCarthy, Chris, *Passchendaele* (London: Arms and Armour Press, 1995).
Persico, Joseph, 11th Month, 11th Day, 11th Hour (London: Arrow Books, 2003).
Sewell, Michael, *Hornsea in the 20th Century*, Volume One, (Hornsea: North Holderness Museum of Village Life, 2004).
Sewell, Michael, *His Duty Nobly Done* (Hornsea: Parchment Oxford, 2003).
Sewell, Michael, *A Dear One Gone Forever* (Hornsea: Parchment Oxford, 2008).
Smith, M. H., editor, *Hornsea a Century Ago* (Beverley: Highgate Press, 1993).
Southwell, G. L., *Hornsea in Picture Postcards* (Oxford: European Press, 1983).
Wilson, Trevor, *The Myriad Faces of War* (Oxford: Blackwell, 1986).
Winter, Denis, *Death's Men* (Middlesex: Penguin, 1978).
Winter, Jay, *Sites of Memory Sites of Mourning* (Cambridge: University Press, 1995).
Winter, J. M., *The Great War and the British People* (Basingstoke: Macmillan, 1895).
Wyrall, Everard, *The East Yorkshire Regiment in the Great War* (London: Harrison Ltd 1928).
Wyrall, Everard, *The Fiftieth Division, 1914 to 1919* (London: Harrison Ltd, 1930).

Index

People

Adkin, John William 9
Allott, Private Thomas 2, 29, 67
Anderson, Private Thomas Edward 24, 38
Andrew, Corporal John William 68-69, 85
Arksey, Private Thomas 25
Aust, Private 5

Barr, Private Thomas 31, 70
Beresford, Colonel 14–15
Binning, Private George Ernest 37–38, 70–71, 82
Birt, Albert Willie 157
Blackburn, Private Francis Henry 10, 71–72
Blanchard, Driver Peter Harold 51, 72
Blanchard, Private Herbert 50, 73
Blanchard, Private Oscar viii, 26, 73–74
Boagey, Bugler Wilfred 26, 148–149
Boddy, Private Thomas 4, 74–75
Botha, General 12
Bourner, Private Harold 161
Bowen, Sergeant Geoffrey 60–61, 75
Bradforth, Private John Bertram 37, 76
Bradley, Private Edward 43
Brighouse, Rifleman Charles Edwin viii, 27–28, 72, 77
Brooks, Private Charles Frederick 78–79
Brown, Lieutenant Robert Henry 161
Brown, Private George vii, 32, 79–80
Bucktrout, Private John Richmond 156
Bulson, Lance Corporal Henry 52, 80–81
Burgess, Private Frederick 14, 17, 81-82
Burgess, Corporal George vii, 14, 18, 81–83
Burrows, Harry Raymond 42
Buttimer, Robert Thomas 3–4

Cannell, Sergeant Walter Cecil 53, 83–84
Carr, Private Harry 4–5, 84–85, 109, 163

Clark, Private W 40
Collinson, 2nd Lieutenant William Holmes 24, 29, 69, 85–86, 144–145
Constable, Lieutenant Colonel Frederick Charles Strickland 44
Constable, Margaret Elizabeth Strickland 13, 15, 19, 26, 42–43, 48, 52, 55
Cook, Private Arthur Barton 155
Cookes, Private Cyril Chester 11, 159
Cooper, Private George William 42, 86–87, 126–127, 138–139, 156, 158
Curtin, Lieutenant Edgar Catley 88
Curtin, Private Alexander 53, 87–88

Dawson, Sergeant Richard Douglas 17, 88-89
Day, Lieutenant Thomas Morris 152
Doyle, Private Thomas 12, 149
Dry, Lance Corporal Richard Alma 43, 90–91
Dunn, Lance Corporal George Herbert 29, 31, 91–92
Dunn, Private Peter Allen 31-32, 91

Eastern, Major C 12
England, 2nd Lieutenant Geoffrey William Seward 13
Evans, Private George Mathew 53-54, 92–93

Fell, Sergeant Herbert James 161
Flanagan, Father 12
Fletcher, Private Conrad Clarke 42, 147
Ford, Private Ernest 50, 93–94
Fowler, Private Thomas 54, 94
Frankish, Private Leonard 56, 95–96
Fridlington, Private John Francis 52, 96–97
Fullam, Apprentice Claude Stanley 36, 97

Galloway, Sergeant Jack 35
Gay, Captain John 27, 149
Gelsthorpe, Air Mechanic Gladwin Webster Thomas 23, 39
Grantham, Private Richard Arthur 43-44, 97–98
Gresham, Lieutenant John Francis 59, 98-99
Griffiths, 2nd Lieutenant Walter Harold 30, 99-100
Grindell, Quartermaster Sergeant Alfred 11
Grummitt, 2nd Lieutenant Hugh Cecil 59, 100-101
Grummitt, Lieutenant Joseph Roland 54, 59, 100-101
Gurdon, Reverend Francis 143

Hall, Corporal John Arthur 27, 162
Hall, Lieutenant George 27, 162
Hamshaw, Private Gordon 102
Hamshaw, Private Joseph 103
Harker, Private Frederick George 25, 103–104
Harman, Private James 28, 104-105
Harrington, Reverend John 16
Heathcote, 2nd Lieutenant Ralph Noel 32, 127
Hedley, Lieutenant Colonel John Ralph 41, 59, 106, 143-145
Hetherington, Private Geoffrey Nevill 50, 106–107
Hill, Private Albert 158
Hobson, Private Arthur Ernest 44
Hood, Trooper Sidney 3
Hornsby, Private Percy 12–13
Hulse, Lieutenant Leslie Montgomery 60
Huntley, Mr Lockwood 63
Hyde, Private Edgar 25, 155–156

Jackson, 2nd Lieutenant Henry Douglas 32, 108-109
Jackson, Lieutenant Harold Willows 38–39, 107–108
Jordan, George 39

Keith, Private Arthur 42, 152
Keith, Private Frederick 110-111
Keith, Private Herbert 50, 151
Keith, Private John 8, 110
Kemp, 2nd Lieutenant Frank 41, 112
Kemp, John Stephenson 12
Kitchener, Field Marshall Herbert 4, 15, 20–21, 23, 25

Loftus, 2nd Lieutenant Kenneth 13, 54, 113
Lonsdale, Lieutenant Arthur John 7–8, 39, 56, 62
Lord, 2nd Lieutenant John Frederick Wilson 37, 113-114
Ludendorf, General 48, 68, 106, 116
Lyon, Private Arthur Stanton 31, 115, 143

Mansfield, 2nd Lieutenant George Stanley 48, 116–117, 144, 160
McDowall, 2nd Lieutenant Hugh Stewart 52, 117-118
Mellish, Private William Henry 56, 147
Miller, Sergeant Richard 41, 118–119
Montgomery, Lieutenant William Oscar 59-60
Myers, Leading Seaman Thomas Herbert 27, 119–120

Norman, Private John William 93, 120–121
Norton, Spare Hand Albert Henry 36, 157–158

Parker, Company Sergeant Major William Reynolds 30-31
Parker, Private Eric 31
Parrott, Gunner Robert 121
Peers, Rifleman George Stanley 48, 116–117, 121–122, 144
Philip, Captain Kenneth 49, 151
Pinchon, Private Gordon 152
Pitchford, Private Cyril Pexton 50, 162
Pooley, Private Arthur 56, 67, 123–124
Potter, Private Montague William 28, 150
Precious, Private Oswald George 156
Preston, Private James Routledge 124–125

Ream, Private Alfred Denis 160
Redman, Claude Stansfield 126
Redman, Trooper James William 125–126
Rendell, Sergeant James 126-127
Reynolds, Lieutenant Roland 61, 127
Richmond, Private Wilfred Norburn 128
Robinson, Private John William 129
Rodgers, Able Seaman William John 61, 148

Saville, Reverend W H 19
Seddon, Private Percy 30, 160
Sedman, Private Llewellyn Frank 129-130, 138
Shaw, Captain Cyril Trevor 19, 130-131
Simpson, Private Herbert Edward 41, 132

Smith, Private Bertram 'Bertie' 11, 133
Snowdon, 2nd Lieutenant Ralph 42, 134
Stephenson, Gunner Charles Waudby
  38-39, 134–135
Steward, Private Robert 12, 149
Sutherby, Private Albert 39, 135–136
Sykes, 2nd Lieutenant Percy Hill 10

Teesdale, Private Albert vii, 3, 157
Teesdale, Private Samuel 157
Thom, Herbert William 136–137
Thompson, Lieutenant Norman L 62
Train, Corporal Albert 24, 130, 137–139

Train, Trooper Hubert 24, 138
Tungate, Corporal Robert 41, 139–140

Usher, Private James Smith 36

Walker, Private William 35
West, Private George Christopher 29, 141, 159
Whipp, Private Philip Stuart 31
Whiting, Captain Thomas 29
Wiles, Private Thomas William 53, 141–142
Williams, Master George Bertram 161
Windle, Private Mark 15

Places

Aubers Ridge 10, 21

Basra Memorial Cemetery 18, 130
British Line 11, 40, 48, 50, 81
Brooklands Military Hospital 59, 100
Brookwood Military Cemetery 54, 113

Courcelette 29, 91, 140

Ellerman Line 52, 117

Flanders 40, 150
Flers 29, 91, 115, 122, 140

Gallipoli 11, 20, 68, 88, 159
German Line 29, 40

Hornsea Bridge Railway Station 37, 76
Hornsea Ex-Servicemen's Club 8, 144
Hornsea Mere vii, 23, 39, 42, 51, 59, 165
Hornsea Recruiting Committee 6, 12
Hornsea Rural District Council 29, 55
Hornsea War Memorial v, vii–viii, xii, 13, 32, 42, 49–50, 53, 64, 69, 93, 97, 111, 130, 138, 143, 151, 155

Jutland 27, 119, 144

La Becque 50, 93
Loos 18, 21, 82–83

Menin Gate Memorial 11, 71–72, 81, 84–85, 88–89, 132–133, 156, 162
Merville 24, 137
Messines 40, 44
Mons x, 3–4, 165

Passchendaele x, 40–42, 44, 87, 110, 126, 139, 165
Pozieres Memorial 48, 116–117, 151

Rolston Camp 3, 5, 16

Thiepval Memorial 29, 31, 41, 69–70, 91–92, 112–113, 115, 121, 123, 128, 140–141, 160

VAD Hospital 12, 26, 42–43, 56, 59, 147, 149, 156
Vimy 37, 44, 129–130

War Memorial Cottage Hospital xi, 60–61, 65, 83, 86, 89, 144

Ypres 4, 8, 11, 13, 20–21, 40–41, 44, 71, 78, 81, 84–86, 88–89, 132–133, 136, 139, 162

Military units and formations

1st Battalion East Yorkshire Regiment 17, 48, 50, 53, 56, 74, 81, 83–84, 86, 116, 123, 151, 157–158
1st Battalion Northumberland Fusiliers 4, 84–85
1st Hull Pals 3, 5, 38, 41–42, 48, 50, 93, 108, 116, 118, 134, 155–156, 160
1st Tyneside Scottish 16–17
1st Volunteer Battalion East Yorkshire Regiment 17, 89
2nd Battalion East Yorkshire Regiment 17, 71, 82, 156
2nd Hull Pals 13, 60, 75, 102, 151, 155
3rd Battalion Lancashire Fusiliers 12, 149
3rd Battalion Manchester Regiment 12, 149
3rd Battalion West Yorkshire Regiment 8, 109
3rd Hull Pals 32, 37, 56, 70, 120, 123, 127, 161
4th Battalion East Yorkshire Regiment 12–13, 32, 38, 42, 48–49, 54, 56, 59, 98–100, 102, 107–109, 116, 134–136, 147, 151, 156
4th Hull Pals 53, 59, 84, 124
50th Northumbrian Division 98, 100, 102, 105, 107–108, 134–136
5th Battalion East Yorkshire Regiment 29
5th Cyclist Battalion 2, 67
6th Battalion East Kent Regiment 31, 69
6th Battalion Northumberland Fusiliers 24, 41, 85–86
6th Battalion Royal Dublin Fusiliers 61, 75
7th Battalion East Yorkshire Regiment 28, 42, 52–53, 87, 92, 96, 104, 152
8th Battalion East Yorkshire Regiment 37, 67, 76, 97, 101–102, 120, 160
10th Battalion Canadian Infantry 11, 133
10th Battalion East Yorkshire Regiment 4–5, 16, 25, 38, 41, 93, 108, 116, 118, 134, 155–156, 160
11th Battalion East Yorkshire Regiment 13, 60, 75, 155
12th Battalion East Yorkshire Regiment 32, 37, 70, 120, 123, 127, 161
20th Battalion Northumberland Fusiliers 16, 44
21st Reserve Battalion Durham Light Infantry 26, 35
26th Battalion Royal Fusiliers 31, 115
30th Battalion Northumberland Fusiliers 27, 149
31st Pals Division 59, 70, 75, 83, 93, 118, 123–125
32nd Reserve Battalion 28, 150
122nd Rajputana Infantry 18, 130–131

Alberta Regiment 11, 132
Army of Occupation 61, 75
Army Service Corps 5, 41, 52, 80, 95, 131

British Army 3, 8, 11, 18, 20, 23, 28, 33
British Expeditionary Force 3–4, 8, 11, 21

Canadian Mounted Rifles 27, 129, 162
Canterbury Regiment 11, 159
Coldstream Guards 3, 24, 29, 38, 41, 91, 110, 139, 157
Collier SS Okement 36, 97

German Army 3–4, 8, 32, 48, 54
Gordon Highlanders 26, 51, 73

HM *Drifter Catspaw* 61, 127
HMS *Blackmore Vale* 27, 162
HMS *Cyclamen* 61, 127
HMS *Defence* 27, 119
HMS *Holderness* 61, 148
Hull Commercials 3, 5–6, 10–11, 16, 25, 38, 41–42, 48, 93, 108, 116, 118, 134, 152, 155, 160
Huntingdonshire Cyclist Battalion 3, 10

Indian Army vii, 7, 62, 143

King's Own Yorkshire Light Infantry 15, 18, 24, 30, 32, 37, 41, 79, 112–113, 137, 159–160
King's Royal Rifle Corps 28–29, 77, 121, 140
Kitchener's New Army 21, 25

Machine-Gun Corps 35, 41, 83, 114

New Zealand Expeditionary Force 11, 159

Royal Field Artillery 19, 38, 51, 54, 69, 72, 80, 105, 113, 121, 134–135, 152
Royal Flying Corps 52, 117
Royal Naval Air Service (RNAS) 23, 39, 51, 59, 163, 165
Royal Naval Division 38, 134

Royal Naval Reserve 2, 27, 37, 152, 156, 159, 162
Royal Navy 1, 27, 36, 61, 97, 110, 119, 123, 127, 132, 148, 152
Royal West Kent Regiment 30, 99

SS *La Cour* 56, 123
Suffolk Yeomanry 25, 103

Territorial Force 1–3, 12–13, 102, 144

West Riding Regiment 31, 60, 161

Miscellaneous

Armistice Day 55, 62–63

Battle of Arras 37–38, 70–71, 84, 102, 107, 113, 118, 134
Battle of Broodseinde 42, 87
Battle of Cambrai 43, 97
Battle of the Aisne 4, 74
Battle of the Ancre Heights 31, 69, 115

Battle of the Scarpe 37, 76, 102, 107
Battle of the Somme 25, 29–30, 32–33, 71, 84, 118, 120, 125, 161

Operation Michael 48, 106

Russian War of Intervention 32, 61, 127

Lightning Source UK Ltd.
Milton Keynes UK
UKHW022120110719
345998UK00004B/533/P